My Best Cellar

All the best Ray gun

Wilf Lunn

My Best Cellar

An autobiography up to the age of eleven ...

and other stuff

Wilf Lunn

© Wilf Lunn, 2008

Published by Shaffron Publishing

June 2008

ISBN 978 0 9556155 1 1

Set in Minion Pro 12/16

Prepared, printed and cover design by:
York Publishing Services Ltd
64 Hallfield Road
Layerthorpe
York YO31 7ZQ
Tel: 01904 431213
Website: www.yps-publishing.co.uk

For my wife, Elizabeth

and

Anna, Dick, Emma, Fiona, Louise and Mandy

Contents ~ Lost in Translation

Doreen with me wearing my exfoliating trousers without underpants.

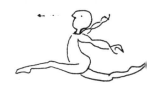

The silence of the Lunns

My younger sister was born in 1943 during 'The late unpleasantness'. She had a birthmark on her arm. It was not a port wine stain or a strawberry mark. We were working class. It was shaped like a sausage, a very small sausage. It was, after all, during the war and food was rationed. Being a war baby, she had her own gas mask and she was called Doreen. Our mother, Irene, wanted to call her Sylvia. Dad couldn't say Sylvia, so they called her Doreen instead. Which I always thought strange, because he couldn't say Doreen either. Dad never learned to talk. When he was a child, measles had made him deaf. So it didn't really matter to him what we were called. My sister could have been called Sylvia or, in fact, anything. Dad couldn't have said it anyway. He just made noises, usually 'Ergogert'. Not 'Hergogert', always 'Ergogert', without an aitch. He was, after all, a deaf Yorkshire man. He didn't have trouble with his aitches; he just never used them in the correct places. Hever! A dictionary on local district dialects by Walter E. Haigh hasn't a section for words beginning with the letter 'H'. The only words in the book spelt with an aitch are his name, Haigh, and Huddersfield, which, of course, are pronounced Aigh and Uddersfield. Curiously, the word aitch doesn't begin with aitch and is not pronounced 'haitch'. We lived in Brighouse, which we pronounced Briggus, leaving out the dreaded 'H'. I still tend to leave out aitches but unfortunately everyday speech demands that you use so many. So I put them back. Usually in the wrong places. I once had to speak on a television programme *What's the Idea?* Or, as I put it, *What's the Hidea?* The show was about hens and eggs or, in my case, 'ens hand heggs'. I was explaining how the hegg came out of the en's rear hend, blunt hend first, hand pointed hend last, thus preventing the en's bottom shutting with a bang. People complained. Not about how I was speaking but about what I was saying. This was progress. They all insisted the egg came out pointed end first. Until then I never realised how closely people watched the private parts of poultry.

Back to Dad and names. If he'd uttered at my christening, I could have been called Ergogert Lunn. I like unusual names, like Brefni Hions, my best friend at junior school. Or Banolo Cabalo. Banolo lived at the bottom of Bramston Street, to the left up Thomas Street. His name could have been Manolo but we all called him Banolo. The last time I saw him, he was outside the Albert cinema watching the people coming out. He told me he wanted to be a psychiatrist and he was studying the effect of the film on the audience. In other words, people pretending to be what they'd just seen on the film. Such as walking like John Wayne or galloping off on imaginary horses with their coat sleeves tied round their necks for cloaks. Banolo wasn't like the common herd, just looking at the girls. Then there was Ada Yinka Dada, a woman I taught with. What about Shlikashluka, a girl I once met in London. She said she was an Eskimo. She certainly behaved like an Eskimo: she wrapped up warm and took anything she could from the surrounding environment. It's called 'living off the land' in the Arctic. A kind person would look on her as an over-dressed kleptomaniac. The police call it something else. Shlikashluka! You don't forget a name like that. Ergogert Lunn would have been fine, but it was not to be.

Dad was called Hubert Berry Lunn. A great name, a real mouthful. I think the year he was born must have been a particularly good blackberry harvest. I can't think why else he was called Berry. To avoid the aitch in Hubert, everybody called him Bert. One woman called him dummy, just the once. She and her family lived in such squalor, it was said, if she'd had a door mat, visitors would have wiped their feet when they left her house. Even as a little kid I knew who the dummy was.

It was decided to call me after my Dad's brother, Uncle Wilf, whose full name was Charles Wilfred Lunn. The idea was to reverse the names to Wilfred Charles. Fortunately they dropped the Charles, so in later life I didn't suffer the indignity of having WC on my school satchel. I could, of course, have had a plain satchel, like Susan Helen Isabel Thorpe. So I understand I was named after Uncle Wilf. I sometimes think Dad was thinking about Pip, Squeak and Wilfred in the *Daily Mirror*. Pip was a dog, Squeak was a Penguin and Wilfred was a rabbit with very big ears. Big ears, get it? I wasn't deaf, but strangely all Wilfred the rabbit could say was 'Gung Nunc'. Dad couldn't say Wilfred or Wilf; the nearest he got to it was to mouth 'Whif'. So he called me Whif. Mam called me Whiferd and everybody else called me Willy.

Dad's school photo
I think he's on the third row up, third from the left.
The only one with any expression on his face.

Question: Why can't a deaf man
tickle nine cats?

Answer: Because he can only
gesticulate.

Dad's teeith

(Father's teeth)

Dad went to Doncaster school for the deaf and dumb poor, where he was taught sign language and cobbling. This was to prepare him for a simple life, where one had only to know the difference between rubber and leather and be familiar with any modern technological advances, namely the 'stick-on-sole' and the 'revolving screw-on heel'. This was a circular rubber heel with a screw through the middle on which it revolved. When it wore down you just turned it to an unworn bit. When the art of pointing at the sole or heel of a boot had been mastered, one could now communicate with the customer and was ready for the world. An added bonus of this type of job was that any strange speech was attributed to having a mouth full of nails. Apparently this is what the craftsman cobbler does, fills his mouth with nails. There was a boot repairer, we pronounced it 'booit', at the bottom of Bonegate Road. He always had a mouth full of nails.

My friend Mike Dews told me that he spat the nails like darts into the boot soles and then hammered them in. I don't know if this was true but everybody called him 'Spithammer'.

Dad could certainly have held a lot of nails in his mouth because he hadn't any teeth. He'd had them all pulled out. I don't think this was to accommodate more nails because, although he always mended our shoes, he never worked as a cobbler. Being toothless made good sense in those days. It was the best way to avoid toothache and further dentist bills. So in 1946, when free dentistry was available on the National Health Service, there was a mass rush for false teeth. People wanted their teeth whipped out quick before the Government changed its mind.

Before Dad had all his teeth removed, Mam said he used to bend iron pokers. She said it as though she thought we were wondering why he didn't bend iron pokers now and, seeing our puzzled faces, she felt obliged to explain. So she'd say to Doreen and me: 'Dad used to bend pokers. Then he had all his teeth out and he stopped.'

I was confused. Did she mean he compulsively bent iron pokers, and having all his teeth out was the only way to stop this irritating habit? Or now, because he hadn't any teeth, he couldn't clench. Perhaps clenched gums didn't give the impetus required to bend pokers. Or did she mean Dad had lost his strength, like Samson when Delilah had his hair cut? Judges 16:17. In other words, Dad's strength was in his teeth.

Had he been to a woman dentist? Who probably didn't know that 'Ergogert' meant 'A light clean please' and not 'Please remove all my teeth'. He should have gone to a deaf dentist who used sign language. But apparently deaf dentists are not popular with screaming, distressed hearing patients, so they're a bit thin on the ground.

Further inquiry into the connection between tooth removal and poker bending was useless. All you got out of Mam was: Dad used to bend pokers and now, with all his teeth out, he didn't. If you tackled Dad about it, pointing at the poker and miming poker bending, he'd smile, shake his head and point at his false teeth. This could, of course, have meant: 'No, last time I did that I over-clenched my teeth so hard they went wobbly and I had to have these false ones'. We will never know.

Dad's false teeth were the colour of ancient ivory. They were that yellow brown tinge that they now paint on pub ceilings. They have to do this because we're not smoking enough to get the mucky look a theme pub, trying to look like a real old pub, should have. Dad achieved this effect on his teeth by simply smoking lots of Woodbine cigarettes. The nightly soaking in Steradent didn't get all the nicotine off. Every night, he'd put his teeth in the glass of Steradent at the side of the bed and his cigarettes under the pillow.

When I started smoking, I'd sneak into his bedroom and gently remove the packet, pinch one cigarette and put the packet back under the pillow. In the morning his teeth would still be there in the glass but one fag would have been taken. When he noticed the disappearances, he told Mam. She, being of a suspicious nature, asked me what I knew about it. I, being a Clever Dick, said it must be the tooth fairy taking the fags because his teeth were in a glass not under the pillow.

Parents told children that if they put their extracted tooth under the pillow the tooth fairy exchanged it for a silver sixpence. Why the tooth fairies wanted the teeth, Mam never told us. We never slept with our heads under the pillow in case the fairies took all our teeth.

Mam told Dad what I said, that the tooth fairy had pinched the cigarette. He signed it couldn't be the tooth fairy. 'It was', I said.

'No', he signed, 'the tooth fairy always leaves money.' He'd got me there. I never did it again unless I'd a thrupenny bit to leave in the packet, then nothing was said.

The cigarettes gave him a terrible cough. His cough was so loud that when he got up in the morning the neighbours used him as an alarm clock. The coughing didn't embarrass us because when he did it he sounded exactly like any normal hearing person coughing up their guts. Coughing, laughing, crying and snoring were the only normal sounds he made. Well perhaps not his snoring; his snoring was unbelievable. I only slept in the same room with him once. It was like trying to sleep with a motorbike at full throttle. If Mam hadn't been deaf she'd have never slept.

Dad would entertain us by pushing his bottom set of false teeth out of his mouth and up against his nose so he looked like an angry bulldog. He'd grab Doreen or me and rub his stubbly chin on our soft faces. It was like sticking your face on a wire brush.

This was fun? He'd remove his top set of teeth and show us how he could touch his nose with his tongue. To me it seemed worth it, having all your teeth out, to be able to touch your nose with your tongue. Imagine the admiring glances you'd get from the girls if you could do that. Oh yes! We made our own entertainment in those days.

With the advent of better dentistry, fun with false teeth will become forgotten and the book will not be written. Tales of bakers crimping the edges of their pies with their false teeth and jokes like: 'My top teeth are fine but the ones in my bottom are killing me.' Or 'Granny's had all her teeth taken out and a gas cooker put in.'

FASTEETH Helps Overcome

FALSE TEETH

Looseness and Worry

All these will become folk memories. Auntie Ethel had all her teeth pulled out. Granny Annie had had her's out much earlier. Mam kept her teeth. One woman we knew had a top set of teeth so slackly fitted that they didn't keep up with her talking. The teeth would stay shut when she opened her mouth. Or, if the teeth opened when she opened her mouth, they would shut before she shut her mouth. It was fascinating to watch her talk. She thought we were really interested in what she was saying. She didn't realise we were mesmerised by her teeth; they seemed to have a mind of their own. We didn't see this effect again till years later in badly dubbed Italian films. Her voice was out of synchronisation with her teeth. If you've seen the creature's teeth in the film *Alien* it was a bit like that, without the drool. She's probably got the drool now. Mam didn't cultivate her friendship; she was impossible to lip-read.

With all these false teeth about, some men had to stop smoking pipes and change to smoking cigarettes. You see, with false teeth you couldn't hold a pipe in your mouth. If you let go, the weight of the bowl acted like a lever and flicked your top set of teeth out of your mouth. Resulting in a loss of cool. Hardened pipe men would hold the bowl at all times and do a lot of pointing with the stem of the pipe whilst talking with their, hopefully, synchronised false teeth. Later in life I designed the pipe stabiliser and the goldfish bowl false teeth cleaner. The pipe stabiliser is made from a loop of metal and a piece of string. It works so well it keeps the pipe firm against the bottom set, allowing you to talk without removing the pipe or having your top set flicked out. The goldfish bowl false teeth cleaner is just a novelty way of allowing your goldfish to eat the scraps between your teeth while you are sleeping.

I had a red gas mask with a tube that made a raspberry noise when you breathed out. Doreen had one made for babies. It was like a haversack with a celluloid window. She was fastened inside it and air was pumped in to her, with a thing like a concertina.

A PIPE STABILIZER NO HANDS NEEDED

WITHOUT STABILIZER

1. Grandad holds his pipe. All is well
2. Grandad lets go of his pipe.
3. Pipe flicks out and if he wears false teeth out they come too.

WITH THE STABILIZER

The stabilizer holds the bottom set of teeth firmly in, allowing Grandad to talk without removing his pipe and even to blow bubbles.

YOU WILL NEED

Stiff wire. approx 30 cm (12")
Elastic approx 20 cm (9")

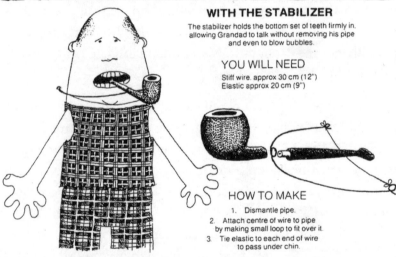

HOW TO MAKE

1. Dismantle pipe.
2. Attach centre of wire to pipe by making small loop to fit over it.
3. Tie elastic to each end of wire to pass under chin.

A HOLDER FOR GRANDMOTHER'S FALSE TEETH

Cheaper to keep than a goldfish

HOW TO MAKE

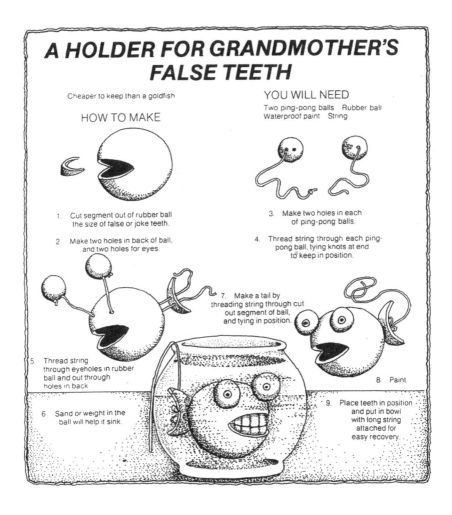

1. Cut segment out of rubber ball the size of false or joke teeth.

2. Make two holes in back of ball, and two holes for eyes.

3. Make two holes in each of ping-pong balls.

4. Thread string through each ping-pong ball, tying knots at end to keep in position.

5. Thread string through eyeholes in rubber ball and out through holes in back.

6. Sand or weight in the ball will help it sink.

7. Make a tail by threading string through cut out segment of ball, and tying in position.

8. Paint.

9. Place teeth in position and put in bowl with long string attached for easy recovery.

11

We never had to use them. A girl from the orphanage told me they all had to sleep in theirs just in case the attack came at night. I suspect it was a way of stopping them talking in bed.

When I was nine years old I was given an old army gas mask. The mask was the type with a tube hanging down to a filter canister. I removed the bottom from the canister. Then I went into the back cellar and stripped off all my clothes. Putting the mask on and holding the canister above my head, I submerged myself in Mam's dolly tub full of water. I thought I could use the mask as a kind of snorkel. When I was under the water, I took a deep breath and, instantly panicking, I leapt out of the tub. There I was, stark naked, the filter canister swinging on its tube like an iron fig leaf bashing my nether regions. The mask had sucked onto my face like an amorous jellyfish. I couldn't breath. It was far worse than an auntie's kiss. My woolly balaclava experience came in handy, and I somehow managed to peel it off. It was similar to the robbery story where the police blocked all the exits but the thief escaped through the entrance. In this case it was the reverse; the water had come in through the air exit. That was the last time I tried on a gas mask. You wouldn't be allowed to wear them now. The filters were made of charcoal and asbestos.

How long is it since you tried on your Gas-Mask?

This should be done every day.

This space is put at the Disposal of the Divisional Warden by H. Marsden, Jeweller. 17, Bradford road, Brighouse.

The smell that can be heard

I never learned sign language. I suppose it was like admitting our family was somehow different. Mam and Dad didn't make any effort to teach us either. I think they felt it was like giving someone a walking stick who didn't have any trouble walking. The only signs I knew were the ones for 'good', 'good morning', 'good evening', 'bad', 'film', 'sausages', 'butter' and the number 'six'. In the alphabet I only knew the vowels and the letter 'G'. The vowels were easy. I didn't know what vowels were then. All I knew was if you put your right index finger on each finger of your left hand starting with the thumb, you had signed 'A, E, I, O, U'. And these letters were the vowels, whatever they were.

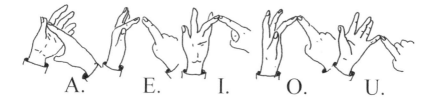

The letter 'G' was much more interesting. If you put the right fist on top of the left fist that was the letter 'G'. But if you repeated the sign it meant 'Bugger'.

BUGGER   OFF

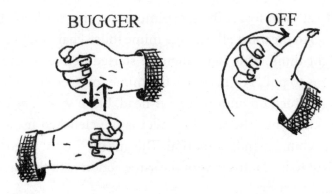

I was told by one of the question setters on, I think it was, *Winner Takes All*, that deaf people watched the show because the questions were written on an illuminated board. They knew this because deaf people had written in to ask if it was possible to flash a light behind the correct answer. Realising they had deaf viewers, they thought it would be a nice idea to set a question about sign language. Unfortunately the question was: 'What is the sign for the letter G?' Which is, as you now know, also the sign for 'bugger'.

The hand sign all the kids in the hearing world knew then wasn't a deaf sign. It was a made-up 'W', for Wall's ice cream. You made the thumb and first finger of each hand into a 'V' sign and put your thumbs together to form a 'W'.

THE WALL'S ICE CREAM SIGN.

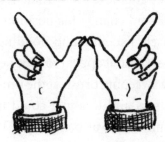

We would do this to passing Wall's delivery vans. Because the inarticulate lorry drivers had to keep one hand on the steering wheel, they'd reply with one hand, using the first two fingers. This was half the 'W' sign. Thus I learned the attitude and the main hand sign in the hearing world.

Oh yes! Let's not forget the most important sign for kids: 'I want to go to the toilet'. It isn't the mime toilet-chain pulling you might think. This sign language started before people had chains to pull. For instance, the mime for 'German' is the first finger stuck up on top of your head, like a spiked helmet, i.e. a picklehaube. The sign for toilet is the clenched fist against the stomach in a winding motion. This meant 'I want to go to the toilet'. Not to be confused with the same action with the flat hand, which meant 'Sorry'.

Very clever, the similarity. The 'I want to go to the toilet' sign could quickly be changed to 'Sorry'. In other words, 'Sorry, too late, I've shat myself'.

Because of my lack of sign language, Dad would mime to me, embellishing his actions with sounds like 'Ergogert' or cod English. He'd use the sound 'Wha' like an actor pretending to be French would make meaningless noises that sounded French. Dad would do the same with English. Often miming two people having a conversation. He would mime incidents at work. With his chest stuck out he would stand at his fullest height wagging his finger and shout 'Wah, wah, wah?' This would be some huge pompous boss telling him off. Like Goliath and David. 1 Samuel 17:48–51. Bosses were always taller because they got more food. Then he would shorten his height, pull his forelock and change his position to look up at the boss. He was now himself, listening and nodding subserviently in agreement with the boss. Or so it appeared. But he was also miming that he was leaning on a sweeping brush at the time. Thus indicating he didn't really give a toss and this guy could talk as long as he liked. While he talked, no work was being done. Who was the fool? Certainly not Dad! He'd then change sides again, increase his height and become the boss again, getting more and more angry. The boss started to look more like Hitler at a Nuremberg rally with the sound turned off. The arms would fly about, the clenched fists banging on an invisible lectern. We'd laugh at the silly man. Suddenly he would change sides, become shorter. He was himself again, calmly leaning on his invisible sweeping brush, nodding. Then he'd be the boss again. It was like watching Jekyll and Hyde. Back and forth, one to the other. Then the boss would grab his own hair with both hands and walk off fuming. He'd change to Dad, nodding and still leaning on the mime brush, watching the boss walking away. He'd have a dramatic pause, as if he was thinking about the situation. Then he'd straighten up to his full height and, gripping the invisible brush, he'd slowly mime sweeping the floor. It was a mini-epic. He was now walking off into the sunset, the hero; he'd won. I didn't know what the argument was about but I got the gist.

It wasn't always easy getting the gist. He would look at me with a puzzled expression on his face, shrug his shoulders and, with his palms upwards, say: 'Wah, wah, Whif?' This could mean 'It looks like rain'. Or 'What the hell are you talking about?' Or maybe 'You are a great disappointment to me Wilf'. You see, various interpretations could be put on what was being expressed. You may think this was peculiar to my Dad, but it's quite common. When interpreting the Bible, for example, or looking at contemporary 'Quack' art. You can take offence or be pleased with the same thing. 'Would I lie to you gorgeous?'

If you see any old Edgar Lustgarten crime films, there's always a scene in it that reminds me of Dad. It's the 'Looking for the suspect' sequence, where you can't hear the voices. Dramatic 'Looking for the suspect music' is playing over the scene. The detective mouths something to a guy. The guy shakes his head. The next scene, same thing, the woman shakes her head. Various people are shown, all being questioned and all shaking their heads. This signifies a long painstaking search was made. Just when you're getting bored with all this, a chap nods his head and points up the street: the detective's found his man. Dad could have played all the parts, including the woman.

In 1942 I won first prize in a war baby competition. I think it was because I was shaped like a bomb. At that time I could only communicate with my deaf parents when they were looking at me. Crying was useless if they weren't looking my way. Only visual signals, vibration or smell would attract their attention. Combining two of these methods, namely in a reverberating fart, would have been extremely useful. Unfortunately this ability came to me later in life when it was no longer generally considered an asset. Apart, that is, from allowing me to do Dad's old trick. He would point a finger at you and indicate he wanted you to pull it. When you pulled it he would instantly let forth a loud fart. It was a great mystery to us as to how this should be, since no amount of pulling our own fingers produced the same effect. Mam and Dad didn't use the word fart; they mouthed the word 'Trump'.

I think the word originated from a bum note played on a trumpet. The hand sign for 'Trump' was right fist held horizontally then quickly dropped, as if knocking on a door, at the same time mouthing 'Trump'. Try it, it's very graphic.

Joke
A little boy was hiding under a table on which his parents were playing whist. His mother asked: 'What's trumps?' A little voice from under the table squeaked 'Poops'.

I had to rely mainly on smell to communicate. Dad had yet to ruin his sense of smell smoking Woodbines, so it worked some of the time. I sometimes wonder if Dad deliberately called me Whif, meaning smelly, not Wilf. Did Mam call me Whiferd, a euphemism for fart, 'The smell that can be heard'?

A lady, who shall remain nameless to conceal the noise of her flatulence, would cough loudly at the same time. Folk soon realised that her coughs were always followed by a strong smell. It could have been thought she had the worst case of coughing halitosis known to man. Whether she farted or not every time she coughed, people automatically moved away.

Graffiti in a penny toilet:
'Here I am broken hearted, paid a penny and only farted'.

RASTRICK WEDDING

Interesting Ceremony at Matthew's Church

A pretty wedding, which attracted a great deal of attention, was solemnised at the St. Matthew's Church, Rastrick, on Saturday afternoon, the contracting parties being Mr. Hubert Berry Lunn, the youngest son of Mr. and Mrs. J. B. Lunn, of 63, Mill Moor-road, Meltham, Huddersfield, and Miss Irene Shaw, youngest daughter of Mr. and Mrs. C. W. Shaw, of 99, Thornhills-road, Rastrick.

The ceremony was performed by the Rev. A. J. Ashley, and as both the bride and bridegroom are deaf and dumb, Mrs. Smith, of the Halifax Deaf and Dumb Institute acted as interpreter.

The bride, who was given away by her father, wore a white satin gown with a quilted bodice and puff sleeves. She wore a long flowing embroidered veil and white shoes, and carried a bouquet of pink carnations and a lucky horseshoe.

Her five attendants were Mrs. R. Hunter, Miss Evelyn Shaw, Miss Pauline Shaw, Miss Kathleen Holdsworth and Miss Christine Pratt (nieces) Mrs. Hunter was attired in a dress of taffeta in blue, with posies of pink and white flowers, and wore silver shoes. The two elder bridesmaids wore dresses of pink taffeta trimmed with blue, and had pink muffs and veils, and the two young attendants were in blue dresses trimmed with pink and carried posies of anemones. They wore blue Victorian bonnets.

Mr. Hubert Lunn (nephew of the groom) was the best man, and Mr. Mills Shaw (nephew of the bride) was the groomsman.

The bride's mother wore a grey coat and blue silk dress, with hat and shoes to tone.

A reception was held at the Co-op. Cafe, about 40 guests being present. There were many beautiful presents from relatives and friends and a telegram was received from the bride's brother who is serving in the Forces.

For the time being Mr. and Mrs. Shaw are to reside at 99, Thornhill-road, Rastrick.

Mam and a tata to town
(Mother and a trip into town)

Mam was a hypochondriac. She enjoyed ill health, so she was actually a happychondriac. A hereditary illness had made her deaf. She always said she was deaf because when she was a little girl, a nail was poked in her eye. Perhaps a childish crucifixion game that went wrong? This is interesting, because if you look at those old phrenology busts, language, verbal memory and verbal expression are all centred round the left eye. I don't for a second think it's true, but she was profoundly deaf and had very bad eye sight that gradually got worse. Eventually she had to use a red-and-white striped stick. The usual joke was 'Is it a stick for a blind barber?'

Folk often asked if Mam and Dad had been deaf all their lives. At the time I'd say, 'Not yet'. They'd also inquire why my parents didn't wear 'Deaf aids'. I would point out they didn't need anything to aid their deafness, they were deaf enough. In fact, they were too deaf to wear 'Hearing aids'.

Mother was always called 'Mam'. It's obviously more suitable than Ma, Mum or Mummy; Mam being short for mammary, an aptly visual and tactile name, so you knew it was her and which was the front in the dark. Pretentious kids, such as girl horse riders,

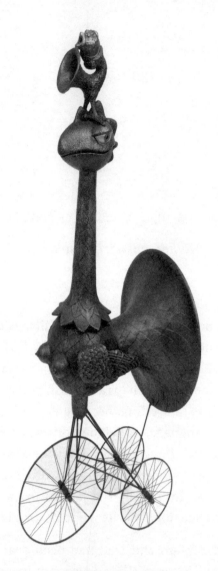

Megaphone bird.

By speaking into the bird's mouth the voice is amplified through the bird's tail. On the bird's head is a smaller bird swallowing a fish, it's a 'halitosis indicator'. When you breathe into its tail, your breath is blown back at your nose, Thus indicating if your breath is suitable for making a speech. The breasts are so you can tell which is the front when it's dark.

called their Mams Mummy. We were happy with Mam. After all, isn't that what they call the Queen? Mam went to Odsal House School for the deaf, where sign language was very much frowned upon. In fact it was totally forbidden. You weren't even allowed to point at things. The idea was that you were deaf but your vocal cords were all right, so you could be taught to talk. It was called 'Oralism'. In theory it seemed all right and for some it worked. Mam was taught to lip-read and to talk, after a fashion. Friends and relatives were the only ones who could really understand her. I eventually taught at Odsal House with my mother's old headmistress, Miss Plant. Well, my Mam called her Miss Plant; all the kids at the school seemed to call her Miss Plant, so I called her Miss Plant. Until she realised I hadn't the excuse of a speech impediment, and then she informed me forcefully that she was called Miss Bland not Miss Plant. There was nothing bland about Miss Bland. She was very strict. There was only one way to do things, and that was her way. She had very deep-rooted opinions that could not be shifted. So to me she will always be Miss Plant.

Mother picked up this totally black and white attitude; everything was either right or wrong, no shades of grey. Her favourite word was 'Selfish'. We were constantly being accused of being selfish. By which she meant we had a total disregard for her own selfishness. Things had to be done the right way: her way. It had to be, as she said, 'The fashion'. In other words, exactly like everyone else. Despite the fact it is totally forbidden in the Bible; Leviticus 21:5.

They shall not make baldness upon their head, neither shall they shave off the corner of their beard, nor make any cuttings in the flesh.

I hadn't had my ears pierced and I was still alright in the beard department, but Mam made me have my hair cut once a fortnight in the right style, which meant short back and sides. So when the two weeks growing time was up, off we'd go for a trip to town, or what was called a 'Tata' to town. Folk would say, 'Are you going for a tata to town?'

A bit baffling because 'Tata' usually meant 'Good bye'. On one of these occasions it was raining and I hadn't a raincoat. I'd probably grown out of it and Granny Annie would have taken it immediately to cut up for the family rag rug. We had to break with 'The fashion'. I had to wear my sister's raincoat.

It fitted me because it had been bought larger so she could, as they say, 'Grow into it'. When she wore it you couldn't see her hands. I remember leaving the house wearing the coat; it was buttoned up and belted the wrong way. A terrible dread came over me of being spotted wearing a girl's coat that buttoned the other way, the girls' way. It could only have been worse if it had been patched. Only poor people had patches or wore odd clothes like their little sister's raincoat. Poor

Why do men button coats left over right?

In the days when men carried swords, the sword was fastened on the left. A man buttoned his coat left over right so it wouldn't flap or get in the way of his sword as it was drawn. It's said women buttoned the opposite way because they usually carry babies in their left arm, it's easier to unbutton and feed them that way. Buttons in the past were expensive and only the rich could afford them. Wealthy ladies did not dress themselves. Buttoning right over left was also easier for the servants.

people, where the last child to get up in a morning had to wear what was left or they didn't go to school. The kid wasn't just 'Sans-culotte'; the last out of bed could be 'Sans the lot'.

It was said one family were so short of clothes, when it was washday the naked kids would take it in turns to wear their dad's flat hat to look out of the window. Now kids are not so sensitive about odd clothes, but then the prospect of having to go to school in three woolly balaclava helmets and a snake belt was scary. I say balaclava helmets because people had been knitting them since the

First World War and, since rationing was still on, we were short of everything except balaclava helmets. Everyone had loads of them; they were very fashionable. Nowadays older folk attribute children's stuck-out ears to not wearing a balaclava helmet from an early age. (n.b. Prince Charles.) On this day though, I wasn't wearing a balaclava because I was going to have my hair cut. I wished I'd worn my balaclava so I could have pulled it over my mouth to disguise me. To make things worse, the coat was green, exactly the same colour as the ones worn at Whitcliffe Mount girls' school. All the local lads knew Whitcliffe Mount girls kept their handkerchiefs in little pockets stitched to their matching green knickers. We'd been told this by jealous girls, who didn't go to the school. Everyone knew girls' green raincoats always went with green knickers. Fortunately the indignity was not added to by having to wear 'Idiot mitts'. Idiot mitts were woolly mittens attached to a long string that went up your coat sleeve, across your back and down the other sleeve. When you took them off they just dangled from your sleeves. Thus making it impossible to lose them. Hence the name 'Idiot mitts'. It was said that if you were caught with one mitten off and an unkind person pulled the loose mitt very hard, the mitten you were still wearing would punch you in the face. We were constantly on the look out for kids with one mitten off. Some kids tried to get out of wearing idiot mitts by breaking the string. Their Mams just tied the string back together, thus shortening it. Kids with tied-up short idiot mitt strings were easy to spot: their shoulders were always hunched up.

Mam and I set off to the barbers. I was terrified of my mates seeing me wearing the dreaded, green, girlie Mac. I tried to conceal my shame by walking slightly behind Mam, between her and the wall. If anyone approached us, she would move in front of me, letting them pass on the pavement edge where they couldn't get a good look at me. This was terrible, because I was on the wrong side of Mam. Being a boy I should, of course, have been on the roadside of Mam. That was 'the fashion'. Everybody knew gentlemen always walked on the outside. Where she'd picked up all this Nancy Mitford 'U and Non-U', I don't know. Perhaps Miss Plant had taught walking up and down etiquette. 'Always walk on the outside of wife.' I had to walk on the outside. It was absolutely ingrained into me. Even from being a toddler, I would always walk on the outside, especially when walking with Dad. This was not because it was 'the fashion' but because his deafness affected his balance and he would suddenly veer off, like a drunk, into the road. I was there for him to trip over, a sort of biological safety barrier. The raincoat incident was so stressful. Fortunately I never had to go through it again. When it rained Doreen wore her coat; my hair waited for fine weather and the purchase of a new dark-blue Macintosh. Just like the gasman's, only shorter. The sleeves, of course, were long so I could grow into it.

On these trips from Rastrick to Brighouse we went down Capel Street, and turned left, past the little wooden hut at the bottom of the hill. The sweet shop. I don't know what the shop was really called, but we always called it 'The wooden hut' or 'The sweet shop'. I'm sure it sold more than sweets, because I remember a sign saying 'Please don't ask for credit as refusal often offends'. I can't imagine kids asking if they could pay when they got their spending money, for two ounces of 'Pontefract cakes' weighed out in a little white paper bag with a pointed bottom. We'd buy kali in those little bags; it was like coloured sugar. You'd eat it by dipping a licked finger in the bag and sucking the kali off. When you'd finished, you had a yellowish brown forefinger that looked like a nicotine stain. This was very desirable because it made you look like a heavy smoking adult, particularly if you had some sweet cigarettes for dessert. A liquorice pipe was not considered as sophisticated; anyway they were all floppy and very unrealistic, even from a distance. The other way to eat kali, avoiding a yellow finger and giving the game away to your Mam, was to bite the point off the bag and allow the crystals to pour into your upturned mouth, like feeding a pate de foie gras goose with a funnel. Kali was not to be confused with sherbet, which was sold in cardboard tubes covered in yellow paper with a liquorice straw stuck in the end. Miss Pring told us that on the Holy crusades a chap called Saladin had saved King Richard's life by giving him sherbet. She didn't say anything about the liquorice straw and I didn't ask, but I nearly mentioned that Saladin had a mill across from the sweet shop up Bramston Street. Fortunately, for once, I didn't say anything. The mill was actually called 'Sladdin's'. Giving someone sherbet when they were ill seemed a better idea than 'Fennings' Fever Cure', even if it didn't work. I didn't suggest it to Mam because Saladin was obviously crackers.

Miss Pring told us King Richard had said his big straight sword was better than Saladin's little curved sword, and he proved it by chopping down a tree with one swipe. Saladin then threw a silk scarf in the air and, as it floated down, sliced it in half and said: 'Your sword can't do that'. Of course it couldn't, but why would you want to chop a silk scarf in half? And anyway, what was he doing with a silk scarf? I thought he'll get in trouble with his Missis.

♪♪ *We three Kings of Orientar, selling chocolate threepence a bar.*
Sherbet sev'n pence, Kali leven pence, following yonder star.
We three Kings of Orientar, one in a taxi one in a car.
One on a scooter blowing his hooter, following yonder star. ♪♪

Walking down Bramston Street, we went past Wright's brandy-snap works. Broken brandy-snaps were available in big white paper bags at a reduced price. The thought that they might just contain illicit alcohol made brandy-snaps very popular. I could never get enough brandy-snaps; this was more to do with lack of money than rationing. My dream of ultimate luxury was crunching brandy-snaps till they pushed my gums up so high you could see the cuticles on my teeth.

Further down the road, on the other side, was a fish and chip shop. Years later I remember older lads at this fish shop. They would buy three pen'orth of chips and fill the paper bags with as much vinegar as they could get away with. When they got outside the shop, they would tear a small corner off the bags. The vinegar would stream out in a fine arc, as if peeing. No matter how often this joke was repeated, they'd laugh; it was a ritual. Then, when the bags were drained, they'd proceed to eat their vinegar-sterilised chips. Sometimes they'd sing a little ditty: 'Milk, milk, lemonade. Round the corner chocolate's made'. Whilst singing, they'd tap each breast for milk; 'Milk, milk'. Then, holding the leaking chip bag by their crutch as if peeing, they'd sing 'Lemonade'. In conclusion, they'd point to their bums and sing 'Round the corner chocolate's made'.

The ditty's probably local, because our Ben Shaw's lemonade was yellow, the colour of pee. The rest of the country drank colourless lemonade. Because we only drank Ben Shaw's lemonade, for years I thought all lemonade was yellow. When I inquired why the rest of the country didn't have yellow lemonade, I was told it was because it was only available within the distance a horse could walk to deliver it from Ben Shaw's pop works. The connection between horse and yellow lemonade was noted. I took every opportunity to mention this to put people off drinking lemonade so I could have more for myself. I would hold the glass up, examine it like a vet, and say 'The horse that delivered this is not fit for work'.

I think this shop was the first to have a refrigerator. I do know he was the first to sell ice lollipops. He didn't have a proper lollipop mould, so he made frozen pop ice cubes with a stick. Who would have thought this simple confection would eventually develop into Woolworth's exotic 'Lolly Golly Choc Bomb'. The fish-shop lollipops were a penny each and a much longed for treat. You could suck all the pop and colour out, leaving a colourless, spongy ice cube. We dared each other to go and ask for money back on the

sucked empty ice cube. You could get money back for
empty pop bottles. If you were lucky enough to get a
soda siphon to take back, you were rich. The deposit on a soda
siphon was considerably more than the soda water cost. It was
rumoured that they were so valuable because crooks melted
the tops down to forge half crowns. Soda water was unheard of
in our house. We had to be content with the money from empty
Ben Shaw's pop bottles.

We got all our pop from Mrs Jones at the next house down, across
the ginnel. She sold pop from her house; nothing else, just pop.
You knocked on the door; she'd open the door, take your order
and disappear into the house, reappearing with your bottle of pop.
It all seemed slightly illegal. My favourite was 'Dandelion and
Burdock'. It was the same rich dark brown colour as 'Doctor Dan's
Health Drink' from the Huddersfield market.

In the fish and chip shop there was a sign with a picture of a
lighthouse informing you that this guy was a member of the FFF. So,
don't mess with me or you'll answer to the 'Fish Friers' Federation'.
Perhaps the Federation was formed to keep up standards, but I
don't think they ever caught the chippy chappy who put his fish
through a wringing machine to flatten them so they looked bigger.
Federations were scary. Wasn't the FBI something to do with
it? They didn't have a secret handshake, you just counted their
fingers. They usually had fingers missing because they'd lost the
rhythm putting the potatoes under the chipping machine. This
machine had a lever that, when pulled down, pushed a metal block
divided into squares down onto the potato, thus cutting it into
chips through a grid of sharp blades.

The chipped potatoes dropped into a bucket underneath. The
rhythm was: potato in, hand out, lever down, chips in bucket.
Potato in, hand out, lever down, chips in bucket. This was done very
quickly to the rhythm. Potato in, hand out, lever down, chips in
bucket. Or, on a bad day: potato in, lever down, finger in bucket.

If you have an arm chopped off, it's called mayhem. But in this case, the act of pruning a finger, I think it is called secateur. Apparently Japanese gangsters perform the act of secateur on their little fingers by way of an apology. They must think our chip-shop chaps very sorry people.

Some fish and chip shop men had what appeared to be a nervous tic in their eyes. This was the 'Batter blink', caused by closing the eyes when the batter splashed off the fish as it hit the hot fat. When the shop closed at night, I think they used to put the shop's takings for the day and the secret batter recipe in a tin and sink it in the beef dripping fat. When the fat cooled and set, no one could pinch the tin without taking the complete cooker.

We only bought lollipops, not fish and chips, at the Bramston Street shop because, although it was near home, there were two fish shops nearer. The one at the top of Thomas Street, near the Co-op, which for a time was owned by Uncle Tommy, and the one at the bottom of Castle Avenue, owned by Alderman Harry C. Nobbs. He was also caretaker of Rastrick Grammar School and became Mayor of Brighouse in 1959. This was the fish shop we usually went to. I thought it was the best because folk came from miles away. I don't know if they really did, but a sign subtly implied this. It said: 'Extra wrapping is available on request for customers having long distances to go'. Walking back home, I had to hold our fish and chip parcel away from my body because, if I didn't, the chip grease soaked through the one sheet of newspaper then onto my clothes. This early form of waterproofing clothes, I think, preceded the 'Barbour' waxed coat method. Even so, Mam was not pleased if this happened. Extra wrapping would have solved this problem, but they wouldn't give me extra wrapping because I was local; it was really for the carriage trade.

I loved to watch the assistant when she started a new pile of white wrapping paper. She put her index finger knuckle in the centre of the paper and, pressing down, would describe small circles. Magically

the paper would make a beautiful fan, separating all the papers so they were easier to pick up. When she'd finished she'd look up and say, 'Yes?' 'Fish n' chips four times,' I'd reply. She then always said, 'W' bits?' These were the little bits of crozzled batter that had dropped off the fish. I always replied, 'Yes'. Because you felt you were getting more for your money.

There was always a queue, which I didn't mind, unless there was a girl in front who would produce a cardboard box she'd managed to conceal about her person. She'd be from the mill. A sigh would go up from the queue because they knew it would be a big order, a long wait, probably involving two changes of beef dripping fat and the Whitby fleet having to go to sea again. The mill cunningly sent different girls each time and cleverly disguised them by making them take their wrap-over pinnies off. Otherwise they knew the people in the queue would grumble.

One day I was in the fish shop queue and the chap at the front ockered [stammered]. He started, 'F, f, f, f, f, f, f'. 'Fish and chips?' the assistant asked, trying to help him. He shook his head, 'F, f, f, f, f, f, f'. The assistant leaned closer to him and looked him straight in the face. When he did speak, she wasn't going to miss it. 'F, f, f, f, f, f'. He took a breath. 'F, f, f, f, f, f, f, f'. The queue was getting restless; this could go on forever. He paused, then quickly said, 'F, f, fuggerit, I'll 'ave a bottle o' pop'. There was silence for a moment. We all thought, please don't ask him what kind. She did; we waited. He took a deep breath, and said 'Dandelion and Burdock'.

Just past the Bramston Street fish shop there was a pin works. If the door was open, you could see great parcels wrapped in sacking, like Egyptian mummies tied with string. They rolled up and down on the flat bed of a big machine. If the door was closed, you could sneak into the yard, break the rust crust covering a pile of iron fillings and pinch a handful. When you got home, you'd throw some on the fire so you had a sparkler fireworks display. Years later I read about some workmen who'd put iron fillings in a mate's

Stammerer's c-c-c-cycle

tea. The article said this was extremely dangerous because the iron reacted with the acid in the stomach and he could have exploded. If we'd only had that information when we were kids, who knows?

After the pin works, you went past the butchers and the paper shop. To the left ran Scotty Bank up the hill, leading back to Thornhill Road where we lived. To the side of Scotty Bank ran the railway viaduct; Bramston Street ran under it to Brighouse. The ultimate dare was to go along the ledge that ran along the viaduct high over Bramston Street. I never heard of anyone doing it. Under the arches, to the side of the street, were lots of rusty old oil drums tightly packed in rows. Some had rusted through and you could see they contained what looked like solid beef dripping, very strange and mysterious. What would the Fish Friers' Federation have to say about this secret hoard of dripping?

One day we were playing on top of these drums. I fell between them and found a suitcase full of chocolates. It turned out these were stolen. Rationing was still on, and chocolate was like gold. A real 'Famous Five' adventure. The police came to our house, and so did all the neighbours. We had a house full, all being helpful and friendly. Friendly being a euphemism for nosey. I was asked to sign a statement; they all laughed when I said, 'I don't do joined up writing'. I still don't. I never got a reward, not even a chocolate; in fact, I never heard anything more about them. I suspect it was like my donation of chocolate watches to the horology collection at the British Museum. When I inquired about them, I was informed they had been eaten. They're obviously not paying them enough, so I've sent them more.

Going under the viaduct, the road led to a little humped back bridge over the river Calder. On the outside of the right-hand bridge wall was a big pipe that ran high above the river. Crossing the river, walking on this pipe, was 'A dare' and I'd done it. When you'd crossed the bridge you were in Brighouse, and Bridge Road lay straight in front of you. We called Bridge Road 'Pong Alley'. It wasn't really small enough to be an alley. We called it an alley because they had alleys in films and in the Gracie Field's song, but we didn't have a single alley in Brighouse and we didn't want to be left out. We christened it 'Pong' because it ponged. It stank awful. The smell came from a crab dresser, down the alley, next to the canal. Why there should be a crab dresser so far from the sea in Brighouse, I don't know.

Off Pong Alley, to the left, was Atlas Mill Road; down there was 'The Destructers'. We didn't bother with fancy euphemisms then. This was where I understood you took things to be destroyed: unloved cats, dogs, foul-mouthed parrots and awkward budgies, etc. 'The Destructers.' It sounds much more final than 'Put down' or, if American, 'Euthanized'.

The scout hut was also on this road, I still have the scar on my leg from when I fell off the roof. The scouts here were not fine-weather scouts, like the Rastrick Grammar softies, who took pressure cookers camping. We didn't even have a pressure cooker at home. The only concession to modernity was getting the 'Woodcraft Badge'. Instead of rubbing two sticks together to make a fire, we were allowed two matches. If that didn't work, we used our cigarette lighters. While camping in Bradley Woods we were told the next day we would be learning to track. The thing we were tracking had a name something like 'woofanpuss'. I've forgotten what it was really called. The Scoutmaster was very mysterious about it. It was a beast I'd never heard of. The next day he appeared with it on the end of a piece of string. It was a chair leg with nails hammered all over it like a hedgehog. We were not thrilled. He set off. We counted to a hundred and easily followed the track of combed grass. So, if a dangerous lunatic escapes dragging a nail embellished chair leg, I'm your man. I left the scouts when I was told that when Prince Charles joined, he got all his cub and scout badges already embroidered on his jumpers. I don't know what he'd done, but he was even given a medal at 5 years old. He wore it at the Coronation.

Before you got to the scout hut, you went past the fairground site. Some of the fairground kids came to our school for a while. We thought it very funny when they always called the female teachers 'Marm'. We thought they were very old fashioned and out of touch. We stopped laughing when one lad brought his Jetex-powered air plane to school. A thing not only way beyond our pockets, but we'd never even heard of them. We were the ones out of touch; we stopped laughing and started envying. It didn't seem like such a bad thing to be stolen by the gypsies. Then we were informed they were the children of 'Show Men'. Travelling fairground people, not gypsies, like Mam thought. The chance of me being kidnapped by gypsies could have been a reason, apart from the crab dresser smell, why Mam never went down Pong Alley if she could avoid it. I don't know if she went down with Doreen, but with me she always went the long way round. We'd turn right at the sweet shop and go on Briggate, past our barbers. Mam said my hair was curly because of the way the barber held it between his two fingers before he cut it. When I was old enough to choose, I of course went to the more fashionable 'Eddie Taylor's' for my hair cutting. Where I would get a D.A. The hair at the back of your head was combed together so it resembled a duck's arse, a D.A. I remember being disdainful when someone said, 'It won't be long before a haircut will cost ten bob [50 pence]'. I thought the guy was an idiot.

Afterwards I'd go to the Zona Bar, which had a jukebox and sold coffee and herbal drinks, including Zona beer. Girls would be posing round the jukebox. Actually, the lasses were lurking. You'd casually walk up to the jukebox, put your money in, and as quickly as possible make your selection. It usually wasn't quick enough. One girl would press the letter button and another the number. Their selection got played and you had no chance.

A sideline of this herbal emporium was what was called 'The continental condom'. They had all sorts of protuberances and frilly bits on them. The owner told me he was the first to import them. He had drawings of them printed on small squares of paper, just like the ones you get in a chocolate selection box. A friend of mine's mother found one of these papers in his coat pocket and asked him what they were. He said 'Pipe cleaners'. The drawings did look like pipe cleaners, because I suppose in a way they were. I always thought women who preferred this kind of rubber stimulation must have a deep desire to return to the sea, because it's rather like making love to a sea anemone.

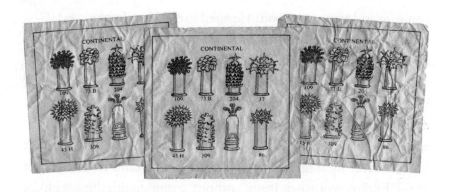

After passing the barbers we'd stop at the music shop, where Mam would always tell me and Doreen the cautionary tale of how the owner of the music shop had blinded himself whilst undoing a knot in his shoelace with a fork. With a fork! I later wondered if she meant a large tuning fork; how else could he be blind in both eyes? He surely hadn't knots in both shoes and done it twice. The implication was that, if you do things the wrong way, terrible things happen. You do not undo shoelace knots with a fork. Especially on the table next to an open umbrella on Friday the 13th, even if you have thrown salt over your left shoulder. I understand the proper thing to undo knots with is that dreadful spike on a Boy Scout's penknife. The one that they always tell you is for removing stones from horse's hooves. They tell you this so you don't undo knots with it. Because if you stuck that in your eye you'd skewer your brain and give yourself an instant 'Ice pick lobotomy'. You'd stop worrying. No music shop or anything for you then. The spike is still on the knife, because very few people know its secret purpose. They still think it's for taking stones out of horses' hooves. What are the chances of coming across a horse with a stone in its hoof? Thorns in elephants' feet are more common. Well, certainly in stories they are.

I sometimes wonder what the orange peeler on the Swiss Army knife's secret purpose is. It can't really be for a Swiss warrior to peel oranges, can it? I have always had a fascination for things used for the wrong purpose. How did they make a limpet mine from a condom and an aniseed ball? I longed to be able to make a radio from a pencil, a razor blade and a safety pin, like prisoners of war did. I read that spies and prisoners concealed secret messages in metal tubes in body orifices. I had an empty metal container used for propelling pencil leads; it was shaped like a liquorice torpedo. I thought this is what they must have meant. I could copy them. Although I didn't have a secret message, I had a metal container and an orifice just the right size, so I stuck it up, without, I might add, the benefit of Vaseline. I thought I'd go out and challenge my mates to find my secret message container. Before leaving, I looked in the mirror and saw that, not only was my nose wider on the right, but you could see the tube end shining up my nostril. I thought the Germans must have been pretty stupid not to spot it. Of course, I'd got the wrong type of tube; it should have been an aluminium cigar tube. Then I would probably have realised I'd got the wrong orifice. I hope the prisoners didn't have the same trouble getting their tubes out that I had.

Pencil lead tubes
Scout knife with fid,
Swiss army knife with orange peeler
and Wilf Lunn's Taxidermist's
companion.

O.O.O.: Acronym for homosexuals, Other Orifice Orientated.

When I couldn't get a grip on the round end, I started to panic. The tube was stuck fast. Then I realised one of my useless bits of knowledge was that when we breath down our nose, we do it for 20 minutes down one nostril, then we automatically change to the other. I was obviously breathing down the empty nostril. I'd less than 20 minutes before breathing swapped over to the other nostril and death. This was serious. I ran to Mam, pointing to my nose. She panicked with me, but she managed to pull it out with her eyebrow tweezers. She did it in time. I breathed a sigh of relief and then realised I was breathing through my mouth. I lied to her about how it got up my nose. She never understood why the big boy on Brooke Street had done this strange thing to me. She eventually tired of pointing at big boys and me shaking my head. It was like Edgar Lustgarten's 'looking for the suspect'.

I did once manage to make a rain detector for a washing line, from a funnel, clothes peg and sugar lump. Using things for the wrong purpose can be dangerous. As I found to my cost when someone used woolly thread, string and a large nut and bolt, all tied to a Jacquard handloom, as a clothes dryer. When I pressed my foot on the loom treadle, the woolly thread broke, releasing the steel nut and bolt, which smashed me in the eye. The agony was unbelievable. My eye felt like a liquorice Pontefract cake, black and flat. The lecturer, Mark Sykes, had to fill in an 'Accident form'. He found describing how the accident occurred so complicated that he simply wrote 'Tripped over loom fitting'. Fortunately I didn't go deaf like Mam, with the nail in her eye, or blind, like the music man with the fork.

Despite the cautionary tale, I still use things for the wrong purpose. I cut my sandwiches with scissors. It works great, particularly with the cheaper meat sandwiches. I don't wear safety goggles whilst I'm doing it, but I do wear elastic-sided boots.

I can't forget Mam and the music man who blinded himself undoing the knot in his shoelace. We'd stand looking in his window for ages, hoping to see him. We never did. His window display never seemed to change. In it were Jews' harps, now apparently called Jaws' harps, next to what appeared to be nicely polished sheep rib bones. He probably got them from the rag and bone man. These things were much desired by older boys. They held a pair between their fingers and rattled out a tune. Some rich kids had them, particularly the sons of fish shop owners with missing fingers. The kids often had two pairs and played in stereo. I think they got them

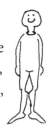

to annoy their dads, who couldn't even snap their fingers. The dads would curse, but if they'd got rhythm in the first place, they'd never have lost their fingers in the chipping machine, would they? I could, of course, have used spoons, which have replaced bones, but to be allowed out with family cutlery was definitely not 'The fashion'. Neighbours might think we were poor and out looking for food.

I did a show once in Geneva with Sylvester McCoy (Doctor Who). He was fire eating and playing the spoons. The leader of the orchestra asked him what key he was playing in. A question he'd never been asked before. Can you get tuneable spoons? Of course not, it's the wrong purpose; spoons are not for tuning, they're for eating with. When you've finish eating, it is acceptable to make music with the leftover bones. Bones, of course, can be tuned.

Next to the bones in the music shop window were pottery shiny green, slug-like things shot through with holes. These were called ocarina. I think because there was always more than one. Otherwise they would have been called ocarinum. Which I now know means little goose. I have visions of the principal of the original instrument being discovered by some unsuspecting diner inadvertently blowing across the parson's nose hole in the end of a goose and getting a note like they do in jug bands, blowing across the mouths of stone bottles. Realising its potential, the diner would play a tune and, before he knew it, the rest of the goose gobblers would have joined in, playing bum notes. Perhaps the didgeridoo was discovered in the same way by an aborigine blowing down a hot, stiff dehydrated snake to cool it before eating. Playing tunes with leftover food is fairly acceptable, but playing with it before you eat is universally unacceptable. 'Don't play with your food' is indelibly engraved on every child's brain. So the pot ocarina was developed probably by pressing clay round a small goose.

Ocarina were fascinating noise makers, but not as fascinating to us as the owner of the shop himself. We looked, hoping he might

ENGLISH
MARROWFAT
PEAS.

SPECIALLY SELECTED.   HAND PICKED.

JAMES S. HARRISON,
❧ GROCER, ❧
Draper, Corn and Provision Merchant,
GREETLAND.

Huntley & Palmer's Biscuits.   Bacon and Hams.
Pickles, Preserves. Marmalades.   Lobsters, Sardines, etc.

RECIPES.

FOR COOKING AS A VEGETABLE.—Soak
the quantity required in water with a little
soda overnight, then put in fresh water with
a little carbonate of soda, one table-spoonful
of brown sugar, a little salt, and a sprig of mint

Boil slowly, or cook in the oven for about
an hour.   Serve with butter, &c., to taste.

FOR SOUP.—Soak the quantity required
in water with a little soda overnight, and then
boil in the soup.   The flavour imparted to
the soup is superior to split peas.

just appear to change his window display. There wasn't a chance we could go into the shop; music figured very low in Mam's priorities. We wondered how he had blinded himself. 'Why hadn't he gone deaf like Mam when the nail stuck in her eye?' we asked. 'When Mam had her accident, was she using a nail to undo a knot in her hair ribbon?' Hair bows were very much the fashion in those days. 'Was he blind in both eyes?' 'Had he stuck the fork in both eyes?' 'Was it a tuning fork?' We'd seen one at school. It only had two prongs. No, she'd say no more; no more information. The man had blinded himself undoing a knot in his shoelace with a fork and that was sufficient information for anyone. What she told you was all that needed to be said about the incident. He'd used a fork, what did he expect to happen?

She didn't say this, it was implied. A friend once told me drunks are like that. They tell the same stories over and over. 'I know,' I said, 'you've told me many times before'. It's so frustrating. Kids did a similar thing, if you asked them why a thing was so. They would reply, 'Cos for'. If you said, 'But why?' they would reply, as if you were completely stupid, 'Cos for'. Life is full of 'Cos fors'.

Attempting to cure narcolepsy with a giant tuning fork

We would leave the shop window and carry on our journey to town, passing to the right of Sugden's flour mill and Mill Royd Street, with the blacksmith's on the left. The blacksmith's door was always open, so you could watch him working. Further up the street was the swimming baths, conveniently next to the town mortuary, with Mellor Mint works across the road. Round the corner we'd come to the 'Bow Window' pea shop. It was called the 'Bow Window' because it had a big bow window made from one sheet of glass. The glass had a crack right across it and behind it there always seemed to be a sleeping cat. A woman called 'Sausage Sarah' opened the shop in 1864. You had to step down into the shop, it was below street level, and was very Dickensian. On the open coal fireplace stood huge iron pots of peas and sausages, bubbling away. The floor was covered in sawdust. You could buy grey peas or green peas. The grey peas were cheaper. My usual order was peas and a muff. If you were really broke, you could have a muff and a dip. That was the muff just dipped into the peas. A muff was a teacake with a slit in it. Cut with a knife, very posh, not like the guy on Rastrick Common, who cut his with his very long thumb nail. We never went there. I suppose it was called a muff because of its similarities to the old fashioned ladies' hand-warming muff. I didn't know, at that time, that this was also slang for an intimate part of a lady's anatomy. Anyway, the muff did keep your sausage warm. It could, of course, just be short for muffin. Mr Edmund Stakes, the chef and owner, squeezed the muff in his left hand, so it opened like a mouth, and ladled peas into it. The muff mouth closed on the peas and he handed it to you. It was really more like a purse of peas. A muff like a lady's muff wouldn't really work. It's got a hole right through and the peas would fall out the bottom. The area health authorities would go bonkers if they saw the place today, but we saw nothing wrong with it. After a visit to the swimming baths for a dip, peas and a dip or sausage and a muff were wonderful to eat in the shop or take away. At times there'd be a long queue of people with those enamel billycans, all eager for sausage and peas. Sadly it closed down in 1959.

Bossy Judith Briggs worked there on Saturdays; she earned 2/6d [30 old pence – only 12½ new pence]. She started a club on Thornhill Road, which was weird to start with. We didn't start clubs. We started gangs! The lure to join her were the buns her mother baked. It wasn't enough for me. I couldn't endure the lining up for hand and nail inspection before entering the house. So I never got one of Bossy's buns. My sister Doreen carried on going. They put on plays, these ladies that bun-lunched at Bossy's; very posh. I understand she is now bossing in Barbados or, as it is now called, using her organisational skills. She worked alongside Jean Anderson, also a school friend. Jean lived just up the road at the Anchor pub. I particularly remember her because, on the first day of junior school, we were all asked what our fathers did. We all knew she lived in a pub, so we were curious to hear what she said. Pubs had connotations of being mysterious, wicked places. I don't know what we expected her to say. She caught us all unaware when she said, 'Publican'. The class, for some reason, laughed. We'd never heard the word 'Publican'. It gave Jean a kind of worldly kudos we didn't have. This was later confirmed when she was put in charge of answering the school telephone for Miss Milnes. What did we know?

To the side of the Anchor pub was the other end of Pong Alley. Past Pong Alley, the Anchor Bridge went over the canal. Now we were in the town with the big shops. John Francis Brown's was the ironmongers where you got your fireworks. Now 'Oddjobs'. Along the road was the chemist's shop where Dad once tried to send me with a note for pills. I refused to go because he wouldn't tell me what kind of pills he wanted. I kept mouthing to him, 'Pills – what – for?' He got more and more annoyed, nodding and pointing at the note. He brought Mam to confirm the note was correct. She looked at it and said it was right. All this did was confirm that they both didn't know what they were talking about. Shaking my head and pointing at the note, I mouthed, 'Pills – spelt – wrong'. Dad shook his head vehemently, denying this. I slowly and carefully mouthed; 'Pills spelt wrong, pills spelt P – I – L – L – S, not P – I – L – E – S'. I never went to the chemist that day, and it was years before I realised that he was right. If, at the time, I'd listened more

Boxes of my Christmas chocolate suppositories with a greeting inside the box lid.

Two reusable wooden suppositories. To use them the screw bung was removed and the thing was filled with ointment. The bung was then screwed back on one turn. The device was then pushed up your bottom. When in place, the screw bung was screwed all the way in. This caused the ointment to squirt out of the holes, thus getting the stuff in the right place.

carefully to his natural sound emissions, I might have noticed something was wrong. For men, an embarrassing side-effect of having piles is that they alter the pitch of their farts. They go from a reassuring masculine baritone rumble to a much higher feminine squeak because of orifice narrowing. Now you know.

Past the chemist shop was Thornton Square, from which ran all the streets to great places like Woolworth's, or Woollies. Brighouse, I think, had the first self-service Woollies in England. I remember once being confused by this name. We were about to go out when a girlfriend said to me 'let's go in Woollies'. I thought this very strange, suggesting we change and it was the height of summer. Was I going like Granny?

The place I loved to go to was a shop called Penny Denham's. They sold toys and upstairs they had every boy's dream: Meccano. Here I'd get more lead soldiers to replace the more severe casualties. In my play battles the main injury was decapitation, so most of my soldiers had their heads held on with matchsticks. This meant you could turn their heads to make them look around. Which I thought was a great advantage when approaching the enemy. I would point out this improvement to my chums, particularly when I was trying to do a swap.

Going round the town, I always had to walk on the roadside of Mam. When we met people who didn't know us well, they'd talk to Mam. They'd use embarrassingly exaggerated mouth and tongue movements, like a bulldog chewing a toffee. Or they'd shout. Not realising it doesn't matter how loud you shout at someone who's stone deaf. Mam would nod knowingly at them, as if taking it all in, and they would walk away. Mam would then turn to me and mouth, 'What say?' I'd shrug my shoulders, holding my palms up, Which meant, 'I have no idea'. This usually satisfied Mam because, if I had no idea, this meant Mam wasn't the only one who didn't know what was going on, so that was all right.

'The undesirable person pursuit cycle'

Snobs and the snotrag rat

(Superior persons and handkerchiefs folded to resemble rats)

I remember on one of the trips to town seeing men in Thornton Square with large patches on their backs. I particularly noticed them because Mam had impressed on me that patches denoted that you were poor and were the absolute 'no, no'. Here were men not only with patches in the middle of their backs, but also patches that didn't match their clothes. I seem to remember the patches were lilac coloured. Lilac was a colour never seen on a man in those days. They were, of course, prisoners of war and they seemed to be heading towards Auntie Annie's shop. They wouldn't be allowed in there with patches. We only called in at Auntie Annie's shop once; it was very scary. We felt like the old lady, overheard in Sainsbury's, who said, 'I've been abroad; I won't be going again'. Auntie Annie had a large furniture shop, 'Arthur Hill. 72–76 Commercial Street Tel: 77'. I remember her as a large frightening woman all in black with a lorgnette through which she looked down on us. The one time we visited her brass-knocker house in salubria, we noticed it didn't just have a number, it had a name: 'Lyngarth', very posh. She was the only person we knew whose house had a number and a name. One day, I thought, I'd have a house with a name. I'd call it 'Mullocks End'. Auntie Annie always made us take our shoes off. She considered us very inferior beasts. When I asked Mam why we

45

Auntie Annie

had to do this, she mouthed, 'Furniture'. From which I concluded Auntie Annie thought we were so unused to furniture we might take fright and start attacking it. Rumours of an incident concerning Dad, a poker and a smashed clotheshorse may have got to her ears. We didn't stay long; we thanked her (for her hostility) and left.

Mam would tell us that when she was a little girl she used to give her socks away to poor children. Poor children apparently didn't have socks. Did this mean that Auntie Annie was checking to see if we were poor people and she made us remove our shoes to see if we had complete socks, not just the bit round our ankles. Fortunately our socks were complete, they weren't even darned. Socks were very important to children. You were constantly being told to 'Pull your socks up and get on with it'.

So you had to have socks. If you didn't have socks to pull up, you couldn't get on with it. You couldn't start on the path to success. Socklessness and therefore the inability to pull them up apparently held poor people back. Disguising your socklessness by wearing Wellington boots was all right in winter but suspicious in summer, unless you were constantly tiddler fishing. These kids would develop terrible 'Wellie rash': a red ring round their calves where the top of the wellie rubbed.

The story of Mam giving her socks away was, I think, meant to convey that even as a child Mam had angelic goodness. When I returned home, once, without my woolly socks, I informed Mam that I had given my socks to the poor. I got a severe telling off. She said she didn't believe me and, because I'd returned with a red balloon, she suspected, no, she knew, I'd swapped my socks for the balloon and the rag and bone man now had my socks. She had a deeply suspicious nature, my Mam, and so had I. I never really believed she gave her socks away.

We were told many anecdotes like this. How the neighbours thought she was a snob because she walked with a ramrod straight back. When she mouthed, 'Snob', she'd straighten her back even more, stick her nose in the air put her forefinger level under her nose and flick it forward, as if flicking a drip off. She'd tell us that she walked with a straight back because she'd had nine operations. Lots of operations apparently lead to a straight back; I think the stitches probably tightened up and stopped her stooping.

The combination of Mam's straight back walk and the fact that she didn't speak to anyone made the locals at first think she was a snob. When they realised Dad and she were deaf, the attitude of some changed to one of resentment. 'Why should they come here and live like us?' I imagine the fact that a deaf couple could bring up a family just like they were doing was an affront to their abilities. Mam was quite pleased to think any odd behaviour towards her was because people thought she was a snob, that is, better than they were. Being deaf and not knowing your place can be extremely irritating to some folk. When I was a baby one of them showed their feelings by tipping a dustbin full of rubbish into my pram.

Mam told us about the boy on the road whose hair was allowed to grow long and how he was always dressed as a girl, until he was quite old. She didn't tell us why. We thought that perhaps his Mam wanted a girl not a boy. I later found that this was sometimes done as a ruse, to avoid boys being kidnapped by gypsies. Gypsies, apparently, it was believed, only stole little boys. Then there was the woman who cornered a rat. Her husband had to cut it from her throat with garden shears. So was Mam telling us not to corner rats or not to use garden shears to kill them? Did the woman live? We never found out. Dad would re-enact this story by folding his handkerchief into a shape like a rat: it had two little ears and a tail. He would put it on his left hand and stroke it with his right hand. The snot rag rat would be still and calm under Dad's gentle caresses. Then suddenly it would make a dash for his throat. Dad would grab it in the nick of time and put it back on his hand, to continue stroking it to calm it down. The tension mounted as we waited for the evil rat to make another dash for the throat. When it did, he'd grab it hard, throw it to the floor and stamp on it vigorously. When it was nice and flat and the drama over, he'd pick it up and carefully undo the handkerchief rat without the aid of a fork.

Mam would tell us about the woman who married a black man. As she told it, he'd married her because she had been his nurse and had saved his life. It was as if it was compulsory to do this. It happened in stories, so it had to happen in real life. Why else could they be together? This story was recounted every time we saw this

HOW TO MAKE A SNOTRAG RAT.

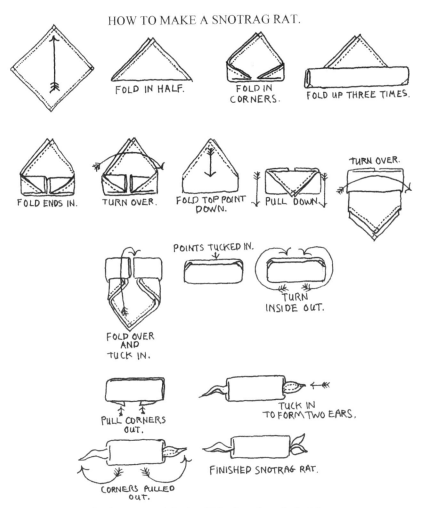

FOLD IN HALF.

FOLD IN CORNERS.

FOLD UP THREE TIMES.

FOLD ENDS IN.

TURN OVER.

FOLD TOP POINT DOWN.

PULL DOWN.

TURN OVER.

POINTS TUCKED IN.

TURN INSIDE OUT.

FOLD OVER AND TUCK IN.

PULL CORNERS OUT.

TUCK IN TO FORM TWO EARS.

CORNERS PULLED OUT.

FINISHED SNOTRAG RAT.

Put the rat on your left palm with the finger tips under the tail.
Gently stroke the rat with the right hand.
Flick the rat with your left finger tips making the rat jump up your arm.
Grab him with your right hand and put him back.

man and woman. He was the first black man I had ever seen and he had a beard. Beards were not the fashion. The only white man I knew with a beard was nicknamed Gillette for obvious reasons. He had a large beard and was scruffily dressed. He seemed to spend most of his time standing in the town bus station quacking like a duck. Despite this duck business, Mam said he only saw water twice a year when they took him in for a bath. Some said he suffered from 'Shell shock'. My Mam said he was like this because his wife had left him. Which is interesting because drakes don't quack when their mates leave. Only ducks quack. Perhaps he felt obliged to take on a female role now his mate had gone. Nowadays it's more difficult to spot the seriously bewildered and yonderly talking to themselves. They disguise their affliction by holding a mobile phone to their ears.

I decided that when I grew up I would have a beard. Black men and beards were great. Whenever I asked, 'Where's my Mam?', the neighbours always said, 'She's run off with a black man'. It must have been wishful thinking on their part. She always came back before I got the urge to quack, and she was always alone. I stopped asking her where she'd been. The stock reply everyone used was 'There and back to see how far it is'. Mam's response was more irritating. She just tapped the end of her nose with her forefinger; this meant 'Mind your own business'. Sometimes she tapped the side of her nose; this meant 'Wouldn't you like to know. I know and I'm not telling you'.

I seemed doomed to only know part of what was going on, never to know the full story. Mam always used the anecdotal, partial information method to tell me about the world and to teach me things, for example how to tell the time. She would point at the numbers on the clock and mouth them off from 1 to 12. Then, pointing at the number 1, she would count up in multiples of 5, pointing at each number in turn, till she got to 30 at 6 o'clock. Then she'd count down in 5s from 30 to 5 at 11 o'clock. Turning to me, she would then nod, signifying 'That's all you needed to know, to tell the time'. I'd say, 'But how do you tell the time?' She would then repeat the 5 times table up to 30 and down to 5. I managed to get the hours, but not the 5 times stuff. Consequently I could not tell the time, but crikey was I good at my 5 times table. Eventually it clicked what she was talking about, by which time I was 15 years old and at Hipperholme Grammar School. At that age I still didn't know the months of the year or the alphabet. I knew the vowels; Mam taught me them in sign language. I was glad she did, it made me appear brighter than I was when the class were asked, 'What are the vowels?' I knew. No one ever asked if I knew the alphabet.

FINGERSPELLING ALPHABET.

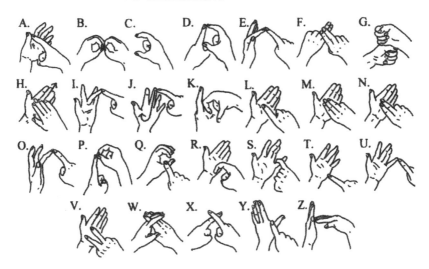

Willy Threewaters

We all lived at 99 Thornhill Road, Rastrick, Brighouse. The road was a bus route to Rastrick, which wasn't a problem except on Mondays, which was washday. The women strung their clothes lines, straining with a week's washing, across the main road. Only their better stuff was put out on the line. Anything not up to scratch was dried indoors. You had to keep up appearances. The bus would stop at the barricade of wet washing. The driver honked his horn. All the women would rush into the road and help each other to hold the washing up with the clothes props so the bus could pass under. They wielded the props like the pike men of old and were just as scary. Fortunately the bus was always a single decker. All this was done quite amicably; after all, the washing had been hung there long before the bus route started.

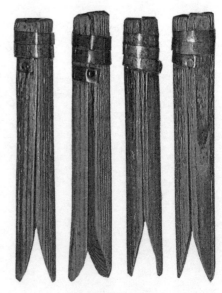

Gypsy clothes pegs

Monday was washday but it was accepted that the bus must get through; the dustbin wagon was a different matter. It once turned up on Monday and all hell broke loose. These women were creatures of cast iron habit. Monday was definitely not dustbin day, 'Wash on Saturday wash in need, wash on Sunday sluts indeed'. Everyone knew that. You had to wash on Monday and nothing was going to change that routine. The washing was now done and out drying; only rain could make them take it in now. No mucky dustbin wagon was going under it. They were not afraid of burly bin men; as they put it, 'Wi noan flayed ut bin men'. The bin men recognised the womens' body language, the folded arms across an ample pinafore covered bust. The body language was saying 'Watch it, keep back or we'll unfold these arms and reveal our even scarier busts'.

The men knew, just touch any one of them there busts and, before you knew where you were, you'd be up in court for the dreaded offence of 'Grope'. You don't seem to hear much about 'Grope' now, but then it was spoken of in whispers. The ladies' arms stayed folded and the dustmen and wagon retreated from the row of threatening elbows.

The women shouted after them, 'Sling yer 'ook barmpots'. That is to say, 'Please go away you mentally challenged chaps'. The last defiant cry came from the retreating driver. Safe in his cab, he shouted 'You'll be getting a letter'. Back came the women's instant reply, 'You'll be wasting a stamp'.

The washing won the day and the women carried on 'Kalin n' calling'. 'Kalin' was gossiping and 'Calling' meant saying unpleasant things about people behind their backs. They savoured their victory while they watched for the next bus or rain.

Fortunately for the neighbours, Mam, with her deafness and bad eyesight, didn't have to watch out for buses because she didn't hang our washing across the road. Our washing was hung across the ginnel at the back of the house. We used gypsy clothes pegs. These were made from two pieces of carved wood held together with a nailed-on strip of tin can. These pegs were gradually replaced by metal springed wooden ones.

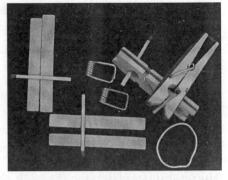

I found that if you took the spring off the peg, the little groove it rested in just fitted a matchstick. With a box of matches and a few dismantled pegs it was possible to join them together.

Two matchstick flickers made with elastic bands and spring pegs

I made a model of Donald Campbell's 'Blue Bird'; Miss Pring was really impressed. The bit I liked best about washday was bringing in the clothes line. Mam taught me how to wind it in a figure of eight loop between my thumb and elbow. The end was wrapped round the middle and pushed through the top loop to hang it up. I thought I looked like a pretty slick cowboy winding in his lasso.

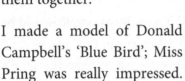

Question: 'How do you make a lasso?' Answer: 'You nip her bum'.

The bit I hated most was folding the cotton sheets. These were all ironed with a flat iron heated on the gas cooker wiped clean with a damp, hissing, knitted string dish clart [dish cloth]. Mam would give me one end of the sheet, I'd take a corner in each hand and back away from Mam to stretch the sheet out. Every time I would be holding the wrong corners and there would be a big twist in the middle. Mam would look up to her God despairingly and I would swap the corners over. She never got it wrong. It was always me. We'd pull the sheet taut, fold it in two longways, then in two again.

I would then walk to Mam and hand her my end, then I'd pick up the end hanging down. She would then fold it in two again, before handing it to me to put on the table. I then got the next one. It was all rather like a square dance with only me dancing. It all comes back when I see American soldiers on TV folding the flag to give to the widow.

Line from an American Square Dance chant:
'After the clap, change partners.'
Which I always though was a good idea!

The washing was done in the back cellar. On the gas stove would be a saucepan of bubbling primeval glutinous soup; this was boiling salt water in which would be the week's stiff, snotty handkerchiefs softening. Germs had to be given no chance. All the water was boiled on the gas stove and put with the clothes and Oxydol or Rinso soap powder in a galvanised dolly tub. It was then agitated with a posser. Our posser was a stick with a copper bowl shaped thing on the end. Held upright, with the bowl at the top, it looked rather like an Olympic torch. This copper thing had holes in it, so when you plunged it up and down, the water squirted through and it made the soapy water frothier. The action was akin to a chanting native crushing corn in a mortar; only I don't remember anyone singing a happy possing song. Some older possers were all wood and were similar to a five-legged stool with a handle on top to push the stool legs up and down and twist in the tub. This visual image of five phallic shaped legs plunging up and down in a tub full of ladies' underwear led to the expression 'He's as leet geen as a posser 'ed in a tub full 'o' knickers'. Which roughly translated means he was more interested in sex than he should be. In other words, randy as a rabbit, politely put in the Latin 'Accensus libidine'.

Even at Christmas we couldn't avoid the obsession with washing, we sang: 'While shepherds washed their socks at night, All seated round the tub, A bar of Sunlight soap came down and they began to scrub'.

Women were such slackers then.

Mam would complain about washing my mucky clothes. She'd hold them up dripping in front of me and, shaking three fingers under my nose, would mouth 'Three waters'. This meant she had to wash the item in three lots of clean water, rub it up and down the rubbing board with a bar of hard soap, and rinse it till it was clean. The rubbing board was a wooden frame with a small sheet of corrugated galvanised metal fixed in it. All the stuff was then put through the big iron mangle and squeezed almost dry. In the holidays, when I was tall enough, I had to wind the handle. The glamour soon went out of that job. Mams would say: 'The kids are hard on their clothes'. None of them ever thought they were wearing the clothes out in the washing. White washing was made to look optically whiter with a hint of blue, put there by using a 'Dolly Blue' in the water. This was a small cloth bag of blue stuff tied on a little stick. I suppose it was called that because it looked like a little wooden doll with a white crinoline.

The Dolly Blue was also used to treat fleabites and bee stings because the Dolly Blue was alkali and neutralised the acid bee sting. Wasp stings are alkali, so they were wiped with vinegar. We children were always advised not to move and to keep very still when wasps and bees were about. If we did this, we were told, they would go away. Because I had very bright orange hair, I tended to attract butterflies, bees and wasps. I think they thought I was some kind of geranium that needed pollinating. One day a wasp approached me. I remembered the advice and stood still. Because I wasn't moving, I think this confirmed in the wasp's mind that I actually was a large geranium. The wasp hung around to reconnoitre. I stood very, very still while the wasp circled my head; like the plane flying round the Empire State building in *King Kong*. My mouth relaxed and fell open. The wasp, like a spacecraft circling an alien ship, must have thought that's the entrance, and he flew into my mouth. This instantly triggered in me some deep animal feeding instinct and, before I could think, I automatically closed my mouth. The wasp, realising the door had shut, turned and stung the door. Whereupon I opened my mouth and he flew out. I ran to Granny screaming in agony. My bottom lip was now slowly inflating. She gripped me firmly by the hand and, dragging me into the back cellar, picked up the Dolly Blue. 'Was it a bee or a wasp?' she asked. I now looked like a plate-lipped woman from Africa, with a super sulking lip. 'Wathsp, wathsp, wathsp', I lisped. 'You sure?' 'Yeth, yeth, wathsp.' She put down the Dolly Blue and grabbed the vinegar bottle.

It wasn't real vinegar; no one had real vinegar. It was acetic acid dyed brown. It added some acid flavour but its main function was to drench and kill anything that was still alive on or in your food. 'Oh no!' I cried, and shut my mouth tight; but it was no good, my lip was stuck out, exposed like a shelf. Granny liberally splashed it with vinegar and, picking up the Dolly Blue by its stick, waved it at me threateningly and said, 'Are you sure it wasn't a bee?' 'Wathsp. Wathsp', I said, with my lip wobbling as I tried to spit the vinegar off furtively on the 'Thsp' in 'Wathsp'. I was used to vinegar on my lips, Mam used to dab it on my cold sores to dry them up, but not in this quantity. Granny was trying to pickle my lip; it was like an over-seasoned uncooked sausage and getting bigger.

A day later, just before I thought I was going to have trouble looking over it, the lip started going down. I was told what a lucky boy I was; if I'd been stung on the tongue it would have swollen and choked me to death. For days I wouldn't leave the house without a rolled up newspaper. The slightest buzz would send me running in a panic, even the sound of someone walking past in corduroy trousers.

Which would you rather bee or a wasp?

59

Duffers

(Frightened persons)

The back ginnel was unmade and very stony. Along the side where the houses were, there was a flagstone path. Over the years, the ginnel had been slowly rain washed and worn away, so the flags were undercut at the kerb edge. A bloke moved into the end house. He had a large motorbike, which he insisted on pushing along the pavement. The weight of the bike was causing the stone flags to subside even more. Dad would mime to this bloke that the path was sinking and would he please push his bike on the road and not on the pavement. The bloke would smile and nod to indicate he understood, and just merrily continue to push his bike on the collapsing path. It was quite clear he had

Doreen and me sitting with Lassie, the dog Granny said was a 'House agent' (Alsatian). This is the path Dad built the wall across to stop a neighbour pushing his motorbike along it.

no intention of taking any notice because he thought Dad couldn't do anything about it. Till one morning on his way to work, he pushed his bike as usual, along the path, and was confronted by Dad's traffic-calming solution.

The Chinese had done it. The Romans had done it. Now my Dad had done it. In the night, he'd built a small brick wall across the path. The bike bloke was beside himself with fury. He couldn't get through. The wall was only a foot high; you could step over it, but you'd have to really struggle to get a motorbike over. Of course this meant everyone who lived at the end of the row had to step over it, going to and fro, and they weren't pleased. The ginnel was unlit at night and the little wall was a worse hazard than a big wall; you don't trip over big walls. They all insisted he remove the wall.

The bike bloke thought he'd won the day. Dad removed most of the wall, but left a section against the house. He explained it was a step for Mam to reach the hook for the clothes line. Everybody thought this was quite reasonable. The bike bloke could still push his bike on the path but, because of the clothes line step, he could only do it if he walked very awkwardly in the road. He soon tired of this and started using the road. I went back recently to see if the step was there. It's gone and the ginnel's been covered in concrete.

Ginnel Enders are seldom guinea lenders.
(E. A. Lodge 'Odds and Ends')

The house was a three-storey end-terrace one. It was built into, not on, a steep cobble stone hill called Capel Street. Because it was so steep it had to be cobbled. You needed the cobbles to get a grip coming up, even in fine weather. Going down, you definitely needed them to stop you developing too much momentum and running into the traffic on Bramston Street, the main road at the bottom of the hill. It was so steep you didn't need snow to sledge down it.

One winter, the father of a boy called Garth gave me a small purple sledge. What a wonderful man he was, giving his kid a great name like Garth. Garth was my 'muscley' strip cartoon hero from the *Daily Mirror*. True, my name was in the *Mirror*, but it didn't seem quite the same as 'Pip, Squeak and Wilfred'. I was thrilled to bits with the sledge. Needing childish instant gratification, I'd got the sledge, now I needed a hill. Where was the nearest hill on my way home? Capel Street, of course. I thought I'd sledge down to our house and show Doreen my prize. So I lay down on the sledge and instantly I was off like billio [very fast]. It was like being on a pneumatic drill going at a hundred miles an hour. The cobbles almost rattled my teeth out. Before I could think, I'd not only gone past our house but I'd crossed the main road at the bottom, mounted the pavement, coming to an abrupt halt when I hit the rocks round the gents' toilets in the recreation ground. I'd missed the traffic crossing the road.

View up Capel Street

I couldn't believe I was still alive. I was ecstatic and fed up at the same time because no one but the cursing motorist on his way to Rastrick had seen me do it, and he probably thought I was a fast-moving hedgehog. This lack of an audience happened again later in my life when I saw the UFO outside the Junction pub in Marsh and there wasn't a soul about to tell. You get those knowing 'Oh yes, pull the other one' looks.

I had sledged down the hill and so I dared my friends to do it. 'You do it first,' they said. I told them I'd already done it, but no one had seen me, so they insisted I do it again. I, of course, declined. I'd done it once and once was one more time than them. They were 'duffers'. If you didn't do the dare or what we called a 'duff,' you were a duffer. This lot might be duffers but they were not daft duffers.

Across Bramston Street, at the bottom of Capel Street, were three recreation grounds. They were bordered with strips of ground planted with bushes, privet, holly and rhododendrons, what we in later days called homofoliage round the toilets in Greenhead Park. Armed only with a matchbox, I'd go hunting the dreaded Colorado beetle (*Leptinotarsa decemlineata*). There were posters in school saying if you found one you had to take it to the police station. These striped invaders from America were threatening our potatoes. 'So what?' we thought, till someone pointed out chips were made from potatoes. This made it serious. I longed to find one, but I never did.

Once I found an amazing 4-foot high dandelion growing through one of the bushes. It had forced its way to the light through the branches, which helped to support its long thin stem. I had my doubts that picking dandelions caused you to wet the bed. If it was true, this lanky lad looked like he'd cause you to leak a lake. Better safe than soaking, so I left the mutant where it was. Nowadays we'd blame it on radiation from Chernobyl.

The park borders were edged with large rocks. The soil was often dug over and weeded, leaving nice clods of earth. We used these dried clods as pretend hand grenades. When they hit the back of some unsuspecting kid's head, they exploded beautifully into clouds of dust. Saturday, the day after bath night, was the best day to bomb kids. It was doubly satisfying knowing the kid would get a further shouting at because his hair had only just been washed.

The bottom recreation ground had the swings and roundabouts. There was the roundabout called the 'Witch's hat'. It was a cone-shaped open metal frame, balanced on a pole. Just like a witch's hat on a stick. Round the base of the cone there were plank seats where the brim of the hat would have been. We'd stand all round it and, gripping the seat, we'd try to lift it off the pole. We never managed to do it, so we had to be content just to use it as a roundabout.

The other roundabout was a heavy wooden disc, low to the ground. The top of this was divided like a cake into sections by waist-high handrails. Doreen would hold one of these handrails and push the thing round. Sometimes she'd hold the rail and, with one foot on the roundabout, she'd use the other to push us round, rather like propelling a scooter. That was the lazy way; I preferred her to run round pushing it. Sometimes she got it going so fast that she couldn't jump on. While she did this, I would be lying down in one of the sections and leaning over the edge holding a piece of sandstone against the concrete base. This was like a giant angle grinder. The stone was ground nice and smooth. We were making miniature tombstones for any dead creatures we might come across or tread on.

We were very fond of playing proper burials. I loved making those tombstones but Doreen wasn't too keen. When she was enthusiastically pushing the roundabout, I suspect she hoped the centrifugal force would throw me off and we could have a big boy burial.

Blessed be the Father, the Son and in the hole he goes.

Another device on the rec. [recreation ground] was an evil-looking thing called the 'Rant'. Why we called it the Rant is a mystery to me. It was a long thick plank of wood, which you sat astride holding onto a looped metal handle. The plank was supported at each end by swinging metal bars attached to supports. The whole thing was in fact similar to a swinging battering ram. To make it swing, kids would stand on the end of the plank holding onto the bars. They'd lean backwards and forwards, pulling and pushing against these bars. This would cause the plank to swing back and forth horizontally, like a ram. Perhaps Rant was a corruption of ram. Girls were usually passengers. Not because of the weaker sex thing, they were reluctant to do the swinging because their skirts blew up and you could see their knickers. I understand that on posher recreation grounds young ladies rode the Rant side-saddle. The middle seat on this thing was ominously called the 'Coffin' because it was said that if you swung it high enough, the occupant of the Coffin would hit the top cross bar, smashing in his head.

Knowing this, it was generally thought a good idea to persuade smaller kids to sit in the Coffin. It would take two kids if they sat back to back and, looking round, it was clear there were plenty of little kids to spare. The kids would be promised, with much crossing of hearts and swearing to die, that the Rant would not be swung too high. On one occasion I was that kid. That day the rec. wasn't too busy. Most of the kids were at the Rant. Being curious, I gravitated towards where the action was. The seats on the Rant were all occupied except one. It was like 'All aboard the Skylark'. 'We're ready to go, just one seat left.' 'Get on kid', they said. Then, to reassure me, 'We're not going too high, swear to God hope to die'. I didn't want to appear scared in front of those older kids so I got on. The kids on either side were facing inwards, towards me, which was strange. They were watching me with great interest. Then I realised I was in the middle. I was in the Coffin. Slowly the 'Rant' swayed back and forth. Should I get off? It gathered momentum. Then it dawned on me, could this be the day they intended to find out if the legend of the Rant was true? It was now too late to jump off. All my cries of 'You promised' and 'God'll get you' were ignored as, crouched as low as I could against the handle, I swung towards the head-crushing crossbar. 'God'll get you, God'll get you', I shrieked.

It looked like God would be getting me first. Swinging up closer and closer to the bar was terrifying but swinging back, which you'd think would give temporary relief, was worse. I was swinging backwards towards the other bar that was swiftly approaching the back of my head, unseen. I closed my eyes waiting for the end. Then suddenly I realised I was swinging away from it, back down. The relief; I was alive. I hadn't hit. I opened my eyes. It wasn't over; I was swinging back to the other bar, right up close. I'd then swing away, down in an arc, and backwards up to the other crossbar. Up close I could see, on either side of the bar, were metal plates thick with black grease, except where they rubbed against each other they were shiny, like the blades of new scissors opening and shutting. Back and forth I went. 'The pit and the pendulum' had nothing on this. The lads working the Rant had now got it so high that they were almost bashing their heads on the kids crouched in the end seats. On the ordeal went, back and forth, back and forth. They really tried, but they just couldn't get my head any nearer the bars. They used up all their strength and eventually had to give up to rest. Gradually the Rant slowed down. Not waiting for it to stop, I lifted my leg over as if I was on a moving horse and, on the forward swing, jumped off. The momentum caused me to run in the direction of home, so I continued that way without looking back. I knew it wasn't beyond this lot, now they'd smelled blood, to tie me on and have another go. They were, after all, from Brooke Street. Much later I realised the metal plates were a kind of governor that made it impossible for the Coffin to smash against the bars.

There was a sign on the swings saying no one over the age of 14 could use them. In the earlier days, they were all chained up at night. So 15-year-old kids couldn't sneak out and swing in the dark. Happiness was rationed too.

One day, in the summer of 1951, two workmen appeared on the bottom rec. and started building a large mysterious object with green metal tubes, setting them into concrete. This activity gathered a crowd of kids fascinated by this strange construction. We couldn't work out what it was. We all debated in loud voices what it might be, hoping one of the workmen would hear and tell us. The men appeared to be hard of hearing and just carried on building. So we started shouting suggestions. 'It's a rocket launcher.' 'No! It's for hanging bandits.' 'It's for hanging clothes. It's a clothes drier.' This last remark shut us all up. We turned to look at the little girl who'd said this and, in the ensuing silence, one of the workmen turned and said, 'You're all wrong, it's a wim-wam for ducks to perk on.'

This completely baffled us; none of us knew what a wim-wam was. I had never ever seen a live duck anywhere, not even on Uncle Bob's farm, and what on earth was 'perking'. The workmen ignored all further pleas for information. We all were desperate to know when the ducks were coming so we could find out what perking was. All we got were smiles, knowing nods from the workmen, and an occasional 'Wait and see'. Two days later it was finished. The workmen silently walked away and left it, like the Trojan horse. We all stood round looking up at it in wonder. The less worldly wise amongst us thought the men had gone to fetch the ducks. Others said that was stupid and were looking expectantly to the sky, waiting for the ducks to fly in. We older ones realised they waited in vain. The ducks would not be coming. The men had fibbed to us. This 'wim-wam for ducks to perk on' looked suspiciously like a large playground slide. We looked at it, wondering what to do. Daring each other to climb the steps and have a go. I said, 'I'm not flaid [scared]'. While some of the kids that couldn't believe adults lied, watched out for attacking ducks. I gripped the handrail tightly and slowly climbed the steep steps to the sky. The kids all shouted and cheered me on. When I got near the top, I peeped over the edge and looked down the shiny brass slide disappearing below me. 'Ummer [hell]', I thought, 'it's blooming high'. In the local parlance I 'ockered', in other words I paused to consider. I then retreated down the steps. The kids all booed and said I was flaid. I was a duffer. I daren't go down the slide. I was a 'Scaredycat'. To which I replied, 'One of you sods shouted ducks. Who shouted ducks?'

Before I got a reply, Brefni had set off up the steps. He was quickly at the top and, ignoring my shout of 'Ducks', without pausing he slid down the slide. After that everybody had a go. So Brefni was the first to go down the Bramston Street slide. He was 'Chuffed' and I was 'Sluffed': he was pleased and I was not. No one can ever take that triumph away from Brefni. He was first to go down the slide. But I was the first to come down the steps and no one can take that away from me.

The middle recreation ground, I was told, had been tennis courts. It must have been real hard-man tennis because the ground was covered in crushed red bricks. We called it the red rec. It wasn't used as a tennis court anymore; I wonder why.

They say everybody remembers where they were when Kennedy was assassinated. I don't. I do remember the 6th of February 1952 at junior school, when a lady teacher opened the door and announced King George had died. In 1953 I remember some stranger in the distance shouting to tell me that sweet rationing had ended. What he actually shouted was 'Spice rations off'.

Living amongst the close-packed houses and hills, nothing was a long way off. There was no sense of things far away. We were like pygmies in the jungle. There were no distant views. Adventure, mystery and danger were near. The red rec. was the largest empty space around; it demanded that something should be done with it. So, I was standing alone in the middle of the red rec. sucking an Oxo cube. 'Nature abhors a vacuum.' All our mams knew an empty mantelpiece was easier to dust but it was an abomination and must be filled. Minimalism was definitely not the thing. This large empty space jarred with me: it had to be filled. As a little boy, all I could do to solve this urge was to stand in the middle with my arms stretched out as far as they would go. Whoever shouted to me must have thought he's out of touch, he won't know rationing ended, and I didn't. I set off running to the wooden hut sweet shop, not too fast. If you fell on the red rec. you knew about it. I can't think why I ran. I hadn't any money but somehow I couldn't just stand there. I felt obliged to react to the news.

The Saint John's Ambulance Band used all the red rec., they practised marching and playing. They were the smartest band I'd ever seen, in their black and white uniforms. Our most famous band was, of course, 'The Brighouse and Rastrick Brass Band'. I never heard them, they were on the wireless.

In the corner of the red rec. were the public toilets. The top rec. was the one where football was played. We came down here from Longroyd School to play football. I was goalie once. I didn't save a single goal. I made out I'd let them in on purpose. The truth was, I couldn't concentrate on the game because I was worried. Mam had made me wear my cousin Edward's football boots that he'd grown out of. She'd so put the fear of catching disease into me from wearing other people's stuff that when she said it was all right to wear my cousin Edward's football boots, I wasn't convinced. I suspected she was willing to put my life at risk rather than buy a new pair of boots. All the time I had them on, I imagined little corn and verruca germs attacking my feet inside them. The outside of the boots had to be regularly smeared with great gobbits of some sticky grease called 'Dubbing'; this was supposed to preserve and waterproof them. I imagined all the germs sticking on it like flypaper. Every time I see film credits with the name of the person that does the 'Dubbing', I think of some poor sod greasing everybody's shoes.

Between the red rec. and the football field was a road, which led to the bottom of the steps to Brooke Street. At the bottom of the steps, to the right, was a small building everyone called the 'Old Men's Parliament'. When we moved to Crown Street, there was one on the rec. there too. The old men used to meet there to smoke, read *The Brighouse and Elland Echo* and drink tea. One day they got more smoke than they wanted; in fact, they all got well kippered. We climbed on the roof and put a sod on the coke-stove chimney. We'd seen it done on cowboy films. It worked, just like in the films; all the old men came staggering out coughing. We were disappointed that, being under age, we didn't have access to firearms so we couldn't carry out the second part of the plan and shoot them all. Who said films don't influence kids? We didn't run away, we watched, all innocence. When they asked if we'd seen who'd done it we nodded and pointed up the steps towards Brooke Street. 'I might a' known', one old geezer gasped, looking up the steps. At the top of the steps lived the dreaded Brooke Street gang; anyway, they were dreaded by us. The steps also led to the secondary modern school, Rastrick Common. You need say no more, who else but one of them would put a sod on an 'Old Man's Parliament' chimney.

View down Capel Street, looking towards the recreation grounds, Brooke Street and the cliffs. The large rocks and toilets have been removed.

A Brighouse brick with a rival company's traveller's sample.

Here there be dragons and a blue tadpole

The Brooke Street area was one our gang occasionally, nervously, ventured into, but never alone. To us it was like the land on old maps that was marked 'Here there be dragons'. This area had to be crossed to get to the cliffs caused by the quarrying at Brighouse brick works. It was full of strange things and really tough girls and big scary boys who pushed drinking straws up frogs' bums so they could blow them up like balloons. The frogs couldn't submerge and some kids would fire catapults or throw stones to try and pop them. I never did it because I was worried about which end of the straw had been up the frog's bum. I'd also seen bubbles in the water so I assumed that, like us, frogs farted.

Putting your feet in wellies full of frog spawn for a dare is understandable. I was a bit apprehensive, though, about the friendly older boy we met under the cliffs. He'd remarked on Doreen's empty jam jar. Thinking we were perhaps kindred spirits, he said he no longer filled his jam jar with frogspawn. He filled his jar with worms, then he put his willy in it. The thought that instantly came into my head was, did he wash them first? I didn't ask. People could get very upset if you're critical about their personal hygiene, especially at the first meeting. I also didn't want to show too much interest in case he started inquiring if there were attractive worms where we lived, and I didn't want to watch a demonstration.

Anyway, it would take ages to collect the worms. I did wonder what Miss Pring, at her Friday afternoon hobby class, would have said about this hobby. We made our excuses and left.

A worm expert is an ogliokist, so I suppose he was sexually an ogliophiliac. If, of course, he'd used dead worms, he would be a necro-ogliophiliac. You don't seem to hear much about ogliophiliacs. In fact, I've never met another. He could still be lurking under the cliffs. I hope this doesn't put strange thoughts into any young man's head.

The cliffs were a source of wonder to us. We were told a woman had been chased off the top by a mad bull. We'd look up from the bottom of the cliffs, trying to catch sight of the bull. If he was there, he wasn't looking over the edge that day. So we'd search the scree at the bottom of the cliff, hoping to find her handbag or the dent

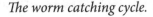

The worm catching cycle.

The device plays on the worm's fear of drowning. It mechanically recreates the sound and vibrations of a rainstorm. The worm emerges from the earth. The cloud visually reassures the worm it has done the right thing prior to being impaled.

where she landed. The cliffs had been quarried away at the base to supply clay for the Brighouse brick works. It was said a tramp was found frozen to death next to one of the brick kilns. He'd slept next to one that wasn't lit. They said the bogies from his nose turned to icicle candles. The thought of it always put me off those long grapefruit lollipops the colour of grey washing-up water.

To get to the cliffs we'd pass the White Horse pub. On the opposite side of the road was Cora Pickle's fish and chip shop. Behind her fish shop was a travelling circus cage. In the cage was a full-grown Himalayan bear called Bobby. He was black with a white 'V' on his chest. Cora told me years later that late one night a clown from the circus at Sunny Bunce's knocked on her door. (It was actually Hope Valley, a similar place near Huddersfield). He told her the circus had shut down and he needed somewhere to park his trailer and Bobby the bear. He said he heard she was in show business, so he thought she might help him out. Cora was the manager of a roller skating rink as well as running the fish shop. She let him park the big trailer behind the fish shop, temporarily. He thanked her and left, never to be seen again.

Bobby the bear stayed with Cora for a long time. He wasn't a great problem, except on one occasion when Cora had a difficult time persuading the ambulance service that she wasn't a hoax caller. Bobby bear had bitten her Dad. Bear bites are unheard of in Brighouse. Her dad had forgotten to knock on the cage door before going in with Bobby's evening fish and chips. He caught Bobby unawares, so Bobby bit him. How many times have you heard, 'Why didn't you knock? I could have been doing anything'. It's not known what Bobby was doing when Cora's Dad quietly entered behind him with the fish and chips. To be strictly correct, you should not knock before entering a room. The assumption is you're knocking because you suspect the person or persons behind the door is or are up to no good. Servants should not knock because their betters never, ever get up to no good behind closed doors. Unfortunately Bobby knew nothing of etiquette.

I eventually wrote a fictional play based on this story and the various attempts to pass the bear on to someone else. Bobby actually ended up in a private zoo. Cora's brother, David Metcalfe, maintains the bear came from Hope Valley at Huddersfield. David was my best man at my first wedding. I remember in the vestry having to sell him a corner cupboard so I could pay the vicar, or the wedding was off. It was a very nice corner cupboard.

Below the cliffs was an old, rusting, vertical boiler, steam crane and two large water holes we tried to sail rafts on, fish for tiddlers and collect frogspawn. By the top pond was a rail track where bogey trucks had been pulled back and forth by a wire rope. This rope went round a big horizontal wheel, which turned to pull the trucks up and down the track. To scare us off, it was said that a kid had been chopped in half between the rope and the wheel. This only made the place more interesting. The top pond was where I saw the big bright blue tadpole. I was so amazed I dived in to catch it, but it got away. It was my own mini Moby Dick; I searched and searched but, unlike Captain Ahab, I never saw it again and, unlike the Loch Ness monster, no one else has ever admitted to seeing one.

Wherever I went, if there was water, I got wet. On one expedition to the cliffs, knowing it was a dangerous area, we decided that, like the Boy Scouts and real expeditions, we had to be prepared. Unfortunately we didn't have anything much to be prepared with, certainly nothing that we could easily smuggle out of the house, like, for example, the coalhole chopper. We had to take something; it wouldn't be a proper expedition without any equipment. Doreen took her usual empty jam jar with a string handle, and I took the tin opener. Why the tin opener? Well how many times have you heard someone with a cigarette say, 'Have you got a light?' I thought there was a slight chance of meeting someone with a tin who might possibly want it opening and, if it was fruit, they might be grateful and share it. It also crossed my mind it could be useful if I somehow got imprisoned in that ominous old steam boiler.

When we got there, I decided that I'd keep away from the water and try to return from this expedition dry. I resolved to climb the cliff. The bull had not been seen, so we assumed it had been taken away to the 'Destructor' and executed for its crime. Its tail would have been made into oxtail soup. The chap at the shop had told me every tin was made from a complete tail. I imagined the rest of him would be nicely silver-papered in Oxo cubes. First I scrambled up the loose scree to the foot of the actual rock face. This placed me quite high above the ponds and my watching mates. The cliff itself now looked no height at all, so I set off climbing, thinking I could always change my mind and climb down if I got scared. I could tell the gang there weren't any footholds; they'd believe that. The climb was quite easy and was going well until I decided to look down. My nerve left me. I'd succeeded in climbing about two-thirds up the cliff, much higher than I intended. It was time to go back. With my face flat against the rock, I looked down to see where the lower footholds were. Because I was panicking, clinging close to the cliff face, I couldn't see anywhere to put my foot. I froze. I didn't want to go any higher and I couldn't go down. The only thing I could do was cling on, till weak with hunger I'd let go and fall off. For some reason, I felt I couldn't shout for help. My face was so close to the cliff I thought the sound could disturb it and perhaps it would shake me off or cause an avalanche. Under my breath I started praying. 'God, if you get me out of this I'll always be good. I'll never ask for anything again. I won't ever climb another cliff.'

I'd been in this position for what seemed like an hour, when the cliff must have thought this is boring, he's not doing anything, scare him on. The little ledge I was standing on started crumbling under my feet. Keeping my grip on the cliff, I tried to move my feet to a more stable bit of the ledge. This made it worse. Suddenly, the ledge fell away completely. My feet went with it; I lost my grip on the rock and the rest of me followed my feet down the cliff. It would be impossible to describe the fear and my emotions as I fell, with my face scraping against the rock. Fortunately the fall was only nine inches. I landed on the ledge below, my face still against the cliff and my arms and legs in the same position, only 9 inches lower. I was nearer the safety of the ground by 9 inches but my predicament was exactly the same. There was only one thing for it; I couldn't go down, I would have to go up. Foot holds and handholds above me were clearly visible, so up I went. Each foot I climbed up was an extra foot to fall down, but there wasn't any going back. I got to within 18 inches of the top. The cliff top was sticking out above my head, all held together with grass roots. Despair set in. I couldn't see how it was possible to get round this overhang. Now, I couldn't climb any further up and I couldn't go down. Then I heard this voice say, 'Hello'.

I leaned my head back and saw this lad looking at me over the cliff top. He looked about the same age as me. I'd never seen him before; he didn't go to my school. 'Hello', I replied quietly. I didn't want an avalanche adding to my problems. I'd seen that happen in cowboy films. 'There's a path that comes up here you know.' It was clear he was trying to be helpful. 'I'm stuck', I said. 'There's a path over there if you want to get up here.' 'Yes, I know. Do you think you could lean over and pull me up?' 'I don't know about that', he said, 'it's easier if you come up the path'. His head disappeared. Risking an avalanche. I shouted, 'If you don't help I'll fall off and get killed'. He was my last hope. I thought he'd gone. Then I heard him say, 'If you think that's best?' He reappeared and gave me his hand. He was kneeling down and, as he pulled me up, he assumed a crouching position. Because of the overhang, I had to lean out from the cliff to get round it. At this point he was holding both my hands. He was holding me with my feet against the top of the cliff; I was leaning backward in mid-air over the drop. We were in a state of equilibrium. Stalemate. He didn't have the strength to pull me up onto the cliff top. He had to make a decision quick, and he did. Being a courteous lad, he let me be first to know what his decision was. With a slightly embarrassed smile he said, 'I'm going to let you go'.

I think he had a good idea what my reply might be, so he didn't bother waiting for it. He let go. I then did something I've never done before or since; I fell, turning two perfect backward somersaults, before I thudded into the ground at the bottom of the cliff. The impact knocked all the wind out of me but I was still conscious. Here the story becomes bizarre. I'd landed next to the eldest Barstow brother who, for some reason, just happened to be sitting at the bottom of the cliff reading a newspaper. He knew exactly what to do: he lifted me by the waist, like a slack string puppet, and pumped me up and down by my pullover collar till my lungs refilled. If he hadn't been there, I'm not sure I'd have recovered. When I came round, my first thought was I'm in deep trouble. I reached down apprehensively to feel the top of my right leg; there was a lump. I breathed a sigh of relief. I still had Mam's tin opener in my pocket. I could safely return home. We could have tinned salmon mixed with bread and vinegar for Sunday tea and I, for once, hadn't fallen in the water.

The top of the cliff was a different land. The lad didn't come down the footpath to see if I was still alive. I didn't go up it. I never saw him again. He probably kept quiet about letting me drop, perhaps thinking he'd killed me. I hope he's gone into the priesthood. Perhaps he's a monk doing penance, pulling people up at that monastery that you can only get to in a basket hauled up the cliff.

View of the cliff I fell off

Auntie Ethel taught Doreen how to whistle but completely failed with me. She bought us toy ukuleles to lift our spirits but that appeared to have failed with me as well. The last memory of Doreen's ukulele was her beating me on the head with it. I don't remember the tune.

Ladies' vice cycle, prevents you falling when chaste.

The best cellar

A lad called Stuart told me he lived in a very nice bungalow. 'The rent is 15 shillings a week', he said. I said, 'That's very cheap for a bungalow'. 'Yes', Stuart said, 'we call them bungalows but most people like to call them prefabs'.

We lived in the lack of luxury at Granny Annie's house at the top of Capel Street. The part of the house we occupied was what I would now call an underdwelling. An estate agent would call it a cellar cottage. Then, everybody called it a cellar. It may have been a cellar, but to me it was the best cellar in Rastrick. It had two rooms. One room was completely underground; this was our kitchen, workshop, coalhole and bathroom, sans bath. Here, over a stone sink, was a single cold water tap. This was our only source of 'Corporation pop' in the house. The water, of course, contained the memory of our free homoeopathic remedy, lead. A well-known brain enhancer. Next to the sink was a huge iron mangle or wringing machine. A geared wheel turned its two splintering wooden rollers. Wet clothes were squeezed almost dry between them. The mangle has long since disappeared from our homes to be replaced by the spin drier. Along with it have gone such quaint expressions as, 'I've never laughed as much since Mam caught her tits in t' mangle'. The same accident with a spin drier doesn't have the same painful visual appeal.

If you didn't count the gas cooker, the mangle was one of the only two machines in the house; the second was the clock. I remember Dad bringing the clock home from Kershaw's and putting it on the mantelpiece. You didn't need ration points for second hand stuff. He was so proud. This was our first bit of modern technology and it was shaped like Nelson's hat. He mimed the shape of the hat with his hands. Since this could easily be confused with the shape of two bananas stuck in your ears, he enlarged on the mime by closing one eye and sticking his right hand in his jacket. This made it clearly Nelson's hat. Not to be confused with a similar mime with the two hands going in a downward arc. This was, of course, a Dutch person's hat, which I also hadn't heard of at the time. The sign for Germans, I've already mentioned, was one finger stuck up on your head like a spiked helmet. A Frenchman was a mime twiddling of a long moustache. If you stuck your thumb in your mouth, puffed your cheeks out as if blowing and, looking very serious, lifted your elbow up and down that was, of course, a Scotsman. The sign for Englishman was the sign you'd make if you were confronted by a vampire and you'd forgotten your crucifix. It was your two index fingers held up in a cross; it actually represents Saint George's cross.

In the ceiling of our room were mysterious, frightening, rusty meat hooks with bits of whitewash flaking off them. Uncle Wilf had similar, nice clean, ones on his upstairs landing ceiling. I remember once seeing a fitch of bacon hanging there. Along the wall opposite the fireplace was Mam's pride and joy, the sideboard. It was a wedding present from Granddad; it was a peculiar thing. When Mam saw it in the shop she said she would have it, but only if they put bowlegs on it. Where she'd got this idea from I don't know. So we had a sideboard that looked like it had rickets. We had two armchairs and a sofa. They were very chunky; dark brown, with black bits where the pile had worn off or had been picked off along with dried-on whatever. Because of their dark brown, black speckled appearance and huge slab construction, they looked as if they were made from great lumps of Christmas fruitcake.

Sitting in these huge chairs was a great pleasure; you could feel down the sides to retrieve other people's lost treasure. All the time thinking about how Granny Annie had come back from Granddad's funeral to find all the furniture slashed open by someone looking for Granddad's hidden illegal bookie money; or so Mam said. So you'd push your hand down further because, as every adult was prone to say, 'You never know'. Or, if you found something nasty, 'So now you know'. 'You never know' meaning, of course, you never know what you might find. The usual 'You never know' advice was to wear clean underwear when you went out. Optimists would perhaps think of a favourable sexual encounter, but it was the dread of being knocked down on the road and found to be wearing dirty underwear that was meant by this advice. I had to be particularly careful since I wore a vest but I was underpantless. When I saw people taking risks crossing roads I always thought they'd be wearing clean undies. Surely if Mams always sent the kids out to play in dirty underwear they'd be more careful and there would be fewer accidents on the road. 'You never know.'

With this thought in mind, I would push my hand further through the rough bristly moquette cushions, like a vet trying to deliver a baby gorilla. When I lost interest in grovelling down the cushions, I would return to grooming the sofa, looking for hard bits to pick off. When this reached a satisfactory conclusion, I'd start an examination of my short corduroy trousers, looking for dried-on food or crystallised, snail trail, snot. This was usually deposited on the trousers while saying, 'Look at those stars up there', You would point with your index finger upwards, making sure it went past your nose, wiping the mucus on the side of your hand. This would distract who ever was with you. Then you'd say, 'Look at those stripes down there'. Pointing to the ground, you'd wipe your hand down your trouser leg, depositing there whatever had been dripping from your nose. You don't see kids now with what we called candles hanging from their noses. Our street kids were veritable walking candelabras. When they snooked up, the mucus vanished up their noses, like frightened tubeworms under the sea. Dried snot had incredible adhesive powers, and picking it off corduroy trousers often removed the nap, creating a kind of corduroy alopecia. When Mam spotted this she would buy more mothballs. I think she thought, under cover of darkness, the moths grazed like sheep on the delicious short, grass-like nap.

When I couldn't find anymore crunchy bits to pick on my clothes, I'd check the condition of my knee and elbow scabs for crunchy bits to pick. These pleasures are now all in the past. I look forward to them again in the future, when I'm an old man spilling my food and falling over. All scabs and crunchy bits picked, I'd maybe look out of the window at the blank wall across the ginnel, the side of Mrs Jones' house. Beneath this window was a rising damp patch, creeping up from the floor, staining the wallpaper with a silhouette that looked like a huge grey mountain. Round the edge of this mountain was a narrow yellow aura, as if the sun was behind it. It was in fact a much, much better view than the one through the window. One day, after a trip to town (probably to buy more moth balls), we entered the house to find the view had dropped off the wall. The damp had parted the wallpaper from the plaster, the plaster from the wall, and the view gave up and dropped off. Very little glue was available in the 1940s; Gloy, Secotine, LePages and rubber cement were all unsuitable for sticking plaster. Auntie Zillah said she always used Nestle's condensed milk to stick the tiles back on her fireplace. Having a tile fireplace was very posh; they lived in luxury, in a council house. We pronounced it 'Nessels' not 'Neslay'. The damp mountain had shattered into too many bits to be stuck back. The bare wall had to be re-plastered. No sooner was this done, than the plaster fell from the ceiling above the door. I think Granny had been stamping in the room above on moths resting on her little stair-top rag rug. The expression 'Stamping ground', meaning where you abide, may come from stamping on various insect life, blackclocks [cockroaches], etc., found wandering round your house.

Fortunately when the ceiling fell down I wasn't banging on the door hook underneath. To explain, whenever I had a screaming tantrum, Dad would take off his big thick brass buckled belt. His trousers didn't fall down because he wore braces as well. Trouser security was very important.

Clothes were rationed and many people didn't have underpants. If they did, they had loops that went round the braces to hold them up; these they showed off, for a bit of swank. For all you knew, they could have been bits of white tape with no underpants. Some men wore their underpants so high that when they went to buy new ones they didn't give their waist size, they gave their chest size. At the time of writing, wearing your expensive underpants high and visible is back in fashion.

Anyway, Dad wore a belt and braces; why he didn't pin his tie to his trousers or, better still, stitch his shirt to his trousers, I don't know. Did this thought process lead to the invention of the coverall, boiler

When serving in India, Uncle Clifford was very concerned about trouser security. For complete security, I designed extra large thigh cycle clips to prevent insects crawling up your shorts.

or siren suit? Knowing his trousers were secure, he would wrap his belt round my waist, buckle it up, and hang me on the coat hook behind the door. He'd point a finger at me saying, 'Ergogert Whiff' and leave me hanging there till I shut up. Which was not very long, I can tell you. He'd take me down, point to the belt, then to the rusty hooks in the ceiling. This was the ultimate threat, 'Watch it, or you'll end up there my lad'. I never did.

Then off to bed in my one-piece pyjamas, that is, with the bottoms stitched to the top and a button-up flap in the back so you could go to the loo without taking them off. Some said the idea came from teaching trousers: the flap was to make access to your bare bum easier for the smacking thereof. This flap was sometimes called the escape hatch, which seems comical now, but in a freezing cold house it was best only to expose the bit that went on the chamber pot, or po as we called it. The best idea was to squat and hover slightly above the po. If you inadvertently sat on the super-cold rim, it was like being branded with a large red-hot iron from the 'Big O' ranch. That's, of course, if you were lucky and got to use a po. The only po in the house belonged to Granny; it was a posing po, a best for show po, so visitors had no doubts we had all the required amenities.

We didn't sleep in the cellar; we slept on the top floor. Before we set off, we had to have hot water bottles, not only to keep us warm in bed but also on the long cold journey up stone stairs without slippers. The rubber hot water bottles were about two-thirds full with boiling hot water from the kettle. Then they were held against the chest and, by pressing the bottle with the other hand, all the steam was breathed out. Before it breathed it back in again, you had to quickly screw the stopper back in. It was a strange feeling doing this. The bottle held against your chest, it was like expelling your own steamy breath and quickly choking your self before you could breath in. Off we'd go with the bottle's sides sucked in like Dad's cheeks with his teeth out. On the way the bottle would come back to life, swelling up with the steam left inside. If you overfilled or forgot to squeeze the bottle, it would swell up like a sumo wrestler about to burst. Panicking, I'd hand the bloated bottle to Mam, and she would gently release the stopper, the bottle would breath a sigh of relief, and all would be well; so onward and upward we'd go to the top floor.

We had to pass through Granny Annie Shaw's room on the middle floor. Because it was her house, she had the best room. Granny's room was level with Thornhill Road, so she had the use of the front door. Out of the front door was a small garden. Stuck up, vertical, in the middle of the garden was an earthenware drainpipe. The drainpipe was the chimney from our underground kitchen. Kids dropped things down it, mainly stuff they had about their person, usually handkerchiefs or balaclavas. Mam dreaded Bonfire night and the now-banned 'Jumping crackers'. The frog season was not fun, because all this stuff fell onto our gas cooker underneath and sometimes into the food.

I remember standing with some kids by a pond. The water was crammed full of frogs writhing in a mad mating frenzy. One kid, John, couldn't understand what was going on. He said to his mate, 'What's happening Norman?' 'Know-it-all Norman' answered, 'It's a war, they're having a battle, John'. 'Why are some on top of each other, Norman?' Norman thought for a moment, then said, 'They're carrying off the wounded stupid'.

Mam would always check the pans on the hob for little gifts, dropped from above. One day she showed us the frying pan. Round the edges were crozzled bits of earlier meals. Dad was going through a craze of frying eggs in holes cut in the middle of slices of bread. So the egg and bread were fried together in one lump. He'd seen a

butler do it in a film. In the middle of these crozzled bits was a disc of virgin white solid fat. The fat usually cooled flat and unmarked. Mam pointed mysteriously into the pan. You could see the first furtive tiny footprints on the edge of the fat, as if testing the surface of a frozen pond. Finding it safe, the footprints then went boldly in a straight line across the fat and off the other side of the pan. It was like looking down on a miniature Arctic. This lonely Captain Oates track of footprints was ominous. A flag stuck in the middle would have completed the illusion. Mam looked down at the single track; it wasn't the usual frog track. It was either a particularly large blackclock or a mouse, but was it alone? She furtively looked from the pan around the cellar. We three formed a protective circle round the pan, like a circled cowboy wagon train, waiting for the Indians. We looked hard and listened; Mam did not fry that day.

When Dad came home from work he was shown the evidence. Dad, being a countryman, was familiar with tracks and he confirmed it was a mouse. We hadn't really doubted it was a mouse. Extremely large cockroaches, small badgers, foxes and rabbits hadn't crossed our minds. Dad knew what to do. He sat up all night in the dim light of a candle, waiting for the mice to wander out towards his irresistible bait of precious Spam. Dad, being a skilled huntsman, then bludgeoned the mice to death with his special silent killing device, a Wellington boot. Come the dawn, before we got up, Dad had left for work. Mam entered the cellar kitchen to find the oven door open and, in it, the huntsman's offering. Hanging in a line by their tails, were the dead mice. This apparently would pass as a joke amongst country folk. Mam was screaming; but it wasn't with laughter.

'We have gas', they used to brag. Granny had a gaslight and we had one in the cellar, and that was it. The gasmen would come every so often to empty the meter; it took 'Bobs', that is shillings; sorry, 5 pence pieces. I always think of this when the name Gascoigne is mentioned. They always came in pairs and wore very long dark-blue Macintoshes. The expression 'A face as long as a gasman's Mac' comes from them. They were always really cheerful blokes. Piling all the shillings up into stacks of 20 to make a pound. One watched, suspiciously, whilst the other would get one stack right and then just make sure all the others were the same height. I thought it was a very clever way to do it. They then put it in a Gladstone bag, leaving a small pile for Mam to keep. Although we had gas, we still had to go to bed by candlelight. This could be scarier than going to bed in complete darkness, because the flickering light attracted moths. These threw huge frightening shadows on the walls. Moths seemed more prevalent then; I think there was more for them to eat. They'd moved into the towns, from the wild of country, for the easy pickings. You see everyone wore wool then. They seemed to laugh at camphor mothballs.

The moth spiking cycle.

The standing joke was you were better off throwing the mothballs or firing them from a catapult at the moths. If you managed to get a moth and squash it between your fingers, they were beautiful and silky, just like talcum powder. You'd have thought that some bright spark would have started a moth ranch and marketed moth talc. Nowadays the moth is not as numerous because we all wear unnatural fibres. The moth, in disgust, has moved back to the wild country to feed on its natural prey, sheep.

When eventually we got to our beds, we had to kneel at the side and say our prayers. Doreen was in Mam and Dad's room. I was on my own in a small side room. I could always hear Doreen and Mam saying their prayers, but never Dad. I don't think for a minute that he did them in sign language. The bedtime prayer was always the same, a list of people for God to bless. The prayer usually started with, 'God bless Mummy and Daddy'. Unless, of course, Mam or Dad were out of favour, in which case we left them out. It was always 'Mummy and Daddy', never 'Mam and Dad; only posh words for God, he was, after all, from the south. I think we probably learnt to pray at Sunday school. We were sent out every Sunday with a penny for the Church collection. We tried to change the penny for two ha'pennies or substitute a suitable sized button, washer or, best of all, a foreign coin. People often tried to cheat Uncle Tommy on his market stall by giving him German marks instead of shillings. He pretended he hadn't noticed because he could exchange them for more than a shilling.

Escaped to Switzerland

Mrs. T. Pratt, of 9, Thomas-street, Rastrick, has recently received notification from the War Office and also from the Red Cross Association that her husband, Dvr. Thomas Pratt, R.A.S.C., aged 28, escaped from a prison camp in Italy when that country capitulated and is now in Switzerland. Dvr. Pratt was taken prisoner at Tobruk in the summer of 1942. He joined the Forces in October, 1940, and proceeded overseas in March, 1941. The last letter Mrs. Pratt received from him prior to his escape was dated August 16, and came from Camp P.G.62/P.M. 3,200, situated in northern Italy. She is now keenly awaiting news from him from Switzerland.

Dvr. T. Pratt.

Uncle Tommy at the market.

The Saint Sebastian, Masochist Dart Club, T Shirt.

Reliquary cycle, with relic of Saint Salio, the hopping patron saint of amputees. NB The single pedal in deference to the saint.

Leruz geruz imbuks

(Shall we get our hymn books?)

Mam and Dad were not 'God botherers'; they never went to church and didn't much care which one we went to either. I'm sure they thought they were all the same. The first one we went to was Bridge End Congregational Chapel, where we were taught 'Thou shalt love thy neighbour as thyself'. Leviticus 19:18. Which, of course, is much easier to do if you have a very low opinion of yourself. We stopped going there when the older boys started throwing darts the full length of the Sunday school hall. I think they were trying to re-enact the martyrdom of Saint Sebastian, using us as moving targets. The trauma of this incident led me later to design a T-shirt for the 'Saint Sebastian Masochist Dart Club'.

The rich masochist demands menaces with money.
The poor sadist takes the money and just walks away.

Saint John's was our next port of call. We were reprimanded for calling people 'Sods', which we thought was a clod of earth. It was explained 'Sod' was short for Sodomite. We were told the Old Testament story of God destroying the cities of Sodom and Gomorrah and turning Lot's wife into a pillar of salt. Genesis 18:16. Furthermore, that sodomy was a rude act between men, very popular in Sodom but not with God. He punished Sodom because of it. The Sunday school teacher didn't even hint at what they got up to in Gomorrah, it was so bad. Even today I don't know what the act of 'Gomorrahy' is and how one got 'Gomorrahed'.

One kid asked if God could do anything. The teacher said he could. Whereupon the kid said, 'Can he make a stone so heavy he can't lift it?' The teacher was stumped. But God was listening and, so as not to be caught out by this Zen conundrum, God made black holes. Black holes, not heard or dreamt of in the 1950s. If that kid had kept his mouth shut, who knows.

The last time I went to a church service was at Saint Martin's, Brighouse. A fellow stood up in the pulpit and announced, in a very loud pompous voice, 'Welcome to the land of pomegranates'. Deuteronomy 8:7–9. I don't know what he said next because, for some reason, I was overcome with uncontrollable laughter (Fou Rire) and was escorted from the premises by a stern-faced elder who was completely baffled by my laughter, which of course made it a lot worse. It never crossed their minds I could have been laughing in tongues or, more fittingly, inebriated. Saint Martin is, after all, the patron saint of drunks and winos.

Dieu est mon cruet.

Salt and pepper set. Lot is the pepper pot.
The salt comes out of Lot's wife's nipples.

Dieu est mon cruet.

Lot taking advantage of his wife's condition to get a better view.

T' lavy

(The lavatory)

Unlike some of our better-off neighbours, we didn't have en suite potties, we had a communal white enamel bucket on the landing and it was strictly for peeing in. This was never said but was strongly hinted at by the fact that there wasn't any paper. Before I was born, the pee used to be collected for the mills to scour the cloth. The workers at the mill all pissed in the mill pot, so the mill owner owned it. Thus the expression 'They all piss in the same pot'. In other words, they work and support the same boss. The urine was called 'Wheeting', meaning wetting. I was told that a chap collected it in a bin on wheels called a 'Wheeting cart' or 'Sig Dilly'. The bin had a grill on the top to stop kids chucking bricks in and splashing him. The workers who walked up and down in the stale urine, pressing the cloth down with their feet, were called 'Walkers'. That's where the name Walker comes from. The collector paid a penny a bucket and a penny ha'penny if you were a red head; it was thought to be better quality. I would therefore, at that time, have merited a separate bucket; some are born special but at the wrong time.

Then, we were only a one-bucket family, but it was sort of still traditional for us all to piss in the same pot and not contaminate what used to be a potential money earner with solid waste products.

Anyone who did use it for anything else never confessed. That would have involved you in the indignity of carrying the bucket all the way to the outside lav, down three floors of the house; which wasn't too bad. Out the back door, turn left along the ginnel at the back of the houses. At this stage you could meet anyone. Turn left again down the yard, down the steps to the row of lavs. The bucket had a thick wire loop handle with a turned wood grip threaded on. When you held this grip it swivelled so you had little control over the swinging bucket. You tried to hold the wobbling, slopping, smelly bucket as far from your body as possible, trying to counterbalance it with the big iron key to the lav door in the other hand. Lav security was very important; you didn't want anyone sneaking in and putting his or her germy bottoms on your lovely lavy seat. When you unlocked the door, it always opened inward, so when you were sitting on the loo you could hold the door shut with your foot. Unlike a coalhole door, that always opened outwards so you could get more coal in and the door wouldn't get stuck. They knew about design in those days.

The loo itself was a pristine white-washed little room. The effect much desired in New York loft conversions. Above the toilet was an orange-coloured lead-lined wooden box. This was the water cistern; stencilled on it in black letters was the word 'JAPKAP'. After flushing the contents of the bucket down the lav, one might take advantage of the facilities to hide out and have a read. I always think my eyes have been affected by these sojourns. Not by what adults normally suspected young boys did in toilets, which was said to make them go blind. Suspected kids had big tubes pushed up their pyjama sleeves over their arms and hands. It was said the tubes prevented them scratching, but it was really an early form of emission control. No, my eyes were not affected by this 'Secret vice'. I always suspected they were affected by the toilet paper. This was neatly torn squares of the *Daily Mirror* hung on a nail behind the door. Mam once, to my delight, used torn-up *Dandy* and *Beano* comics. This episode was short lived; Auntie Ethel informed Mam this was definitely not the fashion. Not because I liked it, but apparently the colour came off on her bum. So we went back to using newspaper. It was always hung by the left-hand corner so it was at an angle. I would attempt to read the sloping lines on hanging squares. Now my left eye is slightly higher than my right. The consequence of this is that when I look forwards everything's normal, but if I look upwards I have double vision. This means that I have twice as many black clouds in my sky but in fine weather I have two suns. So I follow the Duke of Bedford's example and rarely go out when it's wet.

I once went to Woburn Abbey to talk about an exhibition of my model cycles. The invitation letter instructed me go to the front door and ring the bell. I don't know why I thought this strange. I arrived at the front door and rang the bell. The Duke didn't open the door; it was a superior guy I'd never seen before. Before he could say, 'Tradesmen's entrance round the back', I said, 'I've an appointment to see the Duke'. Then I suddenly realised I'd left my briefcase in the car. 'Hang on a minute', I said, 'I've left my briefcase in the car', whereupon I turned and went back to the car, leaving him standing holding the door open. I retrieved my briefcase and, looking back, saw he was still standing by the open door. I don't know if I thought there was a time limit to his services, like an automatic lift door, but I felt obliged to hurry back; so I started running. Just before I got to the door, I tripped and fell full length. I struggled to my feet, to find my white linen suit covered in mud. I didn't want to appear at all concerned in front of the smart flunky. So to be casual and distract his attention from my muddy suit, I pointed at the iron boot scraper at the side of the door and casually said, 'Is that where the Duke scrapes his wellies?' To which, he replied, 'His Grace rarely goes out when it's wet Sir'. As a consequence of this incident, I now like to hold doors open for old ladies, particularly if they are a long way from the door, for example at the end of a long corridor. They always feel obliged to hurry so the polite man is not kept waiting. Try it … it's great fun.

All that afternoon at Woburn, no one mentioned my muddy suit, not even the woman filling the brown sticky paper machine with Perrier water. They knew I'd come from the north. On leaving, I looked at my suit; the mud had dried a light brown. I brushed it off with my hand. It came off easily, there was not a mark left on the cloth. Even the Duke's mud was nicer than ours.

Later when I met the Duke, he was waiting to greet me at the front of the house. He was wearing a light-coloured expensive suit and holding a baby lion. The lion pissed on his suit and, unlike Woburn mud, it had a strong unfamiliar aroma. I was informed that the lion had pissed on his Grace. I assumed I was told because I came from the north and, being unfamiliar with nobility, they didn't want me to think that they normally smelled that way. This is another part of my adult life; the story involved a loaf of bread disguised as a parrot with an Oxo cube tied to it's head (to give the meat flavour), which was a publicity stunt that I did for Woburn Abbey during a meat shortage. It offered an alternative food for the hungry lions.

Granny, like the Duke, was also reluctant to go out to the lav in the wet. She had an old teapot that had lost its lid, so she peed in that. This ruse saved her a long walk to the outside lav. She just threw it out of the back door. Anyone watching thought she was throwing out tea. A normal occurrence in these parts, because you didn't want the tea leaves blocking the sink. She could, of course, have poured it down the sink. There was no chance she would do that; all sorts of diseases were about. Everyone was terrified of germs then. Even now, people don't like pee down their sink.

Granny wasn't the first to think of this personal potty idea. Upper-crust ladies used a similar method to Granny's teapot for pee disposal. They didn't use teapots, they used a specially designed container. It's sometimes seen on dining tables being wrongly used as a gravy boat, which it strongly resembles. Called a Bordeloue, it's named after a Jesuit priest, Louis Bordeloue (1632–1704).

Photo Duke Bedford crutch cycle

The Duke and Duchess of Bedford, with myself holding a 'Crutch criminal cycle'. The cycle punishes only the part of the body that commits the crime. The Duchess is activating a 'Tonsil kicking anti-thumb sucking device'.

A non-electrical 'Crutch criminal cycle'.

He gave such long sermons that the desperate ladies were obliged to use this device in their pews. They were able to do this discreetly because they had long dresses and wore split crutch knickers aptly named 'Ever Readies'.

Granny's old tea pot.

A 'Bordeloue' and a pair of 'Ever Readies'.

I thought of Granny when I came upon a market stall; on it were dozens of teapots, not one of which had a lid. I asked the stallholder what had happened to all the teapot lids. She looked at me as if I was stupid and said, 'Teapots, teapots? These are planters'. Some hotels without en suite toilets have the sink plumbed in at chest height to stop you peeing down them. In these rooms, the chairs always have cane seats, which give way if you stand on them. A broken cane seat in the room is a sure indication that some short guy has been standing on it to pee down the sink. Peeing down sinks is, of course, a man thing. Peeing in teapots is a lady thing. Granny would swirl the contents round the pot before throwing them in a great arc. Every drop shot out with great momentum, like an amber rainbow. That was the recognised way cold tea was always thrown. If I were told to chuck out the real cold tea dregs, I would stand with the pot at crutch height and pour it out slowly through the spout so I looked as though I was having a pee; this would amuse passers by. They'd take a second look, thinking they'd seen someone with a strange willy and an enormous 'Willow pattern' gonad.

Mam caught me once and I got a good leg smacking. She administered this by first grabbing my left arm high up with her left hand, so I couldn't escape. She silently signalled to me by pointing to the teapot and the floor that I should put the teapot down, carefully. This was all done calmly, so she hoped I wouldn't suspect what was coming. Then, when she'd positioned me to her satisfaction in the arena, she exploded in a smacking frenzy. Mam was facing the opposite way to me so she could get a good swing at the back of my legs with her right hand. Her arm swung down like a golf stroke; at the bottom of the swing her hand made contact with my calf and I was being propelled forward and upward. (How much more satisfaction golfers would get if the ball squealed when they hit it.) Mam's grip on my arm combined with me trying to escape just meant we went round in circles, a kind of centrifugal flagellation. I was like a dancer swinging round a

Maypole with Mam as the Maypole, she beating the rhythm in smacks followed by my cries of 'Oiya! Oiya! Oiya!' Her evil hand followed my legs like a swat following a fly. If the smack missed my legs she'd get me the next time round. Red legged, sobbing, I went bob, bob, bobbing around. When she'd had enough, she stopped and released me. I was indignant. With a quivering lip, I mimed bafflement as to why I was being chastised. This mime involved standing with my palms upwards, my mouth and eyes wide open in a look of astonishment, my head shaking from side to side in disbelief. Picking up the teapot and wagging her finger at me, Mam informed me that cold tea should not be disposed of that way because the leaves always stuck to the bottom of the pot; any idiot knew this, which is why they were laughing at me. If that was right, the punishment was a bit over the top. But she knew and I knew we were both fibbing. I realised there was some truth in what she said. Thus I became aware of the difference between being laughed at and being laughed with.

Sometimes Granny saved some pee to soak her feet in; she said it was good for chilblains. Urine was also considered good for curing deafness, but only deafness caused by wax in the ears. This cure involved persuading a strapping youth to pee in your ears. The warm liquid melted the wax and the strong flow washed it out. Finley Topham, a friend of mine's, mother got a book from the library. She said it was called 'Urinate power'. He thought it was about powerful pee-ers, and I don't mean strong noblemen. The book was actually called *Your Innate Power*. You don't hear about peeing in ears nowadays, but I expect with Prince Charles recommending alternative medicine it will come back, and his ears are built for it.

I understand nits are on the increase. I lived in terror of putting on someone else's cap or balaclava. It was drummed into me I'd certainly get a terrible disease, ring worm, nits, scabies or fleas, and if I broke a mirror while looking at myself wearing a borrowed hat I'd be sure to get the lot. Before modern stethoscopes, doctors used a 'Pinard stethoscope', a short trumpet-like gadget to listen to your heart. They always insisted the Pinard wasn't too short. They liked them slightly longer than the height a flea could jump (7 inches) because, if it was too short, they could easily end up with a flea in their ear. They still use the Pinard today on pregnant women.

In England, being polite, we use many euphemisms for the place we go to defecate: lav, privy, bog, loo, etc. One of the nicer ones is the aptly named 'Nessy', which is of course short for 'The necessary'. This word on one occasion led to some confusion. The father of a young truant received a letter from the school stating that, if his son did not attend school more often, they would 'Take the necessary steps'. When the father read the letter, he remarked 'They can take the whole shithole for all I care'.

THE DOCTOR SAYS:

There's a Simple Cure For This

The proper name for "itch" is scabies. Men, women, children, even babies may ket it, especiall in war-time, when all but itch-mites have a poor time.

The female itch-mites burrow in a little way beneath the skin and come out from their tiny holes when you get warm, on evening strolls. So if the irritation's worst in bed, just think of "scabies" first. The rash they cause is on the chest, armpits, forearms and shows best between the fingers, but no case shows it up on the head or face.

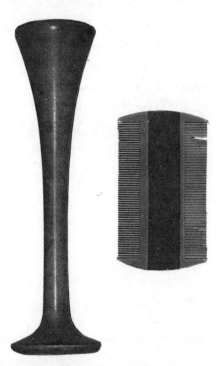

A nit comb, now euphemistically called a dust comb, and a Pinard stethoscope.

106

Wick wi' nits n' oss muck

(Crawling with nits and covered in horse manure)

Every Friday night Mam, went through our hair with a fine toothcomb, looking for nits. But before that ordeal we had to have a bath. All the hot water had to be boiled on the stove. One enterprising chap invented the rocking tin bath, with a curved bottom so you rocked the bath back and forth, economically swilling a minimum of hot water all over your body. But this was not for us; we didn't even have a normal non-rocking static tin bath. We had to make do with a zinc-galvanised barrel called a dolly tub; the same one Mam washed the clothes in.

After our bath we were dried with what are now called 'Exfoliating towels'. Then, all the towels I can remember were 'Extra-exfoliating towels', in other words rough as a rasp. Their function wasn't just to dry but to remove layers of skin with any stuck on germs. The towels were, in fact, more akin to cloth cheese graters than the towels we know today. In fact, I seem to remember Granny peeling new potatoes with one. When you were dried with one of these towels, you weren't just dry, you were a peeled person.

We also used exfoliating hairbrushes. Ours was similar to a hand mirror with a domed rubber bit instead of a glass. Sticking out of the rubber weren't soft bristles but lots of metal spikes, like a

Fakir's bed. I think it was inspired by an ancient folk memory, before brushes were invented and hair was brushed with a dead hedgehog. Mam would vigorously brush my hair with this thing. The spikes would scrape my scalp; the loose skin would fall like snow. Mam would look shocked and say, 'Scurf'. It sounded serious; for long enough I wasn't sure if it was one of her made up words. I couldn't ask anybody, they'd laugh if it wasn't a real word and be suspicious if it was. Even if they didn't know what it was, they wouldn't want to catch it. I'd be shunned if they weren't sure. What if it got worse, would I have to have my head painted with 'Gentian violet', like the kid at school with ringworm? (An early form of biological corn circle.) Then I heard of scurvy: had I got scurvy, was that what Mam meant? Five months without fruit and you got scurvy. My life was fairly fruit free, and the cure was to eat lots of fruit, particularly limes. How could I eat more fruit? I'd never seen a lime. The only lime I knew was the stuff they whitewashed the cellars with. It was years before I found out; scurf was what we now call dandruff.

Mam also used the brush as an information retrieval system. If she wanted information, she would threaten to smack me with the flat side. If she was really serious, she'd show me the spiked side. Then I'd tell her Granny had eaten the biscuits; she wouldn't dare threaten her with the brush. Once I tried to simulate measles by beating my arms with the spiked side, but it was too painful. I daren't do it on my face, I hadn't forgotten about the blind piano tuner.

The dodgy thing about hair washing was water temperature control. The water was boiled in the kettle. Mam's usual method of testing the temperature was to stick her elbow in the water. She couldn't, of course, do this with the kettle. She'd usually test it on the back of her hand, which was not very sensitive, and sometimes she didn't even bother doing that. In other households, if the person you're pouring on starts screaming this is a sure indication the water is too hot. This obviously didn't work with my deaf Mam. So the moment just before she poured the water was always very worrying. Usually she got it right, but occasionally we ended up with glowing, sterilised scalps. The nit comb was very painful those nights.

Hair drying was most fun. The towel was put over my head. I held the two corners at the front, whilst Mam held the two at the back and, by pulling up and down, like milking a two-teat cow, my hair was dry in no time at all. Then I was put in my 'Liberty bodice'. This was like a short-sleeved thick vest fastened up to the neck with rubber buttons. The only thing that was liberty about it was it was too short and your willy was at liberty to be viewed by anyone. Underpants were a luxury item unheard of for little boys in our house. I think the later popularity of the 'Teddy Boy' long jacket style was because of the deep trauma inflicted by the Liberty bodice. Little boys all wanted longer Liberty bodices, in fact drape Liberty bodices. When they grew up, their subconscious memory recalled the indignity of the short Liberty bodice, giving them a deep-seated desire to wear drape jackets.

Actors in tights have the same problem; I remember being advised to make sure you got a long doublet or learn to strategically place a pair of rolled up socks. A clean unworn pair was the best; thus the attraction of the enlarged pubic area was not spoilt by an olfactory contraceptive effect of sweaty socks. Old theatrical wardrobe tights usually have worn out elastic round the top. Once I had to wear a pair of these slack-top tights. A 13-year-old hand at the game said 'I always use ha'pennies on slack tight tops'. This I took to mean you slid ha' pennies round the empty slot and used them like buttons with your braces. I know there are clip-on braces, but we didn't have them then. Unfortunately, I only had two ha'pennies, probably my church collection money. I managed to scrounge a safety pin. The braces I fastened to the two coins at the front and the back I secured with the safety pin. During the performance, I was a demon writhing about on the floor; the safety pin came undone and stuck in my back. I then became the best demon writhing in the agony of hell because I wasn't acting. I was in agony; the pin was firmly stuck, out of reach, at the top of my back. When it came to the part where the demons had to stand up and shuffle off, I noticed I was getting curious looks from the audience. I would have liked to think it was admiration for my agonised performance. I looked down. Because the braces had come off the back of the tights, the front had dropped, giving me an exaggerated crutch. I heard someone chunter 'Over done it a bit with the socks haven't you?'

More than 40 years later, on Sunday 16th of January 2000, I was talking to Ron and Margaret Maris about the trick of using coins on slack tight tops. Ron said, 'I remember, you put a penny in the slot, twist it round to take up the slack, then you tuck the coin and twisted bit in the waist band'. I'd got it wrong. I sometimes wonder if I've misunderstood anything else and it will all come to me on my deathbed, when it's too late.

Friday night, after the bath, was 'Amami' night. Amami was a scented green hair setting lotion. I think it was made from gum tragacanth, a kind of glue. I thought the idea was that if Mam missed a nit, this stuff glued it to your head so at least you didn't give it to someone else. Whilst this was going on, Granny would be outside preventing 'The Angel of Death' and his germs passing over our doorstep. She did this with what appeared to be milk. She didn't use the ancient traditional method of painting a cross on the door. She made absolutely sure by dousing the entire stone step with this milk. She always had a milk bottle of this liquid with her. Later I found out it was the watered-down disinfectant Dettol. She washed the steps in this disinfectant so the germs wouldn't get in. I suppose it worked for the germs on foot but we had to take our chances with the flying ones. We didn't have an 'Air-wick'. That was a bottle that had a disinfectant-soaked felt wick you pulled up out of the top. This covered up smells and killed flying germs. Despite this, not only the first born, but the second born survived. When the steps were thoroughly scrubbed, she then rubbed the edges with a white stone till there was a nice white line round them. That told the germs so far and no further. The main part of the step she'd rub with yellow stone. I suppose this was so if any did get through they would leave tiny yellow footprints. These stones were called donkey stones. Incidentally there's a pub at Manchester airport called 'The Donkey Stone'.

You got your donkey stones from the ragman. Not to be confused with men of the cloth. The ragman came round with his donkey cart shouting; 'Rag, bones. Exchanging balloons and donkey stones for rags'. They were called donkey stones because that was one of the brand names; 'Donkey brand' nothing at all to do with donkeys. You would give the ragman all your moth-eaten woollies, usually cardigans that you couldn't use for the rag rugs or, if your Mam wasn't around, a second-best unloved balaclava. He would give your Mam a white or yellow donkey stone in exchange and you'd sometimes get a balloon. He'd then be off luring moths into the next street, shouting 'Rag, bones.' No one ever gave him bones as far as I remember. Perhaps this is why the knick-knack bones have vanished from the music shops. Some said the bones were for making glue. Perhaps that's why we don't see the stronger hair-setting lotions anymore. Any transaction you had with the ragman was better done quickly. The donkey was usually swarming with flies, carriers of disease. Hadn't plague come up from London in old clothes? They'd had plague in the old days at Hepworth, just outside Huddersfield. Hepworth was a long way off, probably a couple of trolley bus rides away, but who knew where this ragman came from. We all knew he wasn't a local ragman. Ben Shaw's horse could get from Huddersfield to deliver the pop; perhaps a fit donkey could get further. We all knew it was a long way from Nazareth to Bethlehem, 90 miles, but we'd been told a fat lady on a donkey had made it. These donkeys were obviously fitter than they looked. Stood to reason, didn't they use them on the beaches in Blackpool? Nothing second rate in Blackpool. Donkeys were important; hadn't the Germans bombed Meltham and, strangely, the only casualty was Dick Cummins' donkey Daisy. Obviously a great propaganda coup, the Germans must have known that Daisy pulled the ice cream cart.

Wherever the ragman came from, he wasn't trusted. They said he wet the rags and put stones in the pockets so they weighed heavier when he resold them. Not a bad idea, but we couldn't get away with doing the same to him. He only seemed to come in fine weather. Was there plague on the cart? Perhaps there were germs in one of the cardigan pockets? Definite contenders were those unsavoury knicker pockets. This fear of catching things was very real; diphtheria, scarlet fever, tuberculosis, ringworm, polio, fleas, nits and scabies were all about us. We were spared 'Tsu Tsu Gamushi' fever but very little else. 'Coughs and sneezes spread diseases' we were constantly being told, and the solution was to 'Trap your germs on a handkerchief'. Then what did you do, when you'd trapped them? Mam took no chances, she boiled them in salt water. Then there was rickets. I remember seeing old ladies with incredible bowlegs caused by rickets. Unkind folk would remark 'They couldn't stop a pig in a passage'. I suppose their egos were boosted a little by the song 'I love to go swimming with bow-legged women'.

The real scary diseases were the ones without symptoms. You didn't know you'd got it until you suddenly died. There was a lot of that about. Nobody had heard of 'Nut allergy' then. Could have been that, but I don't think so. We couldn't get the nuts anyway. Even in later years our 'Chocolate walnut whips' were seconds, without nuts. We called them 'Eunuch whips'.

Mam told me Granddad would not allow the family to be vaccinated or inoculated against anything. She carried on this tradition after he died. My arms are unmarked to this day, unlike all my contemporaries. We couldn't have 'National dried milk'. He said it was charity. Mam forgot about Granddad when it came to getting that delicious concentrated orange juice and, later, school milk. It was a miracle we survived. Paranoia was our preventative; we had it drummed into us not to put on other kids' hats, drink out of bottles or other people's cups and never to take a bite out of anything already bitten. I remember drinking my school milk and another kid complaining that I'd mistakenly picked up his part-drunk bottle. I'd sucked his straw. I was terrified, that was it, the end. I was like Quee Queg in *Moby Dick*. I just sat down and waited to die. I'm still waiting. When I do die, I know deep down the rot set in when I drank that diseased kid's milk.

*Dad, during the war, looking down the hole that
a bomb made in Meltham.*

Dad, in later years, looking suspiciously at a mine.

Our family was not alone in its paranoia. One woman wouldn't let her children go into public toilets in the town. The reason wasn't like today, in case they met someone nasty, but in case they caught something nasty or, as we thought, something nasty caught them. Wasn't it written on toilet walls everywhere? 'It's no use standing on the seat, the crabs in here can jump 6 feet (183 cm).'

We knew all about crabs, we'd seen huge dead ones at the crab dresser's on Pong Alley and you wouldn't want any part of you caught in the claws of one of those chaps. So this woman wisely wouldn't let her kids go into public toilets. Unkind people said the real reason was that their father wanted the extra sewage for his allotment and the family needed the pee for a severe attack of suicidally itchy chilblains. Their argument was strengthened by the fact that the father had never been known to run out when the ragman's donkey relieved itself outside his house. Horse muck, or in this case donkey muck, was much prized. If it was deposited outside your house there was an unspoken law that said you had first claim to it. It was a sort of 'Droit de dung'. The denizens would rush out, with their third from posh coal shovel and, like dung beetles, collect their steaming prize to spread on their allotment vegetables. Which gave rise to the joke:

Where are you going with that horse muck?

I'm going to put it on my rhubarb.

On your rhubarb! We put custard on ours.

Everyone desperately wanted horse muck, but not the paranoia poo poo family. The donkey muck would stay in the road. The steam from it would drift away; it would cool. Curtains would twitch; they were watching and waiting. The bus to Rastrick would pass and flatten it and return to flatten it again and again. They would wait till dark to be sure he wasn't coming out. Many buses would pass over it, squeezing out the plant-nourishing juices. The dung would spread flatter. Night would fall. In the morning the pizza-shaped poo would have gone. Stolen, to be crumbled up like a dry popadom onto some ailing carrots, or perhaps cut into insoles for some short kid's shoes. Didn't adults always say 'We'll put some horse muck in your shoes, that'll make you grow'? It worked with parsnips, why not with people? The treasured donkey dung had gone. They all went back to waiting for his next visit or, the more frequent summer visitor, Ripley's ice cream cart. He had a pony and came all the way from Hove Edge.

Years later I was listening to the news on the radio. The newsreader was telling us about an earthquake in South America, a famine in Africa and a rail crash in India. He then paused and said, 'And now; some bad news for cricketers'. I began to think of the importance of things and the Thornhill Road fanatical quest for horse muck. This led me to build the mechanical horse cycle I called 'Bad news for rose growers'. The Duke of Bedford bought one and James Mason another.

Bad news for rose growers' cycle

Laikin

(Playing, on holiday or unemployed)

In the valley, at Hove Edge, was a place called Sunny Vale or, as we called it, Sunny Bunce's. I think the chap who started it must have been called Mr Bunce. Whether his disposition was sunny, I don't know. Sunny Bunce's was what was then called an inland resort. During the war you couldn't get to the seaside, so places like Sunny Vale and, over in Huddersfield, 'Hope Bank', were set up. All are gone now. History is now repeating itself; inland resorts are coming back: Lightwater Valley, Alton Towers, etc. I hope this doesn't bode evil.

Sunny Vale had two boating lakes, a scenic railway and a proper hedge maze, with a wooden tower in the middle to spot lost folk from, and lots of fairground attractions. Sunday school trips went there and you were let loose on the site with a yard of paper tickets to go on the rides. My first boat trip was there. Dad took me out on the lake in a small pedalo boat. It was terrifying; the boat had a list to one side, so one revolving paddle splashed almost out of the water. So we tried to compensate by leaning to one side. The boat was awash; I thought from the start we were going to sink.

We set off, Dad pedalling; we travelled in an arc to the middle of the lake. My feet were getting wet. I looked down at the water in the boat bottom. A large frog had appeared, as if to see what was going on and if perhaps we were going his way. He wasn't there when we set off and I hadn't seen him jump in. So I instantly assumed he must have got on board through a hole in the bottom of the boat. A hole in the bottom of the boat; this confirmed in my mind that we were going to sink. I knew holes in boats didn't let water out and I hadn't got my swimming certificate yet. A return to dry land as quick as possible seemed in order, which I tried to indicated to Dad by waving my arms, pointing at the frog and the shore. Dad, being a countryman, couldn't understand why I appeared to be so scared of a frog and why I wanted to take it back to land. He smiled and nodded in the direction of the frog as if to say, 'It's OK, frogs can swim'. I looked down, the frog had gone. This was worse; the frog had abandoned ship, probably back through the same hole he'd come by. The frog had gone. He knew we were sinking. Dad was determined to get his money's worth and carried on casually peddling and paddling. When the water started washing the fluff and bus tickets out of his trouser turn-ups, he realised we were actually slowly sinking. Then his heroic efforts to get to the bank were a sight to behold. The paddle sticking out of the water made us go in circles, but we made it before the boat sank. The frog was nowhere to be seen. He'd done his job, warning us of impending doom, like the dolphins saving men at sea.

When I was about 8 years old, Dad went to Brighouse. When he came back home, he announced to Mam that we were all going to Blackpool for a week's holiday. She then told us what he'd done and I was totally amazed. We usually only went for a day and that was all organised for us on the work's trip. What surprised me was he'd just gone out and arranged it. I couldn't understand how he'd done it so easily. I thought these things took time. A holiday at the seaside for a week must be a complex thing to arrange and was ostentation beyond belief. Dad had done it, no fuss, he'd just done it; I was so proud. I kept telling everyone we were going on holiday for a week and Dad had just gone out and fixed it, just like that.

It wasn't the holiday that I expected them to be surprised at, but the fact Dad had arranged it so easily and I thought he couldn't. I couldn't understand the 'So what?' looks from the adults. They didn't seem to share my admiration of Dad's ability to fix it.

The day to go came and we were off to Blackpool. On the way we played the usual game, trying to be the first to spot the tower. When we got there, we were met by a hoard of young lads with carts on old pram wheels. We called them bogies, nothing to do with nose contents; others called them lorry carts. They were there to take your cases to your bed and breakfast accommodation. Going in a taxi was not even contemplated then. I'd only been in a car once and that had been embarrassing because I had to sit on Mrs Hodinot's knee whilst her pretty daughter Ann sat in the back. These lads charged you but, what the ummer, we were on holiday and the lad knew Blackpool better than us. Dad showed the lad the address written on a piece of paper. The lad loaded up and off we went, following the cart. We proudly looked round for admiring glances from folk who couldn't afford a cart. We were like royalty following our butler to a picnic. He took us on an unknown route to our bed and breakfast place. A route that only a native of the town could have followed. Like a rickshaw man in an exotic eastern town, he took us past many temptations.

The shops were full of gifts; Blackpool towers made in every conceivable material, lots of stuff covered in little seashells and things in brass for the tiny space left on your mantelpiece. Most of these objects had cheap little red liquid thermometers stuck on them. This was because before VAT we had purchase tax that varied from item to item. A bowl would have one tax but, if it had a groove, it was an ash tray so it had a higher luxury tax. If an object could be said to be for medical use, there wasn't any purchase tax to pay, so they stuck thermometers on everything they could. I don't think this rule applied to egg timers, but where there wasn't a thermometer there was an egg timer. We seemed to be a nation in dread of not knowing exactly how cold or hot we were and over-boiling eggs.

Mam hurried him on, telling us that we could come back later. It wasn't that we were particularly strong willed or Mam was keen to get there quick. I think she suspected the lad dragging the cart could be on some sort of a meter. Some weaker willed families were tempted. They were lured into the mock auctions. They ended up spending all their money. I heard of one family that spent up and had to go home before they got to their bed and breakfast.

I don't remember us being charged extra for 'Use of cruet'. Or the overflow on the bath being a few inches from the bottom so you couldn't use too much water. These were vile rumours, probably put about by Scarborough landladies. Our landlady was very nice. This was a memorable holiday for me. I had my first look at contemporary sculpture. Some of Epstein's work was being displayed in an arcade on the sea front. We were not impressed but we didn't feel that our money was completely wasted because there were some shrunken heads to look at. We went on the beach and I made a sand sculpture of Davy Crockett. Dad pointed to the Epstein arcade, shook his head, pointed to my Davy Crockett and stuck his thumb up. He thought my effort was better than Epstein's stuff.

Further on the front there was a caravan parked with a washing line displaying very small ladies' underwear. We paid our entrance fee and Mam, Dad, Doreen and me trooped round to the other side of the caravan to see what was going on. If I remember rightly, the other side of the caravan was cut away to reveal an interior full of little artefacts. Standing in the middle of all this small stuff was a very small lady. She was in fact about the same height as Doreen and me. We all stood in a line and stared at her in embarrassed silence. She stared back and eventually, looking up at Mam, she suddenly said 'Good afternoon Mrs'. Mam was taken aback. She looked down at me and mouthed 'What did she say?' I looked back at Mam and mouthed 'Good afternoon'. At the same time doing the hand sign for good morning, because I never knew the sign for good afternoon. The little lady instantly turned her attention to me. I was on the same eye level as her.

'What's up with her?', she said to me.
'They're deaf and dumb', I replied.
'Who are they?'
'Mam and Dad', I said.
'Oh! You brought them here on a day trip have you?'
'No, Dad brought us here for a week', I said proudly.
'What have you been doing today?'
'Looking at shrunken heads.'
'Very nice.'

She didn't seem too sure about this, probably thinking we looked on her as a living exhibit of the same thing. 'Why aren't you deaf?' 'Don't know.' 'Are you not deaf at all?', she said, very quietly. 'No I'm not', I replied loudly. I was getting a bit fed up with this. Her questions went on; she was obviously fascinated by us. We'd paid to see her and we'd become the exhibits. Other people were coming in and watching this inquisition; they were getting extra value. They were all standing with the little lady looking at us. Dad kept pulling Mam's arm, wanting to know what was going on, and Mam kept pulling mine for answers. 'Do some of that deaf signing thing', she said. 'No', I said, and dragged Mam and Dad out before we got offers of a world tour with her. I then had to go back for Doreen, she was still getting her money's worth looking at the little lady.

Further on the front we came upon a stuffed lion; we had our photos taken sitting on its back. At the time I thought it might be the lion that Uncle Tommy had told me about. The unfrocked Rector of Stiffkey. Unfrocked literally, he earned money by posing nude in a barrel. He entered Freddy the lion's cage collecting empty bottles and, unlike Daniel 6:16–23, the lion ate him. He was the last Christian to be eaten by a lion. Perhaps like Cora's Dad entering Billy bear's cage, he forgot to knock and Freddie the lion took exception.

NB The Rector of Stiffkey, Harold Davidson, was actually killed in Skegness.

This turned out not to be the lion that ate the Rector of Stiffkey.

The dreaded donkey.

We then decided to go back on the beach. From the raised position of the promenade, we could see the beach was absolutely packed. But strangely, right on the sea edge, in a prime position, there appeared to be a large empty space. So we fought our way through the crowds to it. When we staggered into the open space, the reason no one was sitting there was because it was the donkey ride pitch. So people wouldn't think we hadn't known it was a donkey pitch all the time, and to avoid the embarrassment of struggling back, Doreen and I each picked a sullen donkey to ride. We mounted our donkeys, Dad took a photo and off we sidled. My donkey didn't seem enthusiastic about going anywhere. In fact I got the distinct impression the glamour had gone out of this donkey's job. Having paid, I was determined to enjoy myself, but the donkey wouldn't join in and I couldn't achieve that certain cowboy feeling that I wanted from this donkey, he just sedately ambled along. I thought just a little more speed would help the mood. So I held the reins high and shouted 'Hi Ho Silver!' I dug my invisible spurs into his sides. I don't know what I expected to happen but, whatever it was, I didn't expect the donkey to instantly accelerate from 0 to 60 miles an hour. He shot from under me. I fell off and he would have left me behind but my right foot was caught in the stirrup. So I had to go with him. Off he went like a rat up a pump, dragging me behind. I wasn't shouting, I wasn't screaming, I wasn't swearing, but I was quietly mumbling the words of the really severely distressed. 'Oh! Dear, Oh! Dear.'

I think the donkey was a clock-watcher and my shout, like a factory whistle, must have made him think it was time to knock off work and head for home. He was thwarted in this because he couldn't cross the beach to the promenade, it was packed with holidaymakers. So he belted along between them and the wet bit. My short trousers, acting like a scoop, quickly filled with sand. This slowed him only slightly. I often wonder if someone sat on the beach saw this and thought 'That looks like a good way to slow down jets'.

People shouted as he went past, so he veered towards the sea. My fantasy of the cowboy hero wounded by Indians and being dragged by his horse in the soft sand of the desert to die faded quickly, it looked like it was going to be replaced by the true-life story of 'Boy donkey teaser drowned by donkey'. I held my head as high as I could, with my chin pressed against my chest. I pinched my nose with my thumb and forefinger ready to enter the water. Wet sand was now being packed up my trousers, making me heavier. The donkey slowed down and stopped. He must have thought 'Hang on a minute I don't usually come this far and where are the other guys?' He turned to look back and, embarrassed, began a slow walk back to his mates, still dragging me. I was shaken but unhurt. I'm told nowadays in Bognor Regis you are required to wear a crash helmet on the donkeys.

The donkey man gave me a bollocking for upsetting his donkey. Mam, seeing I wasn't hurt, started enthusiastically battering the tightly packed sand from my trousers and, with a swift smack for good luck on my calf, we sidled off. We'd had enough excitement and expense, so we spent the rest of the day sun bathing. I staggered round the beach playing a French legionnaire dying of thirst in the desert. By evening I was genuinely staggering about, I had sunstroke.

On my back were pale yellow watery blisters the size of old pennies. I had to spend the rest of the holiday in the bedroom with the curtains drawn. All this of course helped to instil in me a dislike of holidays involving sun and beaches. From then on I always wore a hat and I never rolled my sleeves up, I always wore them down, just like the cowboys in the films.

The countryside inspires similar feelings. I always feel it's a good idea not to go too far into it or, better still, not to leave the car park. In other words, for safety's sake, stay with the crowds and don't go near the view. Views can be dangerous, especially ones you can fall off or down. The view is always best left in the distance. Anyway, there's only another view when you get there, so why bother. While you're walking towards the view, you are wearing the bits out between the views; you have to walk through all sorts of unpleasantness, nettles, brambles, thistles and thorns. On top of all this, everything in the country leaks, from machinery to cows. You're always in danger of being bitten, stung or trampled on. The very least you can get is a peck, and if you go abroad, well!

I always get the feeling that farmers want to spread muck from their farms thinly all over England. Rather like the guys in that prisoner of war escape film carrying soil from a tunnel down their trousers and spreading it round the camp. Humans in the past employed a lot of thought and effort so we all could leave the discomforts of cave and country to live in town communities. For some strange reason, ungratefully, lots of people want to move back. When I was a kid, I was reminded, we all ate indoors and went to the outside lav. Now we have the lav indoors and it's smart to eat barbecues outside. Kitchens have distressed paint; Belfast sinks with curtains beneath concealing a white enamel bucket. They call them quaint designer country kitchens; we called it poverty. I notice they don't go all the way and have just the one cold tap. This nostalgic desire for a sanitised version of primitive living baffles me. Laurens Van Der Post informed us that the Bushmen have instincts that we westerners have lost. All I can say is I'm glad I've lost these instincts because they obviously don't embrace the instinct to move away and stop living in a hut smeared with cow clap. I was glad to get out of our cellar with its cold water sink.

Town planners can't return the towns to the country so they do the next best thing and try to return it to a previous age. When I suggested they could get more of a feel of Victorian England if they employed anorexic girls to flog matches in the streets, they were not amused. Or perhaps people wearing jodhpurs could pretend they had rickets. I saw that pristine new cobbled streets didn't have the authentic covered in horse muck look. So I designed the Mark 1 Artificial horse dung pile with electric flies. The Mark 2 was intended to steam but no one showed any interest in the project so Mark 2 was never built.

No flies on Wilf — but plenty on his artificial horse muck

Wilf's latest idea causes a stink

By ALLISON DARLING

WHACKY Huddersfield inventor Wilf Lunn has come up with a creation to make the town's St George's Square look more Victorian.

His idea is artificial horse manure — complete with flies.

Wilf came up with the idea after criticising Kirklees Council for restoring the area around the railway station to its Victorian glory.

Said Wilf: "They want to re-create the real Victorian feel of the town — but the town was covered in horse muck then.

"I haven't been able to come up with the smell, but I have made some horse muck which

would go well with the lamps and things in St George's Square."

He added: "Who wants to live in Victorian or Edwardian cities and towns? It is back-ward-looking.

"They should get some young architects in to design some really striking new build-ings which would attract people to Huddersfield."

Cutting from The Examiner

The rudiments of my feelings about the countryside were born when my Auntie Edith, pronounced Edie, decided to take our Doreen on holiday with her. Auntie Edie lived with her brother, my Uncle Wilf, in Meltham. Mam said when I was a baby she'd tried to get me away from them to go and live with her. This information surprised me because she never seemed over fond of me. This feeling was born out somewhat in July 1976. Cousin Rodney tracked me down to tell me Auntie Edie was dying and urgently wanted to see me. I must admit I'd been avoiding her because when we met she always inquired why I wasn't wearing my watch. She had bought me a gold Rotary watch inscribed with my name for my 21st birthday. I'd lent the watch to my then wife who, in a day, managed to lose the winder, glass face and, I think, one hand. She placed the bits in an antique apothecary jar meaning to have it fixed and forgot it was there. A dealer called at the door and, without thinking, she sold him the jar with my gold watch in it. Needless to say he never came back, it's out there somewhere with my name on the back.

So, wearing very long sleeves, I went to see Auntie Edie in Huddersfield Hospital. I took my new book *Mad Things to make from Vision On*. I didn't really think she'd be interested in making a Quasi Modo coat hanger but I thought getting a book published might impress her. I arrived at Auntie Edie's bedside. Rodney said, 'It's Wilfred, you said you wanted to see him'. I leaned over her and, in a low voice, she said, 'I just wanted to tell you'. She paused, I leaned closer, 'I never want to see you again'.

Her wish was granted, she died; 'popped her little clogs', as they say in Yorkshire. If Auntie Edith hadn't summoned me to her bedside she would, of course, have never seen me again, but it wouldn't have been the same. She wanted to be sure I knew I was in the state of not being seen again. So she had to tell me. It's rather like ignoring a person; you can do this by avoiding their company but it's best if you're with them so they know they are really being ignored. I left the book on her bedside table. It was obviously appreciated by someone, it got pinched.

Auntie Edith Annie Broadbent always gave me the impression she thought I had ideas beyond my station. Art wasn't for the likes of us. I think she thought I was what they called a 'Clever clogs'. Which meant you might think you're clever but you're not. All your cleverness won't pay; you'll still end up wearing clogs. To illustrate how far she'd come, she'd show me her first tiny pair of clogs. They were always kept in full view on the fireplace hearth. These tiny clogs were, I think, called 'Straights'. There wasn't a left and right one, which meant they could be worn on either foot. They were swapped over each day; this meant they wore evenly, which was economical, but it also, I understand, corrected foot problems. They had slightly different patterns on them so you knew which was which. These clogs would then be put back on the tiled hearth. They contrasted somewhat with the fireplace, which at the time was the very latest thing. It had tiles with scenes of pheasants and the very latest innovation, slopes at each end of the hearth so you could sweep dirt straight out. Auntie Edie was what they called 'House proud', she always had the best carpets and dearest wallpaper, by which we meant expensive.

When Auntie Edie dusted, she didn't just use one duster she used two, one in each hand. She dusted with the right-hand one and the left one she used to lean on so has not to leave fingerprints. I found that very suspicious. Her cellar was super-clean, white-washed, gleaming and snow-goggle white. In it were lots of her brother's (Uncle Wilf's) bottles of pop. Meltham is close enough to Huddersfield for a horse to walk there and back, so Uncle Wilf had a cellar full of Ben Shaw's pop, including the local yellow lemonade.

Uncle Wilf always seemed to be dressed in a brown lab coat and wellies. He was constantly cleaning eggs in a bucket with a damp cloth. I remember once meeting him on the road with his empty bucket, probably going for more eggs. He said to me, 'Atta barn tut thouse?'

To which, after pausing for thought, I replied, 'Y'what?', because I had been told 'Eh?' was bad manners. He corrected me, 'Pardon'. 'Pardon?', I repeated. He then enunciated his question very slowly, as if talking to a dimwit, 'At-ta bah-n tut thouse?' Which meant 'Are you going to the house?', but at that time I didn't understand what he was saying. To keep him happy I said, 'Oh yeh'. He then said, 'Will you inform your aunt I will put the porcelain away when I've attended to the poultry'. No he didn't; he actually said, 'Will ta tell yer'aunt a'll side pots when 'ave seen tut t'ens'. I did understand that bit, so I nodded. Which seemed to satisfy him because he walked off swinging his bucket.

Apart from saying 'Pardon?' instead of 'Y'what?' or 'Eh?' the only other advice he ever gave me was that the best bit of a beast to eat was the part that did all the work, so don't bother with chicken brains, go for the legs. Fortunately we never had buck rabbit, I didn't fancy bunny willies.

I don't remember any coal in Auntie Edie's cellar. I think coal would be too dirty for her to have on display. She didn't have anything as common as the mucky old firewood we had at our house. She had higher standards. She used brand new unused beautiful-smelling wooden silk bobbins, which I think she pinched from the silk mill where she worked. If I was lucky, she'd give me a bobbin and, with an elastic band, a drawing pin, a match and a slice of candle for a washer, I'd make a bobbin tank. I thought everyone called them bobbins till I confused an American publisher, who said it should be a cotton reel or spool.

HOW TO MAKE A BOBBIN TANK.

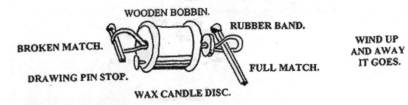

The other thing she had in the cellar was a framework cupboard with galvanised perforated zinc sides. She said it was a 'Meat safe'. Food was valuable and scarce but to actually have more meat than for just one meal was inconceivable to me. I could understand that if it got about that Auntie had extra meat in the house she could have beef burglars breaking in and so a safe would be necessary. But it didn't look all that safe to me; it didn't even have a lock on the door. I remarked on this and was told not to be stupid, it was to keep the flies off the meat. Auntie seemed to have a thing about flies, which wasn't surprising because the house seemed a-buzz with them.

I suppose they followed Uncle Wilf in when he came home smelling of hen muck. Then they were driven mad by the smell of meat they couldn't get at in the Meat safe. Despite all this, I didn't mind going to Auntie Edie's and Uncle Wilf's because I was allowed to stand by the window and listen to the wireless, *Ray's a Laugh*, etc. The wireless was a beautiful veneered floor-standing model. Years later she gave it to us. Mam hated it because she couldn't lip-read it so she was completely left out and, for some reason I never fathomed, she called it 'Tin can'. We, of course, didn't have a wireless at home, which put me at somewhat of a disadvantage when my school chums talked about what they'd been listening to. I'd never heard *Dick Barton Special Agent*.

Mick Walsh told me a kid who lived near the actor who played Dick Barton chucked a stone through his window with a paper message wrapped round it. The message was 'SOLVE THIS'.

For a while, the only way I could listen to radio programmes was on a crystal set. This was a circular black plastic thing. It had to have an aerial and a wire to earth to work. Because we were short of wire, the aerial was attached to the springs of my bed and the earth, because I was in my bedroom, was a short wire attached to a dining fork, stuck in a jar of what we called sal ammoniac [ammonium chloride]. There wasn't a speaker so I had to wear headphones, and to tune it I had to fiddle with a thing called a 'cat's whisker'. This was a little sprung bar that you twiddled till it was on the right spot on the crystal to receive a station. Luxembourg was the station I wanted, it had all the latest songs; it was murder getting it and it kept fading. It was so frustrating I gave up on it.

Later I remembered my crystal set when faced by a girl's breasts. I was wondering what I was supposed to do next. I put her bra on my head like headphones and, turning her breasts with both hands, said 'I think I'm getting Radio Luxembourg'. She was confused. Unlike the waitress in a pub who leaned over me to pick up a glass. Her breast pressed against my ear; to cover my embarrassment, I said, 'I can hear the sea'. Thus making what I thought was an amusing comparison with listening to a seashell. She replied, 'Say that again and you'll see stars as well'.

I wouldn't admit we didn't have a wireless so I had to do some pretty slick lying to join in the conversation at school. Those weekend listening sessions at Auntie Edith's meant I could open the debate so no one suspected we didn't have a set. Auntie Edith didn't approve of sloth and idleness in anyone, especially young boys. She allowed me to stand by the set and listen because it was in front of the window where the majority of the flies and bluebottles congregated in their bid to escape when they realised they couldn't get to her meat. I would stand there listening but I wasn't idle, I was holding a small puffer tin of deadly DDT. Any flies that approached were instantly puffed at and powdered; they'd drop on the window sill, which was littered with dead bodies like icing-sugared currants. The whole experience was very satisfying and could only have been improved on if I been allowed to sit down. I tried always to be on my best behaviour because I knew upstairs, fastened into the landing ceiling, were some of those mysterious scary hooks like the ones we had in our cellar. What were they for? Hanging naughty kids on. Besides, Uncle Wilf frequently gave Doreen and me half a crown each.

Auntie Edie always gave me the feeling that my very existence annoyed her. When I was a student she would constantly ask me, 'When are you going to get a job?' Later, when I was earning money, she'd ask, 'When are you going to get a proper job?' A proper job was, of course, a hard job, one you didn't like and didn't pay well because your final reward was in heaven. It's nice to think that, although girls are no longer called Edith or Edie, a version of Auntie's name lives on. I've heard girls are being christened Ebay.

For the time being, Doreen's reward was a holiday with Auntie Edie; I think they went to London. My consolation prize was a holiday in the country with my other, much nicer, Auntie Ida, Cousin Rodney and Uncle Bob. They also lived in Meltham, on the edge of the view at Upper Owler Bars Farm. 'Owler' is an old word for alder tree; the 'Bars' bit's a mystery. My Dad was born in Meltham so he had no problem with the countryside and its ways. He'd wring a hen's neck, pluck it and gut it, chucking hands full of entrails on the fire, no problem. We'd sit fascinated and watch the feathers and entrails popping and sizzling as they burnt on our open fire. The muse perhaps evoked folk memories of witch burnings or the last moments of Joan of Arc. Or maybe a Roman haruspex priest divining the future from the entrails. We knew the future. Dad would scare us by pulling the exposed tendons on the severed hen's leg; this made the claw open and shut as if alive. Then later we'd be eating the old hen.

I remember him taking just me to the Huddersfield slaughterhouse (no French prissy abattoir name for us). I think he'd worked there for a short period. The floor was awash with blood, piss and cow clap. Dad held my hand while I stood in this slurry, my little wellies made mirror shiny from the goo. His ex-work mates were determined to make the day a memorable one for me. Using a captive bolt gun, they blasted a little hole in a cow's head, pushed a rod down the hole and wiggled it about, so the cow was lobotomised and calm before it dropped dead. For an encore they played a game of skittles with severed cows' heads. Gripping a horn, they'd slide them on the slimy floor like curling stones. The only problem was there was only one skittle and it was me. They were trying to knock me off my feet into the bloody slurry on the floor. Fortunately Dad had a firm grip on my hand and he would lift me up by my arm. The severed heads would slide harmlessly under me. Then Dad dropped me back on my feet, like resetting the skittles in a bowling alley. They never hit me once; the guys were so disappointed. We then went to watch the pigs being electrocuted, after which we caught a trolley bus home.

Strangely, I don't remember being scared or in anyway upset. I think it was some sort of initiation to prepare me for the country life. He was a fund of quaint little country ways. On the pleasant side, he would put a hairy grass seed head or an ear of barley up your sleeve and later you'd find it had crawled up the sleeve and was now mysteriously in the opposite one. He knew how to make itching powder out of the hairy stuff inside rose hips. The best thing for nettle stings I know are nettles, but he reckoned rubbing dock leaves on the stings relieved the pain. All it did for me was give me a green leg. He showed me you could eat young hawthorn leaves. The kids round where I lived were very dismissive. 'We've always known that. It's called bread and cheese.' Their parents had either being deluding them to save money on food or their taste buds had been completely destroyed by rationing.

When out walking Dad would point at a plant everyone called 'Mother die'. He'd cross his arms on his chest like a corpse and look up to heaven, shaking his head, warning us not to touch it. Kids who'd had a good smacking from their Mams, would, intent on revenge, furtively pick it, thinking just picking it would evoke its mortal Mam magic. The plant was actually quite harmless, cow parsley mistaken for hemlock. I don't remember a single Mam dying, they all lived on to smack another day. Picking dandelions was also to be avoided, apparently they made you piss in bed. This power must leave them when they turn into seed heads, or what we called 'Dandelion clocks', because we'd pick them with impunity to tell the time by counting the number of puffs it took to blow away the parachute fairies. This method was completely inaccurate but it did help to spread the dandelions. Dad would put a blade of grass between his thumbs, holding his hands as if praying and blowing through the gap, and the grass would produce a sound. He couldn't hear it but he could feel the vibrations. He would pluck a snapdragon flower head and lightly squeeze it so it opened and shut, like a mouth silently talking. It was a party piece he could never develop; he'd never be a ventriloquist. It's a thought though, a vent's dummy that does hand signing.

So, initiated in country craft, I was sent to Auntie Ida's for my holiday. I was loaned the family camera to record the experience. Owler Bars Farm was a hen and cow farm; anyway that's all I saw there. Uncle Bob was a scary Heathcliffe-type chap; he rarely spoke, in fact I only every remember him speaking to me once. It was at the bottom of Mill Moor Road. He offered me a lift to the top of the hill on his moped. The kindness of this gesture was soon forgotten when I realised the moped had only one seat and I had to ride on the parcel rack. The journey was fortunately short but very painful. Uncle Bob was an object of fascination to me, as he sat silent at the head of the table with his pint pot of tea in which he put six spoons of sugar and, for his health's sake, five saccharins. I recounted this story once to an old friend, Kath Evans, about Uncle Bob's sweet tooth, his hens and how eventually he was electrocuted. Kath said, 'He was electrocuted, they weren't battery hens were they?'

I didn't see much of Cousin Rodney, he was older than I was. He once allowed me to hold a cow's tail while he milked it, squirting a tune on the side of the pail singing. I think it's an old music hall song he'd heard at a pantomime. Anyway, I remembered it when I later designed the pickle onion vice and the square boiled egg machine.

The pickled onion song.

♪♪ *Why don't they make pickled onions square?*
Why do they make them round?
When I stick my fork in to the jar all I get out is the viny-gar
Stab 'em grab 'em, they're nowhere to be found.
Oh why don't they make pickled onions square?
Why are they always round? ♪♪

Cows are not as daft as people think. Most folk believe that cows follow their leader cow into the cowshed. This isn't true; the boss cow is the second cow in the line. The boss cow always allows another cow to go first, just in case there's any danger lurking ahead or behind the door. This could have been the original concept of allowing ladies to go first. If a clever cow is so distrustful of the countryside, I feel my apprehensions are justified.

Hens are different. They have all the worst traits of humans. They are stupid, vindictive, evil feathered fiends. They pick on the weakest. When it's hot they huddle in the corners of their huts and suffocate each other. The farmers try to solve this problem by putting wire netting across the corners. Why don't they just build round hen houses?

Ku Klux egg kosies for white eggs only.

I think Rodney suspected I was bored and, for a treat, he suggested I might like to dig out one of the 'Deep litter' hen huts. 'Deep litter' is a euphemism for 'Let's let the hens crap on the floor till their heads are touching the ceiling, then we'll dig it all out'. Can you imagine a barber who's lost his broom doing that? Warning me not to tell his Dad he smoked, Rodney lit a fag and, with a smile, opened the door of the first shed. I was confronted with a floor covered with a very thick slab of nauseous nougat. It was a sort of beige grey white; an occasional dark fleck broke the surface and the whole lot was bound together with many feathers. 'No problem for a growing lad', I thought, until I stuck the spade into the feathery faeces. The smell it gave off was beyond belief; it was stomach-wrenchingly evil. It smelt worse than the school milk monitor's wiping-up cloth. Rodney had some protection from the smell with his fag, if he needed it. Now, when I think about it, I'm amazed the fag didn't ignite the gas and blow the shed up. I didn't want to lose face in front of Rodney, so I gritted my teeth and struggled

on for what seemed like ages, but it was no good. On the fifth shovel full I had to give up. I made my excuse, which was I'd forgotten to send my Mam a postcard, and left an unhappy Rodney to finish the job. In the village I did buy a postcard and wrote on it what Mam always wrote. 'Just a few lines to let you know, having a nice time. Wish you were here.' She always wrote 'Just a few lines' no matter what. I looked at the card, 'Four views of Meltham', and saw it was printed at 'Leeches' just down the road from where we lived in Brighouse.

The rest of the week I wandered round aimlessly looking for cowpats that had dried hard and could be skimmed like a flying saucer, a sort of early rural Frisbee. Even that wasn't much fun as there was no one smaller to chuck them at. One day I decided, in the heat of the moment, to get my revenge on Mam and Dad for sending me to Meltham. I used up all the roll of film in the camera taking close-up pictures of cows' backsides. I instantly regretted it. Fortunately, when they came back from the chemist, they were all out of focus and, unless you knew what the subject was, completely indecipherable, like out-of-focus Francis Bacon oil paintings. Mam suspected something probably worse than the truth. I was never sent to Meltham again.

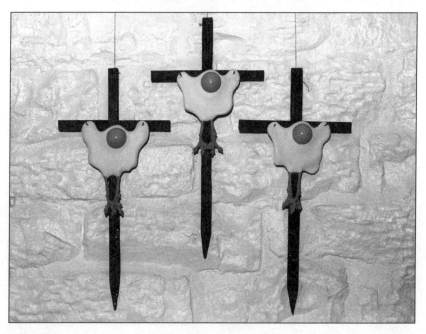

Crucifried eggs.

'Every egg not eaten is a chicken died in vain.'

This device was called a 'Chicken exerciser'. The chicken ran on the revolving ramp trying to get to the food in the box. Why anyone would want a chicken with powerful legs baffle me. I thought perhaps it was because of Uncle Wilf's food Philosophy. 'The best bit of the beast to eat is the bit that does all the work.' I later found out this device was to strengthen the legs of fighting cocks. The reason why it was called a 'Chicken exerciser' was because you weren't allowed to patent anything for illegal practices. It was actually a 'Fighting cock exerciser'.

"Look Mother, we're teaching Willie how to use the Zebra Crossing."
A rub with 'Mansion' will quickly make the floor bright and
healthy again.

MANSION POLISH

your FLOORS FURNITURE AND LINOLEUM

Tins 10d., 1/6d. & 3/9d.

FOR DARK FLOORS USE DARK MANSION

Mansion polish advert

T' lino

(The linoleum)

Lino usually came from Kirkcaldy. Where our wandering lino lads came from I don't know. It wasn't real lino, or to be correct linoleum, it was a kind of oilcloth with a varnished finish and it must not have been rationed. These men would carry great rolls of this stuff on their shoulders, knocking door-to-door trying to sell it. You'd answer the door and there would be a chap holding, vertical, two great wobbling rolls of lino. He looked like a scared Samson. Judges 16:26–30. With his pillars about to fall under their own weight. We never bought any; we were fully linoed, you know.

I always thought what great optimists these men were. They went from door to door looking for the one person who wanted that entire roll of lino in that particular pattern and, on top of that, had the money to pay for it. It must have been like looking for the Holy Grail. I've talked about these chaps in far off Huddersfield and they say they've never heard of them (probably all fully carpeted). Perhaps lino men were only known within the distance a man could walk in a day with a full roll of lino. Maybe they didn't sell full rolls, they sold bits for patching to make their load lighter on their way back to unlucky lino land. I do know some people only had bits of lino covering their floors. Their lino was all different weird patterns, as if they'd cut up a lino sample book. There were geometric ones, like the Art Deco patterns on the trolley bus seat covers, or the pretentious had 'Magritte type', badly drawn parquet. The lino was never plain. With all these different bits of lino, their houses were like working lino museums. Only the occasional rag rug relieved the geometric jigsaw pattern. Rag rugs, of course, are now very much the fashion with stripped pine furniture and distressed paint.

All our paint seemed to distress itself quite happily without any assistance from us. Some vandals once painted graffiti on, I think it was, Stonehenge. An expert said it would take 200 years for the paint to wear off. Everyone wanted to know where they got this paint. I wonder if distressed lino will make a nostalgic comeback. All nicely dried up and cracked, with the sack backing worn into a nice cheap string fringe. Which reminds me of those flying helmets kids preferred to balaclavas; they were supposed to look like leather. It was called leather cloth or American cloth; it looked like thin brown lino. It cracked just like lino and the cloth showed through just the same as lino. I think it probably was reject substandard lino. I don't know where our lino came from; it seemed it had always been there. It was laid on top of an underfelt of *Daily Mirror*s.

Under it lived strange creatures called silver fish. They were less than half an inch long and a sort of shiny silver, white, slippery, leggy thing. They were not at all offensive, so I left them alone. Mam wasn't too happy if she saw a blackclock, the local name for cockroaches or beetles. They were hunted relentlessly. The lino was there to add a touch of class and disguise the fact we had a damp stone flag floor. It didn't fool anyone, the lino had taken on the contours of the stone flags under it. So, on entering, instead of just flagstones, you saw shiny patterned flagstones. The floor was so shiny because Mam polished it vigorously every day with

'Mansion' floor polish. It was the best. Didn't God live in 'Many mansions'? John 14:2. Yes, she polished our cellar floor with the same stuff they used on mansions. Mansion polish was a sort of orangey yellow colour and she put it on the lino with an ordinary white cotton-headed floor mop (I wondered if God had many mops in his many mansions).

Mam always called the mop 'Pom'. Nothing could make her call it a mop, it was always Pom. So she put the polish on with a Pom, then she tied an old vest over the Pom head and polished the lino to a bright shine. She seemed to pay particular attention to polishing the lino at the top of the stairs. This was an area to be wary of because Granny had one of her smaller rag rugs there. If you were rushing and forgot about this rug, and I did on at least two occasions, the rug would slide on the waxy surface with you standing on it. Off you'd fly, like a snowboarder on a floppy board. On one occasion I actually landed at the bottom, missing all the steps. Strangely, when Granny died, she was found at the bottom of her cellar steps.

The mop's white cotton string head eventually turned to the orangey yellow colour of the Mansion polish. In fact the same colour as my hair at the time. When I realised this, I took advantage of my Mam's bad eyesight. I'd lean the orange mop head round the door and Mam would talk to it, thinking it was me. An occasional wiggle made her think the 'mop Wilf' was paying attention and she was happy telling it off.

Joke:
Mrs Elliot's kid's a musical genius,
he's only 6 months old and she
says he's already playing on the
linoleum.

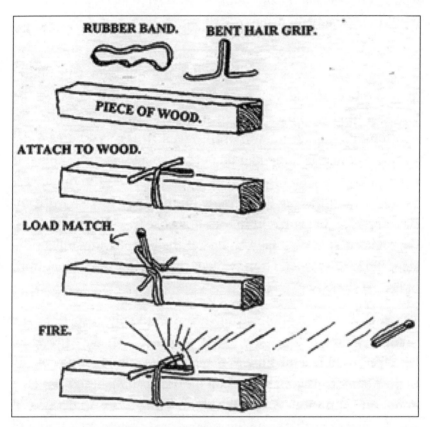

How to make a match stick flicker.

Layin t' fire

(Making the fire)

Making the fire was always called 'Laying the fire'. I suppose because you laid all the stuff in the coal grate prior to lighting it. When Mam laid the fire she would kneel on a sheet of newspaper in front of the fender. The iron fender rested on an enamelled sheet of iron printed to look like an expensive tiled hearth. This would also be covered with paper. She'd riddle the ashes vigorously with the straight poker. The ashes would fall through to the ash pan beneath. The ash pan would then be removed and placed to one side. She'd then remove the larger part-burnt coal clinkers that hadn't fallen through the grate and carefully place them on top of the ash pan. I would then, standing by her like a surgeon's assistant anticipating her every move, hand her a single sheet of newspaper. She would crumple it up and place it in one corner of the grate. I was not considered good enough to crumple. Then, without a sound, her hand would go up. I had to instantly put another sheet of paper in it. Correctly crumpled, she would place this snug against the first one. This continued till the grate was covered, it was like placing apples in a box.

Her hand would go up and I'd smartly hand her a fresh sheet. She shake her hand irritably. This signalled 'I've got enough paper you clot, now get the wood'. She always caught me out; it was her first early morning pleasure, me getting something wrong. The wood came in neat bundles fastened with soft iron wire. This was done with a larger version of the gadget used for tying up asparagus. I, of course, at the time, had not heard of asparagus or the need to tie it. You either untwisted the wire or pushed the middle stick out. This slackened the whole bundle, which fell all over the place like spillikins. I would check if there was a suitable piece of wood that, with an elastic band and a hairpin pinched from Mam, would make a 'Matchstick flicker'. Then I would hand the wood to Mam one stick at a time and she would lay them across the top of the paper like soldiers in a straight line. I would have preferred the log cabin method myself. That is building the sticks up in a square. This was good if you had a fire lighter to put in the middle. You could, of course, start with the fire lighter and build a tepee of wood over it.

'Zippo' firelighters came in blocks like chocolate. When you broke off a section they reeked of sawdust and paraffin. We didn't usually have firelighters and for a while we didn't have wood. Someone told Mam that you could save money by tightly rolling newspaper from one corner diagonally into long tight tapers. These you then looped and tied into a knot and could be used instead of wood. It did work, but what a trouble it was. Thankfully Mam soon gave up on the idea because Doreen and I became amazingly 'kack-handed' at paper rolling and started producing slack tubes of paper. (I still, to this day, find myself unconsciously rolling receipts, bus tickets and bits of paper into tight little tapers and knotting them.)

When the wood was satisfactorily placed, Mam would look at the ash pan and select any clinkers she thought might have a bit of phlogiston left in them. Her fingers hovered over the clinkers as if she was selecting a choice chocolate. With her thumb and forefinger, so minimum contact was made, she'd lift them one at a time and place them carefully on the firewood. I then had to take the ash pan to the dustbin. To this day, in memory of this task, many plastic dustbins bear the legend 'No Hot Ashes'. The journey to the bin was all right if I was just carrying the ash pan, but if there were too many ashes the extra were wrapped in the *News of the World*. The parcel of ashes often split, leaving a trail of ash and me looking like a white-faced Aborigine on a walkabout. Meanwhile Mam would continue kneeling in front of the fire waiting till I got back. She waited because I was required, as the apprentice fire maker, to fetch the coal. While the ash pan was being replaced and the front cover put back, I went with the shovel for the coal.

We didn't have a coal scuttle. The coal was kept in the coal cellar or coalhole, known to us as 'T'coil oil'. I had to delicately select choice pieces of small coals to start the new fire. This had to be done in the dim light coming from the outward open door and the chinks round the coal grate. In the early days at Thornhill Road this wasn't a great problem. Later on, when we moved to Crown Street and Timmy the poodle arrived, it was a problem. They say perpetual motion is impossible because you can never get more out of a thing than you put in. Tell that to someone on diuretics or a dog owner.

When Timmy was a puppy Mam trained him to crap in the coalhole. So all his life, no matter how far he was taken for a walk, he would not crap outside. Timmy could pee in public forever. Like all dogs, he was never empty. He always had a little squirt left, but he would not do a poodle poop in public. He would only crap on coal; he'd only shite on anthracite. He'd save it up until he became absolutely desperate, then he would run hell for leather, dragging me with him back to the coal cellar. It was like holding on to a bull with a chilli pepper up its bum. He'd drag me on the lead back to the house at break-neck speed. At the house, I had to get in front to open doors before he smashed through them in his desperation to get to the cellar. You could almost hear the sigh of relief, or was it steam, when he let it all go on the coal. This was all right for him, but when I had to pick up small pieces of coal in the dark I found it difficult to spot dehydrated Timmy turds. I know a little squeeze would have instantly told me the difference, but I was reluctant to do that in case I picked up a fresh one. Consequently I would end up with at least one on my shovel. Unlike camel dung, dog dung doesn't burn well. It does burn in a good fire but it's difficult to light even if you apply a match direct to one end of the coprolite cigar. Perhaps if we fed the dog liquid paraffin the poop would be easier to light and could economically replace expensive firelighters. I quickly forgot about this idea when I realised that it would also alter the consistency of the doggie dung.

Flying the flag!

**The recent correspondence about dogs and Greenhead Park
Has prompted this witty comment from Wilf Lunn.**
"The problem comes up every year, "he says," and I feel strongly about it.
I've even thought about putting up a sign ' This park does not flush!'"
Perhaps not, but there ought to be a few dog owners' faces which do!

HUDDERSFIELD EXAMINER, AUGUST 24TH. 1983.

A useful doggie dung device.

Altering his diet set me thinking, wouldn't it be a good idea to feed Timmy something to change the colour of his turds from dark anthracite brown to magnolia or even white? Strange, you don't ever see white dog turds nowadays. They used to be quite common when I was a lad during rationing. They were very white; if only the secret of what these dogs were fed on were known. Perhaps it was a breed of dog that's died out and had only appeared during the wartime blackout. White dog turds were a great asset to the walking public. (I've since been told it was because of meat rationing: dogs were fed a lot of bones.) Better still for night time I thought, how about luminous ones? I could perhaps have spiked the dog's food with luminous paint. Or, as we kids, familiar with Blackpool

Illuminations, called it, 'illuminous paint'. Fortunately I never did it. Later I found that luminous paint is poisonous. Clock number painters got a terrible disease called 'Phosy jaw' from licking their brushes. In the meantime, I'm thinking about the production of white luminous poop. I've designed the doggie dung warning flag. I didn't, of course, have these when I stood beside Mam with my shovel of little coals and desiccated dog dung. Even if I had I wouldn't have used them. I would watch her pick up the small bits of coal, waiting for her to pick up a poo piece. Uncannily for someone with such bad eyesight she never touched a turd. They do say when you lose one sense your other instincts compensate. Mam always left the dog do-do on the shovel till last. When all the coal was in place she took the shovel by the handle and tossed the turds on the top. They had to go on the fire. Mam knew that if we didn't burn them we'd end up with more crap than coal. When all this was completed, I would hand Mam the box of matches.

Taking out a match, she would strike it along the sandpaper away from her body. We'd heard dreadful tales of silly boys striking matches towards their bodies and setting fire to their celluloid shirt collars. Separate collars were worn then. The collars would burn fiercely, cooking their heads. Alternatively, if you had celluloid spectacle frames, they could burst into flames leaving you with cracked lenses and a short frizzy haircut, and you wouldn't like that would you. I never saw a celluloid collar. Woolworth's sold thin cardboard ones that weren't easy to light. The only consequence I suffered from striking matches towards me was a slight singeing of the hairs on my woolly pullover. Mam wore glass and metal specs but she still always stuck the match away from her.

When the fire started going, Mam would stand the shovel up in front of it and put a sheet of newspaper over the shovel and the fireplace opening. The shovel stopped the paper going onto the fire. This arrangement caused the fire to suck air from under the grate quite dramatically. The newspaper would be sucked tight against the fireplace opening, only the shovel stopped it being pulled into the fire. Sometimes the roaring fire was so intense the heat would cause the newspaper to catch fire. This was very alarming, a blaze in the living room. Mam would calmly take the shovel and use it to push the fiercely burning paper into the fire, thus saving the day. All this was called 'Drawing the fire'. If this didn't work, I fetched the bag of sugar and Mam threw a handful on the sluggish glimmer and it would burst into flame. The fire had to be seriously struggling before this extravagance was brought into play. When the fire was nicely burning, it was time to clean up. I would hand Mam the push-out brush and small brass shovel from the fireside 'Companion set'. Companion sets comprised a small shovel, coal tongs, brush and a poker, all placed either in a container or dangling from a stand. Whether they were called companion sets because the objects were company for each other or for the owner I don't know. I never found them much company. The hearth nicely cleaned, Mam would put her left hand on the fire surround for support, her right hand on her back to signify the effort she'd gone through, then she'd stand up. That was how my Mam made the fire.

The fire only radiated heat a short distance and the clotheshorse, constantly drying clothes, usually blocked this off. If the clotheshorse wasn't in front of the fire, Granny Annie would be. She'd stand there with her skirts pulled up warming her pink bloomer-enclosed bum. People during the food shortage endearingly called this action, 'Warming dad's supper'. In other words the only person going to have something warm inside them was the lady of the house. If I managed to catch a moment when the front of the fire was clear of bodies, I would stand there myself with my legs apart, hands behind back, like the Lord of the Manor. It wouldn't be long, though, before Granny would say 'Let the dog see the bone' or 'You'd make a better door than a window'. Then I would have to move and Granny or Dad would pinch my place. If Dad did it, I had a way of getting my own back. I'd wait until the back of his floppy long trousers started steaming, then I knew they were really hot. I'd grab his trousers just below his knees and pull it forward. The hot cloth at the back would be pulled against his calves and oh how he'd jump with pain. The effect is known as 'Joan of Arc leg'. He couldn't play the trick on anyone else because he was the only one wearing long trousers in the house. I didn't realise how painful it was until I got to wear long trousers and it was done to me. It was for this reason that Levi had to get rid of the crutch rivet in their jeans. It got so hot by the campfire cowboys burnt themselves. I suppose the trick should have been called Guy Fawke's leg but he was only burnt in image on bonfire night.

Coprophiliac capers

(Fun with sewage)

Weeks before Bonfire night we'd go 'Chumpin' for chumps'. Chumps were any piece of wood or branches and chumpin' was collecting them. We'd go chumpin' in Lillands Wood. We thought

Coprophiliacs' Christmas tree.

nothing of chopping down small trees and dragging them back to the Bonfire. Neighbours would give us Windsor chairs, chaise longues, chest of drawers, which all went on the fire, thus ensuring their antique scarcity value in the future. The fire was usually built with a tunnel to a den in the centre. This was so the fire could be guarded from rival gangs intent on stealing your chumps or, worse still, setting them on fire. I never quite understood the logic of guarding a Bonfire from the inside, 'a pile of chumps with chumps inside'.

The night before Bonfire night was 'Mischief night'. Mam, if she remembered, put a bucket of water on the gas cooker to catch any bangers or, worse still, jumping crackers dropped down the chimney. A very old mischief was pinching people's gates. It's so old it's mentioned in the Bible. Samson did it. Judges 16:3. A favourite trick was called 'Bull-roaring'. We'd stuff as much crumpled newspaper as we could up someone's cast iron drainpipe, then we'd light it. If conditions were right, the paper would burn fiercely like a blowlamp. The drainpipe sucked in air and roared like a rocket. It was quite alarming for the owners of the house but, if they were lucky, their drainpipe didn't crack. Nowadays, with plastic drainpipes, they just melt. The 'Sneck trick' was a particularly unpleasant coprophiliac caper. (A coprophiliac is someone who has an unhealthy interest in poo. Not to be confused with a copoclephillisite, a collector of keyrings.) A sneck is the lever device that goes through a door to lift the latch so you can open the door. You held the handle, pressed the sneck down with your thumb; this lifted and disengaged the latch so the door could be opened. I think the whole thing is now called a 'Suffolk latch'. The trick was to stick a drawing pin smeared with dog muck on the sneck. The dog muck helped to keep the drawing pin in place, 'Blue-tac' not having been invented yet. The unsuspecting person wishing to gain entry would press their thumb on the sneck, thus pricking themselves on the prepared drawing pin. They then would automatically suck the thumb with the dog muck on. I think it was more the thought of it that seemed to amuse. I never saw it actually happen but it's worth bearing in mind if you're in Suffolk on Mischief night.

From 'A Glossary of Dialect of Almondbury & Huddersfield',
Easther. When Mr Franks, Vicar of Huddersfield, was about
to appoint a new incumbent to Slaithwaite, an old disciple well
known for his plain speaking said, 'Yo' mun ha' one 'at'll go to
t'thumb-sneck as well as to t'brass rapper'.
i.e. Call on rich and poor alike.

Another dog-dung jape was to find a fresh lump, preferably not a white one, they tended to be dry and crumbly, and, when you got a good specimen, put it in a paper bag or wrap it in newspaper. Place it on a doorstep, set fire to the whole thing, knock on the door and run away. The householder, on opening the door, sees the fire and stamps it out. Thus getting doggie do-do all over his or her shoes. This prank is particularly satisfying if the dung is from their dog.

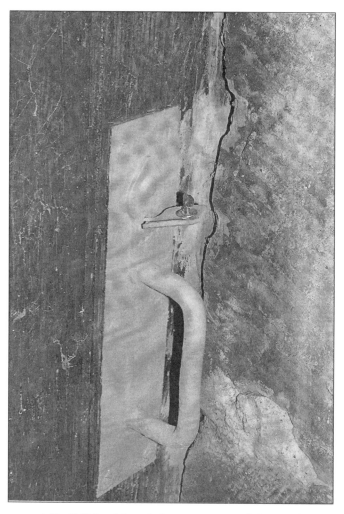

A 'Suffolk latch' with drawing pin and doggie do

The taller boys supposedly indulged in peeing through letterboxes. I never met the legendary lad who apparently peed through letterboxes and, instead of running away, would knock on the door and ask how far it had gone. Tying opposite house's doorknobs together with a clothesline and knocking on the two doors simultaneously needed planning. Knocking on doors and running away was by far the main prank of kids who wanted to irritate for England. It, of course, didn't work at our house if Doreen and me were out. Now, these kids who were good at knocking on doors and running away have all grown up. What are they all doing now? Grown-up japes with a post-rationing cavalier disregard for the cost of comestibles? Are they, for example, jamming potatoes up exhaust pipes, putting smelly kippers on car engines or replacing the gear stick knob with a plum? No, I suspect they are still knocking on doors. Even if you have a door bell it's ignored, they knock very quietly then they walk away quickly and silently but not before they've slipped a card through your letter box to say they've been. These kids have all grown up to become meter readers, plumbers, electricians and telephone engineers. They are still irritating England.

Potted nanny
(Meat paste)

Dad reckoned that he couldn't eat tomatoes because the skins stuck in his false teeth. He wouldn't eat them peeled because he said the seeds sprouted and grew in your belly. Corned beef was banned because he thought it was horsemeat and he knew it was dangerous. This, I think, came from the story of a butcher carrying a case of corned beef tins. He dropped the case on the table, unfortunately his testicles were resting on the table at the time. It was said his scream was heard all over Brighouse. Maybe it's a folk tale but this story had been drastically summarised to 'corned beef is dangerous'. This, coupled with the war time rumour that it was horsemeat, meant corned beef was not for Dad. He had no problem with what was called 'Potted Nanny'. I was suspicious of it; why Nanny? Cannibalism was common in children's stories then, for example Hansel and Gretel. Mainly, it must be said, with children being eaten, not old ladies reduced to meat paste. Nowadays it seems like a good idea with the surfeit of old ladies you see on the buses.

Then, I thought, it was goat meat, that is nanny goat meat. If so, why wasn't there any 'Potted Billy'? I'd never seen a goat but they must have been about because Dad insisted pasteurised milk was

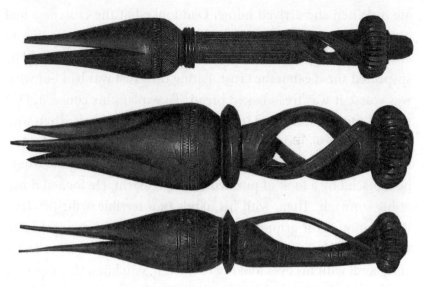

Fiji islands, wooden ceremonial cannibal forks.

goat's milk. Being from the country, he knew nothing tasting like that came out of a cow. The only other milk he knew of came from goats, so he reasoned it must be goat's milk. So was the paste nanny goat meat? No, it turned out it was simple beef paste. Why they all called it Potted Nanny I never found out. Chicken paste was not available then. I always tell the kids chicken paste is the stuff just under the chicken's skin that holds the feathers on.

Dad liked Potted Nanny, it was gentle on his teeth. Apples were not gentle on his teeth. They were always peeled with a knife, cut and eaten in small pieces. He never bit into an apple. His fruit etiquette was good but not his bread etiquette. Which I understand is you should break off a piece and then eat it. Miss Kath Evans, a stickler for correctness, always said, 'I would rather admit my father was a murderer than be seen biting bread'. (I understand the thinking behind this was that only animals bite.) That's how awful it was in some circles. My father had no such qualms, he bit into bread with gusto, but not fresh bread. Fresh baked bread was absolutely not to be eaten. Doreen was once sent to Sim's shop for a loaf of bread. Walking home with the loaf she picked the crunchy crust off and ate it. When she arrived home, Dad looked at the crust-less loaf puzzled. She smiled, mimed and mouthed 'Mr Sims says they're all like that today'. Dad was mortified, despite what Doreen said he suspected she'd eaten the crust. Eating the crust was bad but what was worse it was fresh baked bread. To explain his concern, Dad mimed putting the bread in his mouth and chewing it. Then with a big gulp he would dramatically swallow the mime bread. He'd then smile as if every thing was all right, suddenly his smile would be replaced by a look of puzzlement then alarm. He looked down at his stomach. Then, with his hands in a terrible arthritic claw-like motion, as if gripping a defenceless kitten, he squeezed and squeezed it. Then, sucking in his cheeks, he crossed his arms on his chest and, with his eyes looking to heaven, you knew this was how the fresh bread reacted in your belly, sucking out all your body juices before you died. This left you in no doubt that fresh bread was a stomach-shrinking poison that would suck all the juices out of you and leave you all dried up like a desiccated Egyptian mummy. He looked at us knowingly, shaking his head from side to side and wagging his index finger like a metronome. Indicating don't do it, it's not worth it. We waited for the terrors of the fresh bread to affect Doreen. They never did, but this didn't shake our belief in Dad because Mam said you couldn't trust shopkeepers, it must have been yesterday's bread. Doreen never did it again.

It was all very medieval. I later found that in the old days they had trial by ordeal. They had to grip a red-hot iron bar; if they burnt their hands they were guilty. Suspect witches were thrown into ponds; if they floated they were guilty. This was only for poor people. The clergy were different, they, like our Doreen, had trial by bread. They would call on the wrath of God to strike them dead if they were guilty when they bit into a slice of bread or, more correctly, broke a bit off and put it in their mouth. Being wealthy clergy and thinking there was a very, very slight chance it could be his last meal, he'd probably made it a jam sandwich just in case. Surprisingly I don't think there's a case of any clergyman being found guilty in a trial by jam sandwich. Like my Dad and me, they knew what the secret was, don't eat fresh bread and you'll live.

Eating fresh bread was bad, but what about chewing gum I hear you cry? Well, we were allowed chewing gum even though it irritated and confused Mam with her lip-reading. Chewing toffee was, of course, worse. The chewing gum was all right, it was the consequences of swallowing the gum that was so terrible. To explain the evil of swallowing gum, Dad would mime unwrapping and putting the gum in his mouth and chewing it. All the time he smiled. Smiling indicated only unsuspecting idiots did this. Then he pretended to swallow the imaginary gum and, with his index finger, he traced on his chest the path of the gum from his throat. Strangely it didn't go to his stomach but to his heart. Then stretching his arm out with his index finger pointing downwards he would swing the finger from side to side like an upside down metronome. Clicking his tongue in time to the jerky swing. This indicated a healthy heart beating. The unsuspecting chewing innocent, still smiling, and the finger continued to swing from side to side, in time to the tongue-clicking beat. Not for long though; suddenly the smile would vanish. The finger stopped abruptly, held fast at the end of a swing, stuck. The finger struggled to release itself from the gum. The gum held. The finger struggled harder. The finger manages to free itself. It swings once and sticks at the other side. With superhuman effort it manages to free itself again. It swings back and sticks fast, exhausted. The chewing gum had won. The heart had stopped. Dad's eyes closed slowly. The finger stayed, rigid, stuck. He opened his eyes, looking to heaven as if to say if only I had listened. He paused, his eyes closed, his head dropped to his left shoulder; he was dead. Pausing in his dead pose for greater effect, and because you didn't recover quickly from mime death, his eyes would open and, with his palms upwards; he would look to heaven and hold his hands up as if surrendering to God. Then, licking his index finger, he'd draw a cross over his heart and hold his right hand up as if swearing an oath. This indicated that every one, including God, knew what he said was true. He then pointed at Doreen then me, this meant no excuses, we had been told, so we now knew what happened when we swallowed chewing gum. His warning came too late. He must have been talking about old-fashioned chewing gum because it didn't happen when we swallowed the new stuff.

I was reminded recently of Dad's swinging pendulum heart. Mrs Annie North, my first mother-in-law, suffered from what I call 'Surrealist hypochondria'. She said that the doctors couldn't X-ray her hiatus hernia because every time they attempt to do it her heart swings in front and hides it. She's got a peakaboo organ. How does it know?

Communion cycle

Pigeon catcher.

Meanwhile in Melanesia

Life had order to it then. You knew what was expected of you. You were born, you went to school, you left, got a job, married, had kids, died and went to heaven. This was the road to happiness. That's what every one followed and they were happy, weren't they? To show you were on the right path you had to acquire the correct stuff. The doors had to be flushed. That is, a sheet of hard board nailed over them so they were nice and flat. We were just catching up with the Deco style. Your best room had to have a three-piece suite, a tiled fireplace with a mantelpiece crammed with brass ornaments, and a china cabinet with your coronation mugs and souvenirs. Things like inside toilets, etc., came later.

When you'd got all these things, you could relax, assured you'd done right and wait for the end with a quiet confidence. You could sleep with your flushed doors unlocked, confident that you wouldn't be burgled because you'd nothing worth pinching. Now everybody is confused because the list keeps changing and it's getting longer. People are having to build stone fireplaces with extended mantle pieces to get all their stuff on. The secret's a short list and an achievable, limited palette. Back then, we looked at our betters, the people with good stuff, and we knew that if we followed what they did we were in with a chance of getting more good stuff before going to heaven.

Meanwhile in Melanesia (New Hebrides), in the middle of the jungle, the natives were putting up fences, where there wasn't anything to fence in and building odd, non-functional gates that secured nothing. Forming themselves into lines, they would march up and down with sticks over their shoulders. Having lived on the islands for hundreds of years without doing these things, they now felt compelled do them because they believed that if they performed these meaningless rituals their god, 'John From' (pronounced frum), would send them everything they need. How do they know this? They knew this because they'd seen it happen many times.

The American soldiers on the island put up fences and gates and marched up and down, all for no apparent reason. Then, every so often, an aeroplane comes with a cargo of fridges, radios, toasters, cigarettes, doughnuts, bubble gum and coca-cola. So it was obvious, to the islanders, the reason for this apparently pointless marching and building could only be a form of worship. They concluded that if they do the same things, 'John From' will send them the same stuff, which they believed should have come to them in the first place. Because these people were originally cannibals, Paul Theroux reckoned they were very fond of Spam because it was the nearest thing to human flesh. If they couldn't get Spam they'd eat corpsey flavoured corned beef. 'The Cargo Cult' still exists today and they're still waiting for the goodies.

They now also revere Prince Philip. He's living proof that if you do the right things, no matter how bizarre, everything will be handed to you on a plate. Here they see a man who apparently only walks up and down in fancy clothes and he is given everything he wants. He is living proof that the method works. I imagine somewhere in Melanesia a native is walking up and down with his hands tucked into a pin-striped bark loin cloth, attractive banana skin epaulettes, shell medals and a nice plaited palm sash with a star fish on it. A lesser native might respectfully say to him, 'How was your coconut today sir?' 'Have you ever had a coconut?' Prince Phil would ask. 'Yes', would come the reply. Then the fake Phil, emulating the wit of his counterpart, would reply, 'Well it was like that, now bugger off'.

This may all seem simple-minded and far away, but a chap in Brighouse once stopped me. He'd spotted that I was wearing various finger rings. He informed me that this was not the done thing. His code for success in life was simple, 'If Prince Philip doesn't do it then I don't', he said. The last time I heard about this chap, he was living on state benefits. What more proof do you need that, in a way, he was right?

So we all see the same world around us but arrive at different conclusions, not always wrong but different, for example ballet dancing to a deaf person. One deaf lad watching ballet on television, saw a grown man in tights standing with his feet in the 10 minutes to 2 o'clock position, his arms curved above his head whilst he gazed intently at his extended forefinger. The lad concluded this could only mean one thing, the weird person had just removed some of the contents of his nose and was holding them up to the light to get a better look. This image he had, of something in the hearing world, he thought very amusing and he elaborated on it, when re-enacting the incident to his mates in the playground. First he'd stood in the ballet position with his forefinger up his nose. After a twiddle of his foot, he'd then remove an imaginary bogey from his nose. Holding it up, he would gaze at it lovingly and then start the dance. Bringing his finger to his thumb, he'd dramatically flick the invisible snot into the air. Watching it go up, he'd follow it's flight path with his eyes. Then on it's descent he'd dance forward, catching it in his mouth. Then, with raised eyebrows, he'd look amazed at his empty finger. Which he would then stick back up his nose to evacuate more snot. All sorts of pirouettes, jumps and ballet steps would follow, whilst he extracted copious amounts from his nose. Finally he'd stick both left and right index finger up each nostril. Elegantly removing the fingers he'd extend his arms as if pulling out two long stretchy chewing gum-like bogies. It was rather like the action of a dancer delicately holding out her skirt to do a curtsy. He would bow, with arms out. The silent snot dance was over. It all had a meaning now, so we cheered, various speech impediments permitting.

Extremely repulsive thing carrier.

THE SILENT SNOT DANCE

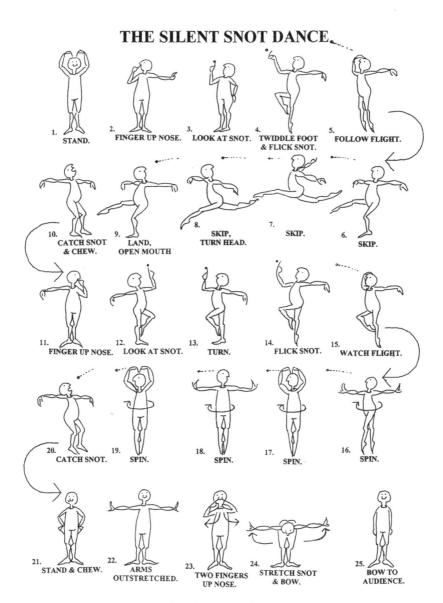

The silent snot dancer.

Put the children on OXO !

Children of all ages love a cup of delicious, beefy OXO. At mid-morning, lunch-time and bed-time hot OXO is always the favourite — and it does them lots of good.

But it's Oxo!

When we eventually got a television, Mam and Dad watched it a lot. They'd watched it with the sound turned up high; they still couldn't hear it. Mam probably thought, if we're paying for sound, I'm having all the sound I can get for my money. Mother told me the deaf had to pay for TV licences the blind didn't. I thought the explanation for this was if you could hear what the chap was saying but couldn't see him it was free, if you could see him but had not a clue what he was talking about you had to pay. So seeing a person on TV was more important than what they were saying. Dad agreed with this, to him most television shows were a load of ducks. To illustrate this he'd hold his hand up and do the action of a duck quacking, then he'd shake his head to show his disapproval. In other words, television to him was a lot of mouths opening and shutting with nothing intelligible coming out. Consequently he liked shows with lots of action, real-life drama and most of all no talking. In other words, wrestling; for Dad it had everything he could understand and he totally believed all he saw. Which for some reason really annoyed me. It was like trying to reason with a Jehovah's Witness. I gave up trying to persuade him that it was all rehearsed, realising that if I succeeded he'd lose a lot of pleasure in his black and white, goody and baddy, TV world.

Mam was very much influenced by television. It was a window that showed her things to add to her list of life, whilst they broadcast she was receiving and, if they advertised it, she bought it. Mam got a red vinyl-covered 'Comfy mat', it took the strain out of tired feet while washing up. The rest of the strain was taken out by making Doreen and me do the washing up. We were lucky, other kids didn't have Comfy mats. I'm sure she was right, because no one bragged about washing up at school, so I never mentioned we had a Comfy mat, no use creating petty jealousies.

The advert said 'Oxo made the best gravy'. Mam took this literally and made gravy by putting one Oxo cube in a gravy boat of warm water. Everyone knows that bad gravy doesn't move on the plate. The trouble with Mam's gravy was it moved too much. If you allowed her to pour this beef-flavoured water on your plate, it turned your mashed potatoes into a thin gruel sludge, which slid through your fork. Smiling, like the lady in the advert, Mam would mouth to me, 'Gravy?' 'No, thank, you', I would mouth back. The 'Thank' involved a very satisfactory sticking out of the tongue on the 'Th', like a rude Maori warrior. Then, in unison with her, I would mouth her reply, 'But it's Oxo'. We went through this ritual every time we had gravy. I always said, 'No'. She always said, 'But it's Oxo'. Because of this, I always refused all gravy and it was years before I knew what real gravy tasted like. Dad, who didn't like to give offence, accepted Mam's gravy. He was crafty though; instantly the potatoes were on his plate he would squash them flat with his knife and draw the fork across them as if ploughing a field. The affect was to corrugate the spuds, so when the watery gravy was poured on it ran off, leaving the rest of his food stuck up like little islands in a black pond. Consequently, because Dad had her gravy, she thought it was all right so she always made it that way. If I copied Dad I was accused of playing with my food; it was easier just to refuse the gravy.

Years later I had a similar experience with a lady called Ada Yinka Dada. She cooked me a meal of roast beef and potatoes and asked if I would like gravy. So as not to give offence, I said, 'Yes please'. She poured it, I tasted it, and the gravy was superb. 'How about Yorkshire Pudding?' she asked. 'Yes please', I replied my confidence growing. To my amazement she carefully poured it, from a jug, onto my plate, as if decanting a precious port. She'd been given the recipe and it was assumed she'd know that it had to be cooked. She didn't. At the time I thought of Dad drinking Mam's gravy and, so as not to give offence, I asked for a spoon and ate it.

I had to be very careful what I said I liked to Mam. Heinz tinned spaghetti was advertised on the television so she bought a tin. I said I liked it, instantly the cupboard was full of spaghetti tins. She now knew what I liked, so she no longer needed to waste her precious time thinking what to feed me. The dog was sorted, he liked Pal. I liked tinned spaghetti and that was what we were both getting for the rest of our lives. Many, many, many meals later, I was like the Israelites who got fed up eating manna for 40 years. Numbers 11:1–6. I couldn't wait 40 years to complain to God, who always answers prayers. Usually the answer is 'No'. So I complained to Mam. I did this by tapping the flat of the back of my hand under my tomato coloured chin, double chin massage style; this is not the sign for full up, it's the sign for fed up. I'd amplify the hand sign by mouthing, 'Fed up spaghetti'. My mouth, incidentally, had the little groove one gets from sucking in miles of spaghetti. 'Fed, up, spaghetti', I repeated. She looked at me with that 'you ungrateful fickle bastard' look, 'I feed you this expensive exotic foreign food and now you say you don't like it'. She then mouthed, 'You said, you like'. In her world you didn't sometimes like and sometimes not like, you just did not change your mind. Things were black or white, no grey; right or wrong, good or bad, no in between. The dog had more strength of character. He knew what he liked and he ate what he liked, the same thing every day. I suppose she thought

I'd be no different. I offered to swap with the dog. She tossed her head in disgust and informed me Timmy didn't like spaghetti. The next time I looked in the cellar head larder there was only tinned dog meat. I thought she'd called my bluff. I hid a tin to see what her reaction would be. She said nothing. The next day there was a tin of Fray Bentos meat pudding next to the dog meat. Did you know Fray Bentos is actually a town in South America?

Which reminds me, one day I walked in and they were absolutely engrossed watching a game of polo, very popular in Argentina. In England, though, it was a sport you rarely saw on television and never in real life. Dad had played hockey at school, so he probably thought it was American cowboy hockey. They were very puzzled; here were men on horseback charging up and down with big hammers. They'd never seen anything like this on the local football pitch. They watched closely and at half time the men and horses left the pitch. Fair enough, but then all the spectators walked onto the pitch and started what's called 'Treading in'. The clods of earth that the ponies kick up have to be trod back down so they have a nice flat pitch for the second half. So Mam and Dad are watching this game in which men on horses are belting up and down a field and suddenly they all stop and trot off the field. Then hundreds of people walk onto the field all looking down. That is the visual image seen by Mam and Dad. Mam turned to me and said, 'Someone lost something?' I, of course, rather than explain said, 'Yes'. Then I added, 'poor people'. She accepted this because the women were wearing headscarves not hats. When they all left the field, before she could ask where they were going, I mouthed, 'Couldn't find it, must have left it at home.' I left the room because I knew what the next question would be.

When I eventually started appearing on television myself, Dad was very proud. When we met anyone, he would draw a square with his two index fingers to represent a television set, point at me, then stick his thumb up. This all meant he's on television and he's very very good. It did my ego a power of good until I found out he'd been watching Mike Harding *The Rochdale Cowboy* thinking he was me. Well, at the time I didn't visit very often. I have actually been mistaken for quite a few people, including Viv Stanshaw, Clive Dunn and Magnus Pike. The worst put down was when I got a letter that started 'Dear Alf, I'm sorry I don't remember your other name'.

I also realised how little notice people took of me in real life when I went into the Studio 58 coffee bar in Huddersfield. I'd been going to the place for years. One day the woman behind the counter said to me 'You've got red hair'. What a strange remark, I thought, from someone I'd seen so often, 'What do you mean?' I asked. 'Oh', she said, 'we've just got a colour telly'.

Photo of me on the Jigsaw set.

Granny didn't have a bouquet so she came as one.

Bother bike.

Chimley chickens and Granny's tuppence

(Chickens used as chimney flue brushes and Grandmother's two pennies)

Granny Annie was my Mam's Mam. She lived in the room above us. My Granddad was dead. All I knew about him was he'd worked for the electricity board and was an illegal street corner bookie and moneylender. Granny said, to commend him, that he never spat in the street. From which I concluded he only spat in the house, for hygiene's sake probably into the fire. There was an awful lot of spitting done then. You don't see the 'No spitting' signs on buses anymore. It seems disgusting to us nowadays that people then needed to be told not to spit. We know it's a foul habit. Of course spit is biodegradable,

'Ee by gum' (as they say we say in Yorkshire.)

unlike chewing gum; we now live in a maculate world, just look down and count the spots.

Granny slept in a double bed that came out of a huge cupboard and stood on iron legs. The cupboard had two very shiny doors, with those strange half and half veneers that look like the folded paper ink blots used in the Rorschach psychiatric test. I must have been very disturbed because all I could see in the swirling grain was two devils swinging two babies round by their legs. She was completely unconcerned by them because the bed was correctly placed for her version of what we now call Feng Shui. This dictated that the foot of the bed should not face the door; her bed didn't. The reasoning was that when you died they carried you out feet towards the door. So to sleep with your feet towards the door was dicing with death. She slept soundly on one side of the bed at the beginning of the week then swapped to the other side at the end of the week. This was considered quite sensible because it wore the sheets evenly. Granny sang to me the first song I ever heard. At the time I hadn't a clue what the song was about. It went like this: 'Who's this coming down the street? Mrs Simpson's sweaty feet. She's been married many times before. Now she's knocking on Edwards's door.'

Granny's first job, she told us, was holding cows' tails while they were milked; apparently you can get a very nasty whiplash on the face from a shitty cow's tail. They later invented a wire device that held the cow's tail, which probably made her job obsolete. Such is progress, now the milker and the milkee's tail holder is gone. It's no fun for the cow lashing the milking machine. Granny was what they called a 'Charwoman'. Her patrons preferred to call her a cleaning lady. She cleaned for ladies in the neighbourhood. Not that their houses needed cleaning or they couldn't do it themselves, it was a status thing. They would actually spend hours cleaning their houses and then have a cleaning lady come in. It wasn't any use having a cleaning lady if no one knew it. So they would slip

Just before we crashed and I got my first black eye.

A perfume brick.

*Granddad's monocle
Used for watching the eclipse
1927.*

Gafas para los muertos (spectacles for the dead).

it into conversation. Such as: 'What a lovely hat you're wearing today Mrs Broadbent'. 'Oh! Do you think so? I'm not so sure of the colour; African violet does seem to clash with my peccary handbag. I'm just wearing it to the hairdresser's. Then when I get back home I'm giving it to my cleaning lady.' Fashion, status and philanthropy all in one go.

Most women's hats were peculiar, more symbolic than practical; they were very small. It was as if they'd taken the crown of one hat and divided it up. Each bit was shaped like the left-over peel of sliced orange. That way, because of the shortages, instead of no hat at all each woman got a part of a hat. So women walked out with what looked like a cloth croissant with a bit of net to keep the flies off. A nice hat was much prized. 'That's very good of you Mrs Broadbent, is it your cleaning lady's birthday?' 'Oh no, we got her a new bucket for her birthday.' They couldn't be letting the charlady get too uppity.

Listening to conversations like this, I overheard that my Granny 'Laid out people'. I thought for long enough this meant she could flatten people with one punch. So I regarded her with greater respect. I'd lurk around when she was having rows hoping to see her flatten someone. Later I discovered 'Laying out' meant Granny sorted dead bodies out. Funnily when I told my grandchildren that grandma laid people out they thought exactly the same.

If the dead person's eyes were open she would close them and weigh the eyelids down with old pennies to make sure they didn't open again. Granny never would give you her last tuppence. They were tools of the trade, you know. Knowing about Granny's pennies I was very much alarmed when on the work's trip to Blackpool I banged my eye riding in a dodgem car. I was getting used to the pain when it was suggested to Dad that he put a penny on it. I didn't realise this was in lieu of a steak. I thought I was on my way out and Granny would be round any minute with another penny for the other eye and her washing bucket. Her job was to wash the body, even if it wasn't bath night, and redress them in their 'Laying out clothes'. These clothes were always kept in the bottom drawer. Kept sweet smelling with a 'Perfume brick'. Women were always ready for the two main stages of life. They had a bottom drawer ready for when they got married and then it was replaced with one for when they died.

Dying was cheaper for a woman; she only needed a nice nightie, a pair of knickers and, for some reason, Granny had a pair of very thick white woolly bed stockings in her bottom drawer. Bed stockings were always very thick and very woolly and totally unsuitable for anything but wearing in arctic bedrooms. You couldn't wear them even inside the slackest wellies. The bed socks were included, I think, because Granny hadn't seen any pictures of coal fires in Heaven. All the coal was of course in Hell and she was taking no chances of having cold feet. Even so, she couldn't have been that concerned because I don't recall her packing a balaclava, although I seem to remember her wearing a pretty white one in her coffin and when I kissed her she was like an ice lolly. Men, of course, went fully clothed. I remember two old chaps outside David's shop. One said, 'Your suit's looking a bit tatty Jim'. 'Yes', Jim replied, 'it'll not see me out, I'll soon have to go to bed'. You see Jim knew it wasn't worth buying another suit because he wouldn't get the wear out of it before he died. He probably ended up buried in a fake suit. Fake suits are the ones that are just a front and tie up the back, like the gowns in hospital. This was the basis of the first play I wrote, *Benny Rolly*. The plot had absolutely nothing to do with the real Benny Rolly. He was an older lad who lived on the road. I just thought it was a great name.

I saw a girl on television the other day she said, 'My sister's very clever she's even read Roger's Theory' (*Roget's Thesaurus*). Granny made the same kind of mistakes, mishearing what was said. (Misheard words are called mondegreens.) I once heard her bragging to a neighbour about my abilities. I think she must have thought I was reading about competitive bakery. She said, 'Yes he's reading a book it's called, *The Currant Teacake Exhibition*'. That puzzled me for a while, till I picked up the book I was reading, *The Kontiki Expedition*. She even got my Dad's name wrong in her Will, she called him Rueben Bertie Lunn. Dad got us a small weird dog. When fully grown, it looked like a fat Alsatian puppy. When a neighbour asked what kind of dog it was, Granny said it was a 'House agent'.

When we got the dog we were told it was a bitch. This information seemed to upset Auntie Ethel. She didn't want to know it was a bitch and she didn't think anyone else did either. To her, bitch was a thing you did, or a bad woman. Auntie Ethel was married to Uncle Ronny; they lived in Sowerby Bridge. When I was small Uncle Ronny used to give me a rolled-up newspaper and hold me up high so I could swat the normally unreachable high-altitude flies, when in season of course. So I was put to work, quite young, fighting disease.

Auntie Ethel came to our house every Saturday. She was very keen on stopping nail biting and encouraging the exposure of cuticles on our fingernails. She would bribe us to push the skin down on our nails with the towel to make the cuticles show. It was also her mission in life to stop us saying 'Eh?' or 'What?' We had to say 'Pardon?' Auntie thought this was correct; she was, of course, completely wrong. She would inform me when I was being naughty but would often not tell me why. I was told not to hum tunes. When I asked why, she'd say, 'It's rude'. Later I found out it wasn't the humming that she thought was rude, it was what I was humming. I didn't know the words. Auntie Ethel obviously knew the words. The song was 'Hitler has only got one ball'.

The very first rude song I knew, I learned at junior school from a lad called Martin Brown. It was sung to the tune of *Blaze Away*. I don't know what it was called but it went like this:

'In't it a pity she's only one titty to feed the baby on.
In't it a bugger it can't have another. Berrom berrom berrom'.

He also had a much ruder one sung to the theme tune of *Desert Island Discs*.

Auntie Ethel's reaction was the same when I started calling people 'Twats'. She wouldn't tell me what it meant, it just had not to be said. I remember her trying to tell me not to say the word, without saying the word herself. She would wince when I said it and look round hoping no one was in earshot. 'You mustn't say that word again.' 'What word?' I'd ask. 'You know, that word.' Innocently I'd look up at her and say, 'Twat?' She'd whisper, 'Yes, stop it'. As if talking about the word without saying it was just as bad and by whispering God might not hear. She asked where I'd heard it. I said a teacher had called me it. That threw her. She said, 'Well, you could knock me down with a feather'. Which threw me; I thought you could only knock someone down with a feather if it was still attached to the chicken. I don't think Auntie Ethel believed a teacher had called me a twat. Thinking back he probably called me a twit. I'm still not sure what either word means. It was rather like the girl who asked what 'Confidential' meant. She was told it was something we didn't talk about. So she assumed it was something rude and never mentioned it again. I was not like that girl. I took every opportunity to tell anyone, whether they wanted to know or not, particularly adults.

Some words are meaningless but sound rude. While I was working on *Jigsaw* I was involved in a scene in which the word 'Wazak' was used. The BBC sent me a letter from a woman complaining. The gist of which was that she didn't spend lots of money sending her daughter to school for her to come home and hear the word 'Wazak' on the television. In future she would make sure that her daughter never watched the BBC ever again. A covering letter asked me what the word meant. I contacted Clive Doig the producer and pointed out that I hadn't a clue what the word meant but I was fairly certain that it wasn't rude. I then asked why the letter had been sent to me, since I hadn't said the word. I'd actual been called 'a wazak' by the puppet Hector the hedgehog. I must admit at the time I thought it sounded a bit off. I think the assumption was that any strange, rude, dialect-sounding words must have come from me. You don't have to use rude words for effect; said the right way, 'Pillow case' can sound very offensive.

Knowing Lassie our dog was a bitch, we took every opportunity to now use legitimately what we knew was a rude word. People would stop and would say to us, 'Oh what a lovely puppy. Is it an Alsatian?' 'No', I'd say, 'it's a bitch'. Two friends, John and Doreen Norris, came round one day; they said they'd told their mother our dog was a bitch. 'A bitch is it', she said, 'and I bet it's a bugger?' We kids thought, great, this must be one heck of a bad dog. Mrs Norris was right, the little sod was a bugger; it would come home with hens bigger than it was. I don't think she liked what we were feeding her. She didn't, of course, have a ration book. The dog had to stretch her head really high to drag the hens home; even then, she kept tripping over them. Why she brought them home I don't know. Perhaps she'd seen Dad plucking a hen and thought that maybe he'd do one for her. We were stuck with stolen dead hens. Eating them would have made us a party to the crime. Granny said, I think jokingly, 'Why don't we use it to clean the chimley?' 'The chimley', was, I later found out, correctly pronounced 'Chimney'.

Granny told us they used to clean their chimneys by tying a shelter brick to a bush and dropping it down the chimney. We always called bricks 'shelter bricks' because all the houses were stone; only the air-raid shelters were brick, so all bricks were called shelter bricks. For a really clean chimney, instead of a bush, a chicken was used, preferably a live one. The brick was dropped down with the rope and the chicken pulled through. The mad fluttering cleaned the chimney, partially plucked the chicken and, if the chimney was hot, part cooked it. The terror raised the adrenaline in the chicken and made it nicer to eat. This was because fear improves the flavour. Don't they all say food tasted better then? It had been common knowledge since the time of bull baiting. Everyone knew, in the past, a baited bull was more palatable. Cannibals understood this pre-cooking terror tip. Baiting and cannibalism are frowned on but there was a scary war on then. Scared food is tastier food. Now we're informed even plants have feelings. So I suppose a scared carrot is a tastier carrot. So don't talk to your plants like Prince Charles, threaten them. I never knew what happened to the dog's stolen hens. Dad never told me. I think he thought I might crack under interrogation. The hens' bodies just disappeared, and so did the dog.

When I was a student I got the worse for drink and returned home with five paraffin road lamps, which I left, still lit, on the kitchen table. When I came down in the morning the smell of paraffin smoke reminded me of my souvenirs. They were nowhere to be seen. Dad had hidden the evidence of my crime. He'd gone out and found the nearest hole in the road and put the lamps round it. It was not the hole I'd got them from. The workmen, I think, were used to lamps going missing but not increasing. Dad was very clever hiding the lamps where you would naturally expect them to be. But where would you put dead chickens that would appear normal. I concluded he must have put them on a Zebra crossing so it appeared they'd been caught unawares on a chicken's day out.

I'm reminded of a woman that I met in a shoe shop. She said she had to buy lots of shoes because her feet swelled up. She said, 'I'm working in temperatures of 90 degrees'. Amazed, I inquired where was she working. 'Elland brickworks?' I suggested. 'No', she said, 'the old folk's home, it's so hot the inmates are par-boiled'. 'I suppose it makes them easier to cook, sorry, cremate', I remarked. I was, of course, thinking of Potted Nanny and the chimney chickens.

Elland brickworks brings to mind Anton, a blind guy, who told me he'd been to Australia. I tried to persuade him he'd been conned, what was the point of sending a blind person on a scenic holiday? They could have saved money by sending him on a virtual reality holiday to Elland brickworks. There they have the heat and the dust. How would he know he wasn't in Australia? They could put his hands on a brick kiln and tell him it was Ayers Rock. They could give him senna pod wine and tell him he was in Egypt. He'd have the heat, the dust and the shits as well. How would he know the difference? I couldn't convince him, he was no fool, hadn't he planned the great escape from Tapton Mount School for the Blind? The escape party consisted of Anton, Colin, Andrew, Kevin and Brian; they all planned to boldly walk out of the school. Not so simple when you're blind. So they wouldn't be recognised, they made masks out of Braille paper. The stroke of genius was that they'd cut eyeholes in them. Any teacher from the school might wonder 'Who are those mysterious masked boys?' Then they'd note the eyeholes and realise they were not from Tapton School because they could see. As the escape approached, their morale was getting lower, so Anton decided to take his mandolin to keep their spirits up. Andrew said Mr Broom was on duty and he would be everywhere watching; it couldn't be done, he wouldn't risk it. Kevin said he wasn't scared but he had hurt his knee and he didn't want to slow them down. Colin said there was no point in him escaping because he was going home at the weekend anyway. Brian said it was a school rule that they were not allowed to cross roads; this meant they would probably end up just walking round the outside of the school until they were caught. Anton pointed out it was also a school rule that they were not allowed to escape. Anyway, he had the mandolin to keep both their spirits up. Then it started to rain; everyone knows what rain can do to Braille masks and mandolins. They regretfully had to call the escape off.

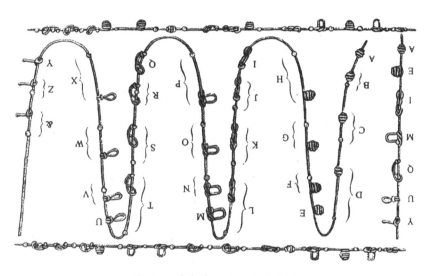

String alphabet, for the blind.
David Macbeath and Robert Mylne of The Edinburgh Blind Asylum
(circa 1850)

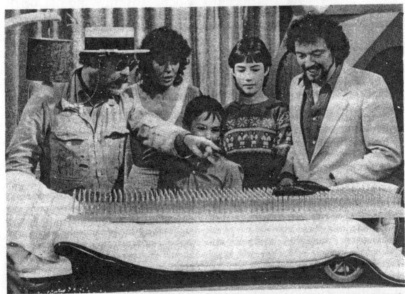

The Saturday Show launched a competition with Pepper Press recently to find the best 'outlawed invention' from a viewer. The competition evolved from publicity for OUTLAWED INVENTIONS by Chris Winn and Jeremy Beadle, and the winner was Paul Bedworth, aged 9, for his 'Uncomfortable Bed for Getting Rid of Boring Visitors'. Here Wilf Lunn (left) of the Saturday Show demonstrates how nails are hidden under the bed, and how a special device pulls rubber slugs up the bed. With him (from left) are Isla St Clair, Paul Bedworth, Sheila Hudson, the runner-up, and Jeremy Beadle.

Schooil

(School)

I understand I first went to Longroyd Nursery School when I was 3 years old. It was said that this was because my mother made a mistake about my age. She later caused a panic by informing them I'd had yellow fever. Jaundice was what she actually meant. I clearly remember having jaundice because during the day I was allowed to lie in Granny Annie's bed in the front room with the fire lit. This luxury was unheard of. I was given medicine that I had to drink through a straw to stop it touching my teeth. I think it was quinine. Usually when we were ill Mam would give us an eggcup full of 'Fennings' Fever Cure'. This stuff burnt the polish off your teeth, which wasn't surprising. I was told later that it was dilute nitric acid. The principle was that it dissolved the top layer off your teeth and throat, killing all the germs. I loved the taste.

I lay there all yellow and they fed me oranges. I didn't actually eat them, I sucked them dry. The skin was pierced and I squeezed and sucked the juice out. The outside lav was miles away, so I was allowed to use Granny's best po, and not just to pee in. I remember looking at the poo in the po and being alarmed; I'd never seen it so close up. Because I was sucking orange juice, my poo was not only orange but also round like an orange. It was as if my body was reconstituting the orange back to the solid. I was puzzled, but it wasn't a thing I ever mentioned to anyone, till now.

It wasn't far to school and I don't ever remember being taken there. I always went with Doreen and the other kids. Mam just pushed us out of the door into the stream of sad kids heading towards the school and assumed that's where we'd arrive. If she pushed us out and the kids weren't trudging past, we knew it was a holiday so we went back inside. Mam would look out to check and then let us stay. Otherwise it was off to school. I loved the summer holiday but I wasn't fond of Christmas. The only present I remember was a Black and Decker drill I got when I was 11. I've still got it. After all this time I can now afford the wood. My other memories are of a strange small Christmas tree that was made of green brushes on a stick stuck in a square red lump of wood. All the rest was trouble. Sentenced to the paper chain gang. The scary caretaker Santa. The jelly bowl I didn't bring back from the party. The tea towel famine because most of the kids had been shepherds in the nativity plays and lost them. All that joy. It was hell.

On the way to school we went through a derelict building we called the Mission. Apparently the demolition of this Primitive Methodist Mission Chapel had been started by a mini whirlwind in 1922. Obviously a sign from God that Thornhill Road didn't need converting. It was here that we often played at night, lighting fires and assisting in God's work by further demolishing the building. The spirit of Jericho, Joshua 8:20–21, and Oliver Cromwell was with us. They now call it vandalism.

After passing through the Mission it was an uphill walk to the nursery. The nursery was at the lower end of the junior school. The entrance was at the top of a huge flight of stone steps. With my little legs, it was like climbing a huge Ziggurat. Then, when we got to the top, what did we do? All I remember is we were given cod liver oil capsules to stop us getting rickets and, I think, a red pill like a 'Smarty'. Then we were put on small camp beds and made to pretend we were asleep. Women walked up and down the ranks of beds looking for any signs of cheating. The women then clapped their hands and we all pretended to wake up and they sent us home. The joy of the kids running home, with their Mac's like cloaks fastened at the neck with one button because we all knew heroes in a hurry always wear cloaks. From the nursery school we went on to the junior infants in the main school. In the morning, when we arrived in the school playground, we'd hang about doing whatever the season dictated, marbles, conkers, dead leg, which involved kneeing someone on the thigh hard enough for the leg to go dead and they'd fall over, or cock fighting, a game which involved avoiding being kicked in the crutch. A teacher would come out of the school furtively and watch silently for any naughtinesses. (Incidentally the word 'naughtinesses' is a crossword puzzle clue for a three-letter word and it's not SIN but it is to do with saving souls.) When the teacher was absolutely sure we were all fully occupied and happy in what we were doing and we had also completely forgotten we were at school, then, and not until then, she blew her 'Acme Thunderer' whistle. Instantly everyone froze as if in a photograph. No movement was allowed till the second whistle. We were kept in these poses and watched to make sure there was absolutely no movement. Because it could be a while between the two whistles, you quickly learnt it was a good idea, on hearing the first whistle, to strike a pose you could sustain. Preferably a pose that was not too exotic, with both feet on the ground. Lying down was suspect and was not allowed otherwise, when the whistle went, the yard would have looked as if a bomb had gone off. I think the whole exercise was originally an early type of health test. If you fell over, you were a possible contagious case. So it was a good idea to spot the sickly before they got into the building. The school didn't use my Granny's doorstep Dettol-dousing method of preventing germs entering the building so they had to be extra careful.

When the 'All-seeing eye' was satisfied that all had been sufficiently Medusa'd, the second whistle sounded and we all, in absolute silence, scurried to our class line. When queuing usually the idea is to be at the front. But on these occasions the reverse was true. No one wanted to be directly under the eye of the teachers. Much discreet positioning and tactics were involved. Suddenly lots of shoelaces needed retying and noses had to be picked. Kids' brains went blank and they walked in the wrong direction, like the zombie dead. These skills came in useful for some later in life when they used them to avoided being first at the pub bar to buy a round of drinks. Eventually we would all settle down and we'd look up and there would be Miss Milnes, the headmistress. She liked to tell us about cannibals and talked with relish about eating chubby children's bottoms. She'd silently emerged from the depths of the school while we were doing the great silent pose. The staff were all now standing like Indians round the rim of the canyon, watching over us unarmed cowboys and girls. She'd nod to her lieutenant with the whistle. This meant she was taking over. Then she would address us, 'Good morning children'. We'd all reply with one voice, 'Good morning Miss Milnes'. Then she would present the 'Good Shield'. It was shaped like a shield of old, in lovely polished wood with shiny silver bits. This jewel was presented to the class with the best attendance. It was usually a lower form where abject terror was still rife. Then came the 'Bad Shield'. Appropriately minimum

The Bad Shield. This shield went to the class with the poorest attendance.

effort had been put into making this badge of shame. It wasn't even shield shaped. It was square, painted black, with a big white question mark on it. As if to say 'What the hell are you slackers playing at?' This was obviously for the shortest queue, usually the queue that people like to be in, but not then. So the good kids that had turned up to school got the Bad Shield. The hostages suffered the shame.

The whistle was blown again and we all filed off to the cloakrooms, assembly and lessons. We seemed to spend most of our time learning our times tables 'Parrot fashion'. One 2's 2. Two 2's 4. Three 2's 6. My favourite, of course, was the 5 times table; 5, 10, 15, 20, 25, 30, and I could do it backwards. This was a product of Mam attempting to teach me how to tell the time.

I had early suspicions about teachers when one lad, Melvin, came in from the yard saying he'd hurt his leg. Our class teacher, a rangy young woman in a cotton frock, said it looked bad because he'd got two large lumps on either side of his ankle. I pointed out that I'd got the same lumps on my ankle and I felt no pain. In fact I got them on both ankle. 'Wasn't I brave?' Others in the class joined in to say they had the same lumps. After a quick check, we found everybody had them, including Miss Cottonfrock. The mystery was that none of us had fallen over in the yard. Miss looked at Melvin's other ankle to compare and found he had lumps on that as well. During the ensuing debate Melvin forgot which ankle he'd hurt. Miss said never mind, all was well, and we must get back to lessons. All was not well. I now had doubts about her infallibility. Then she told us about the Great Exhibition, how all the wonderful things were displayed in a place called the Crystal Palace. It was called the Crystal Palace because it was a great big building made of glass. One kid pointed out if it was made of glass there'd be no need to pay to get in to see the stuff. Miss Cottonfrock was stuck for an answer. Pausing to think, with a smile she said, 'You couldn't anyway, it burnt down ages ago'. A glass building burnt down, not likely, I thought. She liked to tell her stories with a device made from a cardboard box. The box had a window cut in the side so it looked like a television set. This was very forward thinking of her because none of us had ever seen a television set. On either side of the window were wooden dowel rods, which held a scroll of paper across the window. The dowel rods stuck out of the top of the box, each having a cotton reel pushed on it. By turning these cotton reels the scroll of paper moved in front of the opening, revealing a crayoned picture of each stage of the story. This was the third bit of technology I'd come across as a child. The first was the washing mangle, followed by the clock. This wasn't as good as the mangle. Things were going down hill. The story I particularly remember, because it left me perplexed was, John the Baptist and Salome. Mathew:14:1–10.

Miss told the story of how John was imprisoned and Salome wanted the King to chop his head off. All the time Miss was winding different pictures into the frame to illustrate that part of the story. At the beginning of the story, Miss told us that the King Herod had put John in prison because his wife said he had been rude to her. Salome didn't think prison was enough, she wanted his head chopped off. He must have been really rude. Of course there wasn't a picture illustrating this act of rudeness. We had to know what he'd done that was so rude he was put in gaol. Miss realised she would have to come up with an answer. She leaned forward conspiratorially. I leaned towards her, determined not to miss anything. In a low voice she whispered, 'Salome said'. Pausing, she continued in an even lower voice, almost just mouthing it, 'John looked at her knickers'. A stunned silence fell on the class. Here and there you could hear the voices of kids who hadn't been listening or couldn't lip-read desperately pleading, 'What did she say, what did she say?' I think we expected she'd say he'd stuck his tongue out at her, but not this. I wasn't convinced. Didn't they all wear long frocks in the olden days? He'd have had to lie on the floor as she was walking past to look up her frock and see her knickers. She'd spot him straight off, if she didn't trip over him. I suspected that she'd shown him her knickers deliberately and then told on him. I knew girls were like that. This hypothesis was born out at playtime when we lads had to avoid looking at the bolder girls doing cancan-style flashes of their knickers accompanied by the terrifying cry of 'I'll tell Miss on you.'

Trying to ignore them, we lads did what we nearly always did at break. We formed lines with our arms round each other shoulders. Then we charged or skipped round the yard chanting, 'Anybody playing at cowboys and Indians but no lasses?' Others would join the end of line. Sometimes it reached terrifying proportions, gathering would-be players. This was in fact the entire game, we never, ever got round to playing cowboys and Indians. All playtime was often spent in line prancing and chanting. It took our minds off school and it gave us a feeling of camaraderie; best of all it intimidated the girls. It was all very satisfactory. The girls couldn't flash their knickers in front of a chorus line of stampeding, would-be cowboys and live to tell Miss Cottonfrock.

I finally lost all faith in Miss Cottonfrock on the day Melvin informed me that men were in space and had landed on the moon. This was 1948. I knew my family wasn't in touch with all world events. We didn't have a wireless but I thought someone might have mentioned landing on the moon. I said it wasn't true. To prove his point he produced a book with illustration of all these occurrences. I said it was just a storybook. He decided he'd call on a higher power to arbitrate. He chose Miss Cottonfrock, she of the great lumpy leg medical mystery. She studied the book, brought in evidence, very carefully. She pronounced her judgement. Her judgement was, she wasn't sure. She wasn't sure. I was, but I was no longer sure of Miss Cottonfrock. Melvin was sure. He eventually became a vicar.

The next memorable lesson was not with Miss Cottonfrock. It was higher up the school and the lesson was 'Telling the time'. You'll note I didn't say learning to tell the time; I said telling the time. This frightening woman, Miss Torquemada, (not her real name) I'm still scared of her, first made us all stand on our seats. Then, using a white cardboard clock pinned to the blackboard, she would move the big and little hands to a time. She would then walk up and down between the rows of desks, while we quaked.

ADS (Attention Deficit Syndrome) was, at that time, not allowed. Stopping at the side of a child, always on her right, she'd look at the child and ask, 'What time is it?' If they got it right, they were allowed to sit down, if not they had to carry on standing. The situation got more alarming as she got frustrated with wrong answers and we realised why she was walking to our left from the back of the classroom. It was so she could give your left leg a really good smack. She strolled up the rows of bare legs. We all kept our eyes on her, like mice watching a snake. She slivered down my row past me. I think she heard my relieved heart slow down because she paused in her prowl. Turning to look straight at me, she asked, 'What time is it?' I looked from her face, with its slightly evil smirk, to the clock face. The big hand was at 12 and the little hand was at 3. I couldn't tell the time but I knew the hours, Mam had taught me. I was saved. I mumbled 'Three o'clock Miss'. 'Sit', she responded, disappointed at my success. I sat down in a forest of skinny legs. The class knew the way of things now. As she approached them, they instinctively tried to protect their left legs from smacking by lifting them to make a smaller target. So instead of a forest of skinny legs it was like being amongst a flock of flinching frightened flamingos standing on one leg. She'd silently stand by a flamingo who, knowing that standing on one leg wasn't allowed, would, hoping for mercy, nervously lower it back towards the seat. Like a person testing the bath water with their big toe. Thinking it might just be all right if they put the foot down. Then quick as a flash, 'What's the time?' 'Er, er, threety.' Thwack! She smacked them on the calf. Instantly they'd go back into the flamingo position, this time clutching the leg with the mouth wide open, like an empty eggcup, in a silent scream. Audible screaming was not allowed. When morning milk break arrived, the ones that had steadfastly refused to tell the time were allowed down off their rickety legs. The milk monitors would hand out the milk. They'd drink their milk thinking the ordeal was over, but it wasn't. Before they went out to play they were given a nice card with thick rough sisal string tied to it so it could hang round their necks. Printed on it in bold capitals was the word 'DUNCE'. This woman terrorised me for a year, then it was all over.

The rest of my junior school life was great. I was introduced to such luxuries as waxed paper straws and toilet paper printed with the command 'NOW WASH YOUR HANDS'. Pretty scary, because the toilet didn't have a sink. This toilet paper was available only on request from your class teacher. Never more than two sheets; if you needed more than two sheets you were considered ill. The toilets had screwed down seats shaped like a wooden horseshoe so you didn't pee on the front bit. This sign in a Gent's public toilet baffled me as a kid. Shouldn't it have been in the Ladies? 'PLEASE ADJUST YOUR DRESS BEFORE LEAVING'.

The school dinners were wonderful. Before eating we had to say 'Grace': 'For what we are about to receive may the Lord make us truly thankful. Amen'. Or, as we said it, 'Haymen', followed by a whispered 'Straw women'. We were taught how to hold our knives and forks. The fork, in the left hand, was held like a pen. The knife, in the right hand fist with the index finger pointing down it, to give added pressure when cutting. That was the way, no other way was allowed. To hold knife in the left hand was death. To this day I cringe if I see anyone deviating from this style. I really liked school dinners, they had that essential ingredient missing at home, quantity. The puddings were eagerly awaited, such things as 'Baby's arm', a kind of jam rolly polly, and 'Flies' graveyard', a flat pudding with currants on top. Semolina was always served with a small dollop of jam in the middle. When it was served it was customary to recite a little poem to try to put you off eating it. I don't know what the rhyme was called but it went like this:

'Scatter matter custard, green phlegm pie. All mixed up with a dead dog's eye. A worm in the middle to make it look thick. All washed down with a cup of cold sick'.

While this chant was being ignored, you would contemplate the semolina with its luxurious dollop of jam. I never found out which was the correct way to eat this. Did one eat the jam first then the semolina, or eat the semolina leaving a little island of jam? Could you perhaps take a little jam on the tip of your spoon with a little semolina? Some kids, obviously driven mad with indecision, would violently stir the whole lot into a pale pink sludge whilst mumbling 'All mixed up with a dead dog's eye.' If they were caught they were told never to do it again and informed by the teacher that 'If it was meant to be eaten like that it would have been served like that'.

These rebel freethinkers were in the mould of Wilber and Orville Wright, who were told 'If we were meant to fly God would have given us wings'. Or, lower down the scale, 'If we were meant to smoke we'd all have chimneys'. They carried on mixing the jam into the semolina. The only pudding that appeared to be in short supply was prunes and custard. There was always plenty of custard but very rarely more than three or four prunes. This was probably to stop mass visits to the toilet and thus save precious toilet paper. Or was it a conspiracy war propaganda prune pudding? You see, as we ate the prunes we put the stones on the side of the bowl. When we'd finished we'd say a poem counting on each stone to predict what we would be when we left school. Three prune stones meant you were going to be a soldier, four a sailor, five a war profiteer. If you got more it meant there was a fifth columnist spy in the kitchen. The Propaganda Prune Poem:

'Tinker, tailor, soldier, sailor. Rich man, poor man, beggar man, thief. Doctor, lawyer, Indian chief.'

At dinner you had to have what was served. You could ask for a small portion but you had to have some of everything. All food, when it was put on your plate, had to be eaten and you weren't allowed to leave the dining room till your plate was empty. On occasions we all would leave the hall while one sad child would be left gazing at a plate of gristle that looked like the cause of what killed the cow in the first place. Then one day I was that child. I normally ate my dinner with relish and was always first up for seconds. Until the day the cook put too much vanilla essence ($C_6H_3.OH.OCH_3.COH$) in the sponge pudding. Not paying attention, I received a large lump. I just couldn't eat it. When I brought the spoon towards my mouth the vanilla smell made me retch; it was nearly as bad as the worst smell in the world, the milk monitor's manky wiping-up cloth. Like opposing magnets pushing apart, I couldn't physically get the pudding in my mouth. I couldn't get it near my mouth. I tried closing my eyes but the smell was too strong. The smell was the problem. I never got to know the taste because I couldn't get it in my mouth. Now, you may think, why didn't I just give it to someone else so my plate was emptied? We all lived in such abject fear of catching diseases that we wouldn't dream of eating someone else's food. Especially when that person was retching over the plate and what was on the plate may have been eaten once and come up again. The rest of the kids hadn't a problem finished theirs and they all left for the playground. I felt every single eye on me as they walked to freedom. Some kids looked at me encouragingly whilst others were unable to conceal their glee at my discomfort. I avoided the girls' looks.

They all filed out full of the poison pudding. Teachers, dinner ladies and teachers' toadies busied themselves sorting out the room for the afternoon. Nothing was said to me. I knew I had to stay till the pudding was eaten. The tables were all cleared away. The big folding room divider was pulled across, making the hall into two classrooms. I was then sat, with my spoon and bowl, vanilla sponge and custard, at a desk, which was now at the back of someone else's class room. All the organising of the desks and chairs was going on around me. Most of the time I was completely ignored. Occasionally a pitying glance was cast my way but I mainly remember schadenfreude smirks: I had to eat the pudding and that was that. Then I was alone in the classroom. I could hear things going on outside. What was going to happen now?

What had happened to the kid with the gristle? I didn't remember ever seeing him again. Oh no! What had they done with him? The terrible thought crossed my mind. Was Miss Milnes really a cannibal that ate children's chubby bottoms? Looking at the pudding I knew there was no way I could eat it. The bowl had to be emptied. I could, of course, hide it in one of the desks. I knew God was watching me, but was anybody else? Before I could proceed with my plan, the door opened and in walked Miss Torquemada followed by her class. They all stood silently by their desks waiting for the instruction to sit. No one sat till Miss Torquemada sat, then, in a low voice she said, 'Sit'. They all dutifully sat. Except, of course, for the pretty girl whose desk I was sitting at. She was stuck up like a sore thumb and, to make herself more visible, she stuck her arm up and said, 'Please Miss?'

It was like baby bear discovering Goldilocks. This was real life, though, and I knew that real Mummy bears would eat Goldilocks, especially if they hadn't eaten their pudding. Then a strange thing happened; she told me to come to the front of the class with my bowl and spoon. I walked the long walk towards her. My hand was uncontrollably shaking. The custard would have normally spilt but it had congealed, holding the pudding firmly in the centre of the bowl. It was the reverse of Oliver Twist; I didn't want more, I wanted less, in fact nothing at all. She took the pudding and spoon off me. Told me to go to my own classroom and not to forget to shut the door. I walked out, waiting for the bullet in the back. Nothing happened. I was in the corridor and free, although feeling a little peckish after my unexpected pudding pardon.

My classmates couldn't believe it, not of Miss Torquemada, the Genghis Can't of the classroom. They reckoned it was a cruel ruse: I was only on pudding parole. I was being allowed to think I'd got away with not eating my pudding but it would be waiting for me at the next dinner and every dinner afterwards, until I ate it or it ended up like Miss Havisham's wedding cake. That night, after a grovelling pudding praying and leaving out a blessing for the dinnerladies and teachers, I slept fitfully. With the fingers on both hands crossed and touching the wooden headboard I hoped to evoke good luck. Next day, at school dinners I can't remember what the pudding of the day was but there was no sign of the dreaded vanilla sponge. Salvation. I could now brag I'd lived through the pudding persecution and, despite everything, I had dared not to eat my pudding. The incident was now to my advantage. I even hinted I'd done it on purpose. I was not a scared duffer. Granted, some of my kudos was lost when some minor Sherlock Holmes pointed out that vanilla sponge was Miss Torquemada's favourite and she, like all vengeful people, liked it cold.

On a television show, Jeremy Beadle had an invention competition for children. Part of the prize was that I would build the winning invention. The winner was a bed for unwelcome guests, which I subsequently built. I wasn't a judge, but my favourite entry was the second prize winner. A doll designed by Sheila Hudson. The doll had a secret compartment for unwanted school dinners. The problem still goes on.

When, on two occasions, parsnips were served at Hipperholme Grammar School, I'm proud to say I was one of the few that could eat them. If those lads had been in an open boat with just parsnips they would all have died. For once at that school, I felt somehow superior. I'm glad to say my Achilles' heel, the vanilla sponge, was never served. Apart from vanilla sponge and an early aversion to jelly, I could eat anything. Later I found that, if I kept my mouth tight shut and squirted the jelly through the gaps in my teeth, the lumpy jelly was reduced to a liquid and I could swallow it. So jelly was back on the menu. Some of the kids at Longroyd Junior were from the local orphanage. They were brought to school in a large shooting brake car; I was quite jealous. They invited me back to the orphanage for tea. First we played with the vast quantity of toys they had. Then we sat down to tea. On the table was a plate piled high with sandwiches cut diagonally into triangles. This was posh. They all sat there waiting for me to take the first sandwich from the top. I was the guest. After prompting by them, I took the first sandwich. Not one of them took a sandwich. They watched me. I was worried was there something wrong. The kid next to me said, 'Go on eat it'. I thought they mustn't be hungry. I was starving, so I said, 'What the ummer?' When I bit into it, it was unfamiliar, strange and chewy. I liked it. 'What is it?' I asked. They all leaned forward conspiratorially and mouthed quietly in unison, 'It's date'. Then, poshly, one said, 'Do have another'.

I took another; they all watched me eat the date sandwiches until there was just one left on that layer. The atmosphere was tense; I couldn't understand why was I eating alone. I picked up the last triangle. Instantly they were on to the pile like locusts. They were in a feeding frenzy. The layers of sandwiches went down before my eyes. Then, just as quickly as they started, they suddenly stopped. They were waiting and watching me again. I picked up a sandwich from the newly exposed layer and bit into it, a very familiar taste was in my mouth, it was date. The plan was revealed. Table manners dictated that they were only allowed to take sandwiches from the top of the pile; not one of them liked dates. I was their sandwich salvation. I never found out what was in the other sandwiches.

On television one Sunday evening there was an appeal for married couples to adopt children. The man finished the appeal by saying

> *'If you're interested in adopting a child please send us*
> *a very large stamped envelope'.*

Moving up into the higher school had its difficult moments. What I didn't learn at school or pick up from my friends, I didn't know. Not wanting to appear stupid, I often pretended I did know. Some of the things seem bizarre now. For example, when I first heard of fir trees or when the teacher told the class we were going to have a holiday. I thought it was something to do with the prickly holly bushes at the back of the school. Whatever it was, it was secret and we weren't allowed in school while it went on. The word hobbies had me baffled. The teacher said, 'On Friday I want you all to bring your hobbies'. I panicked, what was I going to do? The only hobby I'd heard of was the hobbyhorse in storybooks. I hadn't got one. In fact, I'd never seen one, except in nursery books. The only thing on our road anything like a hobbyhorse was Barraclough's rocking horse and I couldn't see him carrying that to school. Teacher had said, quite clearly, 'On Friday I want you all to bring your hobbies'. This implied all the kids had one but me. They'd all kept very quiet about them. I'd never seen anybody playing cowboys on one. Which I didn't find surprising; from what I could remember they were all covered in ribbons and bells, very girlie. Perhaps they cost loads of money? They had to be kept for best and only played with in the house. Anyway, I thought teachers weren't keen on horses: weren't they always saying they didn't want any 'Horse play' or 'Horsing about'. It confused me because I'd never seen horses playing. After thinking about it, I assumed they meant pretending to be riding a horse, clicking your tongue to make the sound of hoof beats, holding your left hand up as if holding the reins and smacking your bum with your other hand to make you go faster.

What was a hobby? Mam and Dad hadn't any idea what I was talking about. Because I was never sure which weekday it was, Friday came unrealised and I joined the procession to school. I saw various school chums with jigsaw puzzles and books. It must be a new craze I knew nothing about. When I inquired why they were taking them to school, they said had I forgotten it was hobby day? I stood back alarmed; had they all got colds? 'Hobbyday?' I was puzzled, 'but why are you going to school and all taking jigsaw puzzles?' 'Because it's hobby day', they replied, as if talking to a moron. Hobbyday; was it the pronunciation that had changed from holiday? 'Have you forgotten?' they said, 'This afternoon instead of lessons we can do anything we like'. I eventually cottoned on that a hobby was doing something you liked. Or, to be correct, something that you liked doing, and was acceptable to adults. I approached David and said, 'I didn't know you liked doing jigsaw puzzles, Dave?' 'I don't,' he said, 'my Dad won't let me bring my Meccano. He says I'll lose the little bits or get it all pinched'. That was it, everybody hadn't suddenly taken to doing jigsaws. Their parents wouldn't let them out with anything valuable they might lose or get pinched and, unlike David's Meccano, every jigsaw had a bit missing. Some of the girls had wool and knitting needles stuck in corks. I think there was a rumour of a balaclava shortage. The week after I tried to give the impression I'd always had an interesting hobby. I took a battery, wire and bulb, which was a big mistake. I wired up the bulb, it lit up. The girls went, 'Ah!' The boys went, 'so what?' They were right, the rest of the afternoon stretched before me. I hadn't even a back-up jigsaw to do. Miss realised my predicament and suggested perhaps I could just sit quietly and think how I could wire up the doll's house. The shame, I so much wanted to impress.

Other boys would casually make remarks, not realising how impressed I was. A boy across the road had a brother in the army. He came home on leave sometimes. I never saw him. I was totally amazed when I was told he'd brought his mother a box of chocolates. The only brown things I could get wrapped in silver paper were Oxo cubes, which I would suck straight out of the packet. Frequently taking it out of my mouth for some relief from the powerful taste and to admire the sucked rounded corners. Eventually it would end up as a small round black ball. An occasional cough and a spit near a passing adult would get a sympathetic disgusted look for the poor tubercular child.

Remember, this was during rationing. They say Yorkshire puddings were invented to fill you up so you'd eat less meat. A local family that bought chocolate employed a similar idea. They'd break the chocolate into small bits and put it in sandwiches. We all know what a box of chocolates is now but then I'd only ever seen bars of chocolate. This chap was in the army so the box of chocolates I envisaged was a wooden ammunition box. The type I had seen on cowboy films. I dreamt about this box of chocolates. I could see it being opened with a lovely little crowbar specially made for the purpose. Well, they had toffee hammers didn't they? The lid would come off and there, tightly packed, would be rows of chocolate bars. I would look at them not wanting to remove one and spoil the opulent symmetry. It was not for eating, it was for looking at, lusting after. I didn't need to eat it, the very fact that there was a lot gave a kind of satisfaction. Misers must feel that way. I knew I would never have a box of chocolate. I consoled myself by thinking a complete bottle of pop was a possibility. Uncle Wilf had loads of pop in his cellar, a sure sign of a man who'd made it.

So little was available, we were like squirrels, we hoarded whatever we could find. Squirrels will hoard clothes pegs if there are a lot around just because they're there. We collected cigarette cards, cigarette boxes, stamps, foreign coins, rubber bands, silver paper, matchboxes, etc. My collection of matchboxes were all the same. To me it was the quantity that came first, not quality or variety. So strictly speaking it wasn't a collection, it would have been more accurately described as 'A lot of matchboxes'. A mistake frequently made by collectors. I'd push each matchbox drawer halfway out and then join them end to end. The only place I could keep this cardboard tower was under Mam's bowlegged sideboard. When it started sticking out from under the ends of the sideboard, Mam made me stop and get rid of them. I saved a few boxes so I could blow the drawer out at people and for making 'Mickey walks the tightrope' ear phones. One box of Pilot matches I carried with me. By placing my thumb over the steering wheel I could turn the sailor into a well-endowed self-abuser, my first dirty picture. With the Captain Webb box of matches a live match was pushed through a hole in the crutch of his swimming trunks so he appeared to have a little red willy. When you opened the box, the willy extended alarmingly. Mam wouldn't let me start another matchbox collection.

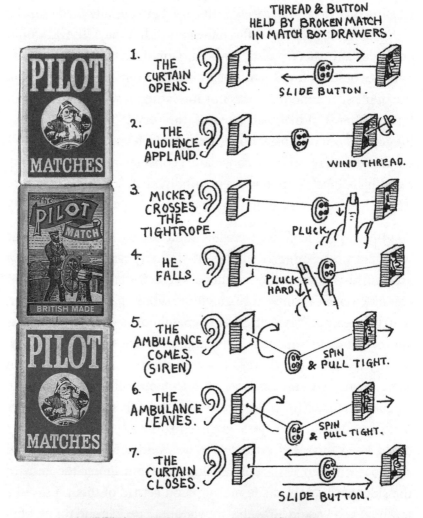

Mickey walks the tight rope

One of the big lads told me that he collected beer mats. I hadn't a clue what a beer mat was. Kids never went in pubs then. He explained that they were the mats they put beer glasses on. The fact that he collected these was supposed to imply he was tough and he wasn't scared to go in pubs. The only mats I knew were the crotchet lacy ones Granny put under all her vases. Pinch one of them at your peril. If beer mats were anything like Granny's, I thought anyone who collected them ought to keep quiet about it. Strange lad; he also told me he had a Sten gun, so I kept quiet about his hobby.

In the park bushes one day, I came upon a construction of flat stones, probably sandstone roofing slates. They were all stood on their ends, forming a series of oblong containers. Each stone container was filled to the top with a different substance. One was full of iron fillings, another with part made pins. Someone had gone to a lot of trouble to carry this lot up from the pin works. The other stone containers held stuff from closer at hand, crushed brick from the red rec., holly berries, leaves and sand. The only container not full held lucky stones, these are beautiful shiny green-striped stones. I took one. The whole thing was very neatly made, a thing to be proud of. Now they would call it 'Installation art'. They would tell you how it spoke of deprivation, of a deep desire to control and possess things. To hoard and to have more than others, yet still to share, by displaying your excess, to elicit admiration at a price. In other words it looked like someone was playing shop. All the stuff was worthless but there was a lot of it and it looked good. Doesn't that mirror life?

I went back later to see if I could catch the creator of this wonderful thing, playing shops. Sadly someone was playing robbers. It was all gone, but I still had the lucky stone I thought wouldn't be missed. This was to be my new hobby, collecting lucky stones. Come next hobby day I took my lucky stones to school. Miss hadn't a clue what to say about these green glassy objects. Feigning interest she said, 'I think you ought to show these to Mr Plimsole'. I walked the empty corridors to Mr Plimsole's classroom, scared stiff. I'd heard rumours about Plimy. It turned out he was really interested. The green stones were a kind of waste slag from the foundries. He told me studying stones was called geology. From then on I wanted to be a geologist. Each week I took different stones to school; he always knew what they were and he never lost interest. One weekend I carefully looked at every piece of coal in the coalhole. Picking each piece up and placing it in another pile so I knew I'd examined it. I was looking for fossils. I didn't find a single fossil but it was worth it because I found a moon-shaped piece of iron pyrites better known as 'Fool's gold'. Whenever I was asked what I wanted to be when I grew up, I said, 'A geologist'. That stopped the conversation stone dead.

I learned early on that when you hadn't a clue about most things it was always a good idea to start the conversation. Then you at least knew what the conversation was about. I don't know if the rumours about Mr Plimsoll were true. I always found him a completely amiable chap. The rumour was that he had a big slipper and if you crossed him he'd belt you with it. I didn't think Mr Plimsoll would sink so low. Mr Dunlop, it was said, had an enormous pump, one of a pair of pumps, the other having been worn out on the bottoms of small children. The scariest one was the teacher that had a piece of wood with a nail in it. I never saw the lump of wood with the nail in it. Occasionally, while teachers rummaged through their drawers, we had what appeared to be accidental glimpses of various dilapidated items of footwear. A murmur would go round the class. The teacher would look up and there would be instant silence. These glimpses kept the rumours going. I never, all the time I was there, met a child that had been punished with any of the implements or smacked. Except for the smacking Miss Torquemada in the lower school, of course.

In the upper school we learnt to write in ink. We were given wooden-shafted dip-in pens and told to suck the new steel nib. This cleaned the anti-rust protective oil off and helped the pen to take up ink. Some kids thought you had to suck the nib after every dip of the pen. They ended up with dark-blue tongues and lips. They took a lot of reassuring by Miss that they weren't going to die. We weren't convinced and added to their misery on the way home after school by telling them so. It was only when they came in the following day like a load of Captain Oates, with paler blue lips, that we thought they had a chance of surviving.

The writing lessons continued. We were only allowed to print. Joined up letters, loops on letters and sloping letters were strictly forbidden. We never had the lesson on joined up or loopy writing. Laboriously printing each letter was the way. This slowed us down, so we could contemplate the saying that was drummed into us daily, 'Think before you ink'. This, of course, went along with spelling tests. It was always handy to memorise a few alien words teacher put in to catch you out. Two, I particularly remember, came up frequently, yacht and silhouette. When learned, they were quickly forgotten; yacht and silhouette didn't fit easily into our everyday conversations. The teacher would wait a while, then put them into a new test with words like separate, disappoint and disappear. Bollockings all round would ensue if we got them wrong.

Other lessons were more interesting. Growing mustard and cress in eggshells didn't relieve the food crisis. In fact, we didn't know we were short of mustard and cress. I'd heard of mustard but I'd never heard of cress. Getting two eggshells for this project was a problem. Not because eggs were scarce. Auntie Ethel had told Doreen that you had to make a hole in the shell because witches went to sea in them. I explained that if witches were so small you could tread on them, then perhaps it was a good idea they went to sea. Anyway an eggshell, full of muck and mustard and cress, would sink. She relented. The mustard and cress was grown. We took it home, cut it with scissors and put it in a sandwich. The general opinion was we hadn't been missing much. Another day we collected all the cream off the school milk. We sat for what seemed like hours shaking it in screw-top jars. It eventually solidified, we added a pinch of salt and we had what Miss said was butter. It wasn't like any butter I'd tasted but then I didn't know that I'd never tasted butter. What Mam called butter was margarine. The sign she used for butter was two finger pointed like a gun, scraped up and down on the open left hand as if buttering a slice of bread. Buttering bread involved spreading it on with the knife, then scraping off as much as you could. Leaving evidence that there had ever been butter on the bread was an unheard of extravagance. After all, the function of the butter was only to provide a damp course to stop the bread going soggy by soaking up too much precious jam. It was known for people to melt butter and paint it on the bread with a paintbrush. These economy methods are not entirely gone; cheapskate cafes use aerosol butter now.

Mam once sent me to the Co-op for butter. The Co-op was right on the end of Thornhill Road, it had a lovely stone carving of bees buzzing round a hive above the door. Our family dividend number was engraved on my brain, 150321. They would write it on small pale-yellow perforated receipt tickets that they'd tear off a larger sheet to give to you. They used copy-ink pencils, which were just like normal pencils till you licked them and they changed and wrote like ink. I asked for a quarter of a pound of butter. The woman cut a lump of stuff off a bigger lump of stuff, wrapped it, then asked me for an enormous sum of money. I hadn't enough; this was unheard of, Mam always gave me the exact amount of money. What had happened? Things were always the same price, it never changed. Fish were sixpence, chips were threepence; it had always been so and would always be so. The woman asked if I was sure I wanted butter. Yes, I was sure Mam had said butter, but the stuff we usually got came in oblong blocks. The woman said, 'I think you want margarine'. I'd never heard of margarine. 'No',

I said, 'butter'. She said, 'I think you want margarine'. I wasn't convinced. I left empty-handed, while the disgruntled woman stuck the butter back on the big lump. I told Mam they'd sold out. We had lard instead; lovely, with a little salt, almost like proper beef dripping.

Years later at Hipperholme Grammar, Dizzy Day, the geography teacher, told us how the people of Tibet put butter in their tea. He painted a vivid word picture of them shivering whilst drinking tea in the freezing mountain air. Their uncontrollable shaking hands spilling the drink down their chests. The buttery liquid would be left to set in the cold Tibetan air, helping to keep out the chill. Come the next tea break they would scrape it off with a knife and slop it back in the teapot. After school I tried it. I made the same mistake once again of thinking margarine was butter. The tea had the molten margarine floating on the top like diesel oil. I drank it. I was left with a faint yellow moustache and I was ever so sick.

Back at school we were now growing a bean between the inside of a jam jar and a piece of soggy blotting paper. It seemed particularly cruel. The idea was to show that the bean knew which way was up. We attempted to confuse it by turning it round. Clever little bean, it didn't know much, but it certainly knew which way was up towards the light. One of the scariest things I ever saw was the day I moved to into an old house. I opened the coalhole door, the place looked dark and empty. I sensed something was wrong. I looked down at the floor and there, reaching for me, were long pale-green tendrils. Had that tortured bean come for me? Panicking, I instantly slammed the door shut. I thought, 'My God what was it?' When I got up the nerve to have another look, I did this by saying to my then wife 'What do you think this might be?' opening the door with her in front. She said someone's left a bag of seed potatoes at the back and the shoots are growing towards the light under the door. The shoots were more than 5 foot long. I thought of Monte Cristo. How sad.

One day the production of coal gas was explained. We were told if you put little pieces of coal in a cocoa tin and punched holes in the lid, then put the tin on a lit gas ring, little jets of gas would come out of the holes and you could light them. After school, the minute I got home, I insisted that the school had said I'd got to do this experiment. To Mam, if school said it had to be done, it had to be done. Authority had to be obeyed. An oblong Rowntree's cocoa tin was emptied and the teacher's instructions followed. I lit the little holes and it worked. The flames were just like the cookers. It was a great anti-climax. Now what? There was the cooker with a little cooker on top. It was like those boxes you open and there's another one inside, you open that and there's another one, and so on. Should I now put a smaller tin of coal on top of the cocoa tin and light that. I thought about it, then turned the gas off and threw the lot away.

I was also disappointed when we were told we were going to be allowed, as a treat, to play on the school stilts. These turned out to be two-pound treacle tins with string threaded through holes in them. The idea was you stood on the treacle tins and held them tight against your feet with the loop of string. This wasn't my idea of stilts. Stilts made you really tall. I wanted to be tall. These were vertigo stilts for kids scared of heights. Which soon I found out I was.

Music lessons were a misery. I think Britain had captured a German freighter of triangles and castanets, because the school was full of them. In every music lesson I was either in the massed triangle section or the massed castanets section. Never got my hands on anything else, not even a girlie tambourine. The castanets were not for the macho type. They were not the ones seen in the films. The ones that stiff-backed Spanish dancers had in each hand. Ours were similar to them, but tied to a stick, probably so we wouldn't lose or pinch them. Despite the vast quantity they were rationed, they couldn't shake the habit. Teacher only allowed us one each. They made the same sound as knick-knack bones but they lacked the panache. School castanets were like rattling your Granny's teeth on a stick. You'd have thought that, with all the school dinners they served, they would have had plenty of knick-knack bones, but no. The only consolation was, when playing the castanets you sort of rattled along most of the time. Not on the triangles though, it was all counting bars. Lots of little mouths, moving silently, counting. Triangles held a-loft, shiny plinker, poised, bobbing in time to the rhythm and the counting. I dreamt of a huge orchestral triangle that made a sound like the cowboys' chuck wagon cook made, bashing a lump of metal, when the beans were boiled. Gabby Hayes wouldn't have been seen dead with my triangle. Hopalong Cassidy would laugh himself silly if he could see me counting up to the plink. You'd think the moment to plink was arriving, then the doubt set in. Were you on the right bar? The uncertainty, the hesitation, I'd looked round at the many poised plinkers dithering and then, Plink! Bugger! Another kid plinked before you. The rest of the massed triangles followed, like lemmings in a cacophony of plinks, with the odd out-of-tune plonk. Some kids just couldn't hold a triangle properly. You look round, self-satisfied and glad it was over. A job badly done, but done. Then surprise, a lonely single plink, crystal clear and perfect, rings across the room. We all smirk, he's late. We all turn and look in the direction of the sound. Damn, it was the kid that always got it right. He'd been demoted for the day for improvising on the drums. He continues, smugly, silently, counting the bars to his next triumphant plink. We were all completely lost; he'd be back on the drums next week, lucky sod.

Other lessons were much more fun. We were introduced to pointillism and colour theory. Mixing yellow and blue crayon dots, we saw that from a distance they looked green. The classroom vibrated with us all dotting our pictures of a thatched cottage. Apparently pointillism didn't lend itself to smokey Yorkshire scenes. That's why it was more popular abroad and down south. We were all being gently persuaded out of the 'Kipper School' of drawing and painting. That is, with both eyes on the same side of the nose, despite Mr. Picasso's attempts to popularise it.

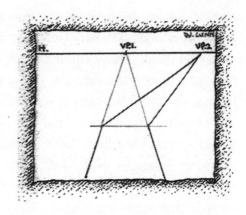

Measured perspective

Measured perspective appealed to those that needed rules. The first lesson was how to draw a road disappearing into the distance with one bend. The class was amazed they'd achieved this artistic optical effect with a ruler. To me it still looks like a Ku Klux Klansman in a wind. My favourite lesson, though, was my introduction to papier-mâché. We had to make a mask. A figure eight was constructed with a clay snake. This instantly made the mask with its eyeholes. We then proceeded to cover this mould with small pieces of newspaper stuck on with flour and water paste, alternating the layers with school toilet paper. Brefni had his mask covered in loads of paste and was smoothing it up and down. The shape was reminiscent of a lady's hour-glass shapely figure. This had not gone unnoticed. He was smoothing the paste up and down whilst giving me knowing winks. Thus I was introduced to eroticism and papier-mâché, an obsession that stayed with me all my life. That is, an obsession for papier-mâché. I don't know though. Brefni, being more in touch with the adult world, told me the second joke I'd heard as a child. It was about the boy that went home crying. His mother asked why. He replied, 'Is Amsterdam swearing?' His mother said, 'No'. He asked, 'Is Rotterdam swearing?' 'No', she said. He then told her the teacher had taken his sweets from him and smacked him, and all he'd said was, 'I hope the sweets Rotterdam teeth'.

The first joke I knew was: 'Adam and Eve and Nipmewell went down to the river to bathe. Adam and Eve fell in. Who do you think was saved?' Of course you'd reply, 'Nipmewell'. Whereupon your bum would be savagely pinched.

The final year teacher at Longroyd was Miss Pring. I came to her attention early when she pointed out to the class that my hair was not ginger, a great surprise to all of us. She meant it wasn't the beige colour of ginger spice. My hair, she said, was the same colour as the painter Titian's. So my nickname changed from Willy and from then on I was known as Tish. It wasn't so bad. It was better than 'Clutchit', the lad who wanted to wee all the time, or 'Peelow' one of the less successful up-the-lavy wall peeing contestants. Ann Gill ended up being called Penelope after a lesson on Greek legend. Girls are called that now; it's usually shortened to Penny but then it was completely unheard of.

Miss Pring told us Brighouse was called Brighouse because there used to be a house by the bridge, thus bridge house, Brighouse. This information gave birth to a life-long interest in how names came about. Most people haven't any interest but you'd think someone living in a place called Chickenly would be curious. I tried to find out from an inhabitant why the place was called Chickenly. Attempting jocularity, I asked if he noticed a lot of huts or chicken wire fences where he lived. 'No.' 'Was it the way people walked?' I inquired. He had no idea why the place was called Chickenly and he'd never been curious to know or thought it at all strange or funny. I considered, how this could be, then I realised I'd done the same thing myself. I would never have thought of asking about hen huts or 'Is it the way people walk in Henley?' I don't know why, but chickens are funny and hens are not. I suppose that's why you can get rubber chickens and not rubber hens.

'There was a cow that wouldn't yield,
it adn't ad its Uddersfield.'

213

Miss Pring's classroom was wonderland to me. It was like a magician's show, when the curtain goes back to reveal a stage set out with things you eagerly wait to be demonstrated. On the windowsills were dioramas of biblical scenes cut out of plywood: Jonah being swallowed by the whale, Jesus walking on water, the tower of Babel. I thought, crikey, we're never going to be able to make such great things. I was right, we never did. We'd ask when we were going to start and she'd say, 'When we're ready'. I suspect the models had been left there long ago by Druid children and she had no idea how to make them. They just stood around as monuments to what you could achieve with a fret saw if you really tried. Trying, that was her constant theme. She'd set a task; you were in the doghouse if you said you couldn't do it, you had to say you'd try.

She would take us to the swimming baths in Brighouse; we'd line up in twos with our towels in home-made drawstring pump bags. All the boys walked with boys and the girls with girls. I was secretly glad of this tradition because, I suppose, I had my first girlfriend at this time. She was called Kay Franklin and she embarrassed me no end. Walking home from school she insisted we hold hands. Imagine walking to the baths holding hands with a girl. Before setting off to the baths, we were instructed that if we met any adults on the way we had to step into the road and allow them to pass on the pavement. Older folk who'd survived childhood made the rules; they must be respected and allowed a longer productive life. It didn't seem to matter that a whole class of kids was put at risk for the sake of manners. We were dispensable. Had it not been so since the days of child sacrifice? So we had to step into the road. The only people we ever met were old women or housewives. The only young men about during the day were either burglars or off sick from work, in which case they had to stay indoors. Old men sat in the 'Old men's parliaments' unsuccessfully trying to kipper themselves against the diseases of old age, by smoking themselves silly.

At the baths the boys had to get changed in the curtained cubicles on the right side of the bath. The girls had to change in the cubicles facing them, on the left side of the baths. This separation failed in its intention because, being opposite each other, it was easy to look under the curtains and see the girls taking their knickers off. That's of course, if you wanted to. The girls would emerge in their one-piece costumes wearing swimming caps almost like rubber balaclavas with a chinstrap. They were absolutely not allowed in the water without them. This was something to do with long hairs getting in the water, I think. Long hairs in the water must have been a serious threat to something, and they were not allowed. The attendant had a long pole with a tin on the end for scooping out old sticky plasters and other bits that dropped off bathers. Mam didn't mind us going to the baths because the water had so much chlorine in it germs couldn't survive. It was clever really, the town was disinfecting its population and getting them to pay for it themselves, thinking it was entertainment. Rather like getting the sheep to pay for the sheep dip. The water killed every thing except, of course, the dreaded verucca, of which I can say nothing. I never got one.

When at the baths, it was the usual thing with Miss Pring. You weren't allowed to say you couldn't swim, you had to say you'd try. After a few, standing, shivering, swimming lessons in the 3-foot end. Strange how all the skinny kids that couldn't swim huddled in the corner at the shallow end, shivering, just like the chickens in a hot hen house. Miss Pring lined us up at the 4 foot 6 deep bit. She informed us we could now swim, and we had to jump in. I had confidence in her confidence, so I jumped in. I instantly learned two things. I couldn't swim and I wasn't 4 foot 6 inches tall. My feet were standing on the bottom but my head was under water and I wasn't floating. I instantly sprang up on one foot and my head broke the surface. I managed to cross the width of the bath in a series of forward hops assisted slightly by a kind of token breaststroke. Grabbing the bar at the other end, I pulled my self out, scraping my chest on the concrete surround. This was my first remembered ordeal at the baths. When you'd did manage to swim three breadths (widths), you could attempt to swim the length of the bath to get your 'Length certificate'. After that, if you were really good, you could enter for your 'Life-saving certificate'. This involved wearing pyjamas and swimming through a hoop under water. A circumstance that I thought rarely occurs in real life. So I didn't bother.

The wartime ban on embroidery had been lifted for sometime. Doreen learned how to do chain stitch embroidery. Wanting to put her newly found skill to use, she embroidered a yellow 'W' on the front of my maroon-coloured trunks. I wasn't too happy disporting myself in my customised swimwear with it's unfortunately placed 'W'. The embarrassment was added to when I trapped my foot in the bath inlet pipe. Later my arm got caught under the bar running round the bath. Every time someone jumped in, the water rose and my head went under. The attendant eventually rescued me, not in a spirit of the 'Good Samaritan' or because he'd heard my screams over the din; he knew by the shade of blue my wrinkled skin had gone (I think he had a shade card) that I'd obviously been in longer than I'd paid for. The final indignity was the day I went to the baths and nothing went wrong in the bath. I managed to get dried and dressed without incident. Feeling confident, I decided to squander a penny and use one of the latest coin-operated hair driers. They had installed two, one on each side of the little wringing machine you used for squeezing the water out of your cossie. The machines were on sprung hinged bars attached to the wall. You put your penny in the slot and it started blowing hot air. Then you pulled it down close to your head. I put my penny in and it started blowing. I reached up to pull it down and, before I touched it, it dropped like a giant mallet on my head, knocking me out. The screw on the end punched a tiny dint in my head. Some bastard had unhitched the spring. The kind of guy who unscrewed the top of the salt pot so you ended up with salt all over your dinner. He'd have been watching me with his mouth under water so he wouldn't be spotted, bubbling with mirth. That was the last time I ever went to Brighouse Swimming Baths to swim.

I did go back as a teacher with a class of kids from Rastrick Common Secondary School. I'm glad to say it was strictly forbidden for teachers to go in the water. At the time Miss Ping was also teaching there. I don't think she remembered me. From the day of the hair drier incident I didn't enter the water of a swimming bath for nearly 30 years, till 1981 in Liverpool baths. I was dressed as an Edwardian bather and was demonstrating a swimming machine invention for television. The machine didn't work and I had to be rescued, exhausted, by Peter Wragg, a special effects guy. He had to continue the demonstration for the underwater shots. On the film, you see red-haired me paddling away on the surface, then it cuts to the underwater shots of a pair of black hairy legs, Peter's. From that day to this I have not returned to the water.

One morning our class didn't go to our school. We went instead up the steps, past Brooke Street, to Rastrick Common Secondary School to do the 'Eleven plus' exam. Miss Pring always encouraged us to try. When we were told of the impending exam, one brave lad told Miss that his parents didn't want him to take the test. I always wondered why. We were all sat in desks one yard apart, to prevent copying. That's all I remember about the exam, apart from the lad that sat to my right. He was called Binns. I passed the exam and opted to go to Hipperholme Grammar School because I was told they taught German. Someone asked Mam if they were paying for me to go. The implication being the children of deaf parents should be too thick to pass exams. It certainly cost a lot to kit me out. Mam was sent a list of things I had to have. It was an official list, so Mam had to get everything new. On the list were underpants, an unheard of luxury for little boys of my ilk.

After the summer holidays I arrived at the school full of confidence. That soon went out of the window. Everyone was clever and most were a lot cleverer. It was misery from the start. I might have passed the 'Eleven plus' but I still didn't know the months of the year, the alphabet or how to tell the time. I was in trouble straight away. I was in Mr Conry's class. I entered nervously. I'd been told he was called 'Killer Conry', which didn't help. The first thing he did was to inform us that he was filling in the class register, in alphabetical order. I started to panic. Then he confused me about Christian and surnames. Was it the 'W' or the 'L' he wanted? Eventually my name was put in the register when he said, 'Anyone I've missed?' I put my hand up; Killer Conry wasn't pleased. Binns, the lad who'd sat next to me in the exam, was in the same class. He not only knew the alphabet but he could recite it belching. Killer Conry, when he heard I was called Lunn, told the class about the bun called a Sally Lunn after the 19th century pastry cook from Bath. From that moment until I left school I was called 'Sally'. For some reason it never bothered me. Unlike the lad called 'Sir', which doesn't seem offensive till you knew he was so called because he was a large chap and it was short for 'Circumference'. All the teachers were addressed as just Sir, except the French teacher Monsieur Viette. We gave him his full title, 'Serviette'.

I remember Killer asking me what I'd got for Christmas. Certain I'd impress him and the class, I proudly said, 'A Black and Decker electric drill'. He then deflated me when he said, 'That's nice, do you think you could make me a piano?' I have the drill to this day and it's still working, I wonder if Killer is? We didn't do German, we did French, with Killer Conry. I was familiar with French because one side of our HP sauce bottle was all in French. Earlier bottles had 'Garton's HP Sauce' on the front. I think this was removed because it spells 'Snotrag' backwards. Killer explained that in French there are two words for 'The'. All nouns are either masculine or feminine, each having its own 'The'. They are le or la. He then told us most feminine nouns end with an 'E'. Our first homework was to put all the le's and la's with a list of masculine and feminine nouns. He'd said feminine ended in 'E', so I reckoned le must be feminine. That's why I got my entire French homework wrong and my first detention in the first week. It was downhill from then on.

Each morning started with a religious assembly; we were stood in lines patrolled by prefects. We were given free Bibles by the British and Foreign Bible Society. These were mainly used by the prefects for bashing you on the head for any minor infringement of their rules, such as looking happy. They would bash you quite hard with their Bibles. Perhaps the idea was to raise lumps in certain positions on your head to make you more intelligent? Was it a way of artificially acquiring intelligence phrenologically? It was, after all, a very old fashioned school. These Biblical bashings caused me to have biblical bumps. I got 'Furunculosis' (boils in my ears). I really did! Job 2:7. Recommended cheery reading when you're down in the dumps. Fortunately the doctor didn't recommend Job's method, scraping them off with a bit of broken pot. I got penicillin in a tube with a long nozzle.

Because I used Granddad's medical books for reference when writing my own school notes, I liked to use scientific words new to me. I, of course, didn't know how to pronounce them. I got caught out when I thought I'd upgrade my cold to 'Nasal catarrh'. When asked, I said I'd had 'Naz-hal cat-harra'. The most sickening time I did this was when I thought I'd use the correct full name for an indicator 'Soduim dimethylamenoazobenzenasulphonate'. I spelt sodium wrong. I seemed to remember all the things that didn't matter, like 'Becker and Stahl's phlogiston theory'. It was all done to cover my lack of knowledge by knowing about things no one else gave a toss about (Anorackiosis).

Joke:
A boy's mother arrived at the school, she said to the master, 'I've come to tell you our Stanley can't come he's got diarrhoea'. The master replied, 'You needn't have come all the way to school, you could have sent a note'. To which she retorted,
'If I could've spelt it I would have'.

We had to learn the school song in Latin. Our class didn't do Latin, so we had no idea what we were singing. I have, on occasions, just as people are about to eat, said, 'Is anyone going to say Grace?' This always causes an embarrassed silence. I would offer to do it. Imagine how impressed they are when I do it at length in Latin, reciting the school song.

They were very strict about school uniform, it had to be worn including the cap. Tall gangling youths could be seen wearing old tiny shabby school caps on the back of their heads like skullcaps. I was the only one that got away with not wearing the school tie. I wore a black one. A master told me after I'd left school that nothing had been said to me because they thought there had been a death in the family. In a way they were right, nobody in the family had died but my interest in this kind of education had.

You learn something new every day if you're not careful.

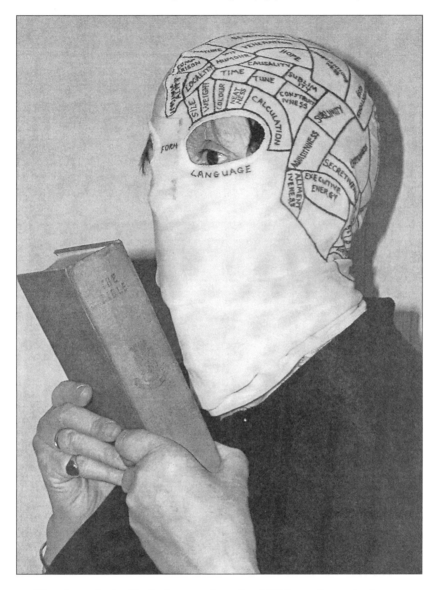

The phrenological balaclava and a school Bible used to raise lumps.

Ritz A.B.C. Minor's trip.
When posing for photographs no one argued with Pat Gott.

Filums
(Films)

If I asked Dad for money to go to the pictures he would draw an oblong in the air with his fingers, point to the wall and stick his thumb up. This was one of Dad's little jokes with language. I meant I wanted to go to the cinema. He was saying the pictures on the wall were very good. He actually meant wall pictures in general because we didn't have any pictures on our walls. The only picture I remember was the little one in Granny's room. It was of Jesus with a lantern standing outside what looked to me like a lavatory door. Granny used to hold it in her hands and cry. The deaf sign for film was to hold your left hand against the left eye pointing like a camera. Then, putting the heel of your right hand against the left, you'd wiggle it back and forth to imitate a camera flicker. To enforce the image you'd also mouth carefully the word 'Filum'. Dad would articulate the word with exaggerated mouth movements to make it clear. Because of this I thought the word was 'Filum' and that's how I always pronounced it. The kids in Miss Pring's class would fall about laughing when she got me to say, 'Filum'. She would look at me and say, 'Fil-m-m-m'. I would look back and say, 'Fil-um-um-um'. The class would all laugh. I was completely baffled; I just couldn't tell what she was on about. I'd say, 'Filum', they'd all laugh and I didn't know why.

Theresa couldn't pronounce her 'Rs'. For a laugh, other kids would try to get her to say words with Rs in them. 'What are those over there Terweeser?' they asked her. 'Twees', she replied. Sniggering, they'd carry on the tease, 'What kind of twees are they Terweesa?' She replied with all the superiority of one talking to lesser stupid beings, 'Werhuden ones, of corwse'.

Brefni was the first to point out to me that the film always started after the director's name came up. I'd never noticed. He was very observant and funny. His description of a film he'd seen always sticks in my mind. It was called *Never Take No For An Answer*; it was showing in August 1952 at the Ritz. All the time Brefni was telling the film's story, about a dying donkey, he dabbed his eyes with his handkerchief. Then, to show it was really very, very sad, he mimed wringing out the tear-soaked cloth on the floor. We fell about laughing. I went to see the film and it really was a lump in the throat choker. The film was about a little Italian boy who made a pathetic living transporting fat people on his little donkey. One day his donkey fell ill. The little boy decided the only way to save it was to have the donkey blessed in the Saint Francis bit of the church. This was where all the children took their sick pets. Apparently they were not as concerned about wheel chair access then and they certainly didn't make provision for donkey blessing. The only way to get the donkey into the Saint Francis section was by knocking down a wall. The priests wouldn't do it. Meanwhile there was mention of Saint Francis's treasure being hidden somewhere in the church. The little boy eventually decided to go to the Pope. The Pope gave permission, what else could he do. The little boy returned to his dying donkey's stable to give it the good news. I remember the scene vividly. The boy enters the stable after all his trials and tribulations and he's too late: the donkey's gone. Is the donkey dead? No he isn't, he's just gone out for a constitutional walk. They knock down the wall in the church and the donkey enters to get blessed. Miraculously the donkey makes a full recovery and goes on to spend the rest of his miserable life carrying fat people. Like Lazarus, it went on to try to die again. The priests find Saint Francis's treasure box in the wall. They open the box, in it are a flower and a feather, which instantly crumble to dust. I left the cinema confused. If only he had taken 'No' for an answer. The donkey would have been put out of its misery. The priest wouldn't have found that Saint Francis was obviously an idiot collecting the wrong stuff. If the truth were known, I bet the donkey just wanted a day off. This film was actually the second feature. I remember it so well but I can't remember a thing about the main film, which was called *The Happy Family*.

My first visit to the cinema was with Granny Annie. I recall walking back home up Bramston Street scared stiff. The only thing I can remember about what I'd seen was the ending of what may have been a serial. The image is still with me; it was of a surgical boot on a clubfoot, limping, slowly, towards me through dense fog. It didn't put me off going to the cinema. I went at least twice a week and sometimes three times on Saturday. We had three cinemas in Brighouse, the Albert, The Savoy and The Ritz. The Ritz was considered the up-market posh cinema. Along the back row there were special double necking seats for courting couples. It also had a Saturday morning club, 'The ABC Minors', where we went to see *Flash Gordon* and, my favourite, *Lash La Rue*. When Lash picked a flower with his whip, I thought if I could do that I'd be irresistible to girls. The best I could do to impress was to use a bit of dialogue from the *Robin Hood* film. When leaving a girl, instead of just saying 'Good bye', I'd say

'I'll pine and fret for your return'.

They weren't impressed. The other lines from the same film that always stuck in my mind were in a song:

'He robbed the rich to aid the poor, a most unusual practice. And now that he's been outlawed he needn't pay his taxes'.

The cinema showed big films and often had displays related to the film. I remember the manager, always in his dinner jacket, watching us as we stared at real spears in the display for *African Queen*. It was on from the 28th of April 1952 for a week (incidentally the boat was built in Lytham Saint Annes). All the best films were put on for a full week. Later that year, in November I sat through *Gone With the Wind*, which was completely ruined for me by a chap sitting in the next row. Every time anyone in the film left a room or rode off, he felt compelled to say, 'He's gone with the wind' or 'She's gone with the wind'. I joined in and the cheeky sod turned round and told me to 'Shush.' Then he continued to do it. The scene that stuck in my mind was the dying horse foaming at the mouth. I couldn't drink milk or eat custard for ages.

One evening in 1952 I sat with Mam and Dad through the film *Moulin Rouge*, with Jose Ferrer playing the very short-legged painter, Henri de Toulouse Lautrec. In a painful scene, where they try to lengthen his short legs, a wag in the audience, familiar with a well-known local cure for shortness, shouted, 'Put some horse muck in his shoes'. The end of the film was a heart-rending scene of Henri dying in bed. If you've seen the film you probably didn't notice, because I certainly didn't, what was going on under the sheets. My Mam explained to me when we came out of the show. She told me that, while Henri was dying, under the sheets his legs were growing back to their normal size. Mam knew when you died God put all your afflictions right. All I could say was it was a bit bloody late. Funny though, 2 years earlier, at the Albert cinema, we'd seen Jose Ferrer playing *Cyrano de Bergerac* and Mam said nothing about God sorting his nose out post-mortem.

I occasionally went to the Albert cinema but my favourite was the Savoy. Sometimes it was unfairly called a fleapit. I never heard of anyone catching fleas or a disease at the pictures, the place was always sprayed with a perfumed disinfectant, sometimes when we were sitting there. At the Savoy they used a big brass pumped garden spray. Of course, if you were really worried you could get a bag of Dr Thomas's pastilles to suck and keep germs at bay. These were always advertised in the local paper, *The Echo*. The pastilles would, of course, stop germs getting in your mouth, but what about the sneaky little chaps getting in the other orifices. For total security I imagine you would have to stick a pastille in all seven body orifices. I don't recall seeing anybody with a couple of them stuck up their nose.

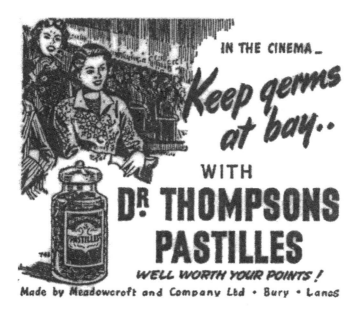

Mr Ambrose Broomhead and Harold ran the Savoy. These two chaps were better known as Sheriff Ambrose and Deputy Harold. It wasn't unknown for kids in the gun battle scenes to shoot at the screen with slug guns. Gats and Dianes were the weapons used. Webleys were more powerful but they were too expensive. Deputy Harold was always on the look out for air guns. To the right and left of the screen, tucked right under it, were the threepenny rush seats. So called because no one rushed to buy them. They were usually empty. Behind them were the rows of sixpenny seats and behind them were the ninepenny seats and then the dearer seats. There was a balcony but I never remember anyone being allowed up there. The plan was always to buy a sixpenny ticket and crawl under the seats into the ninepennies or further back if possible. Deputy Harold was constantly on watch with his spotlight torch. I wasn't successful at this caper, having distinctive ginger hair, and wearing a balaclava to cover it made me look very suspicious. One never wore a balaclava indoors, except perhaps to go to bed. I would often find my self practically alone on the back row of the sixpennies, sitting in front of the packed ninepennies. Sheriff Ambrose was not to be beaten. He removed two rows of seats between the sixpennies and the ninepennies. There was now a gap to crawl across and Deputy Harold walked up and down it. There was a rumour about barbed wire.

After every show, a film of the Queen in uniform sitting side-saddle on a horse and *God save the Queen* was played. Everyone stood to attention. Men took their hats off; some not only stood to attention, they saluted. It was all very serious. No one left the cinema till the film faded and the last note was played. The rot set in when the curtains started to close early, the film of the Queen being projected on the curtains. The projectionists obviously wanted to get home early. At the Saturday children's shows, the children knew it was disrespectful to sit during the Queen and, worse still, to leave during it. There was always a mass rush to get out before the Queen started. If they were not quite out of the doors and the Queen came on, they would freeze in their track as if caught in a spotlight escaping from prison. Slowly they'd turn round and face the screen and guiltily stand to attention. Gradually, when nothing happened to these kids, everyone started rushing out during the Queen. This disrespect was very upsetting to people like Sheriff Ambrose and Deputy Harold. It had to be stopped. Appealing to the children's sense of patriotism was a waste of time. Then someone had a brilliant idea. I'd like to think it was Sheriff Ambrose. The idea was to make it so the kids didn't want to rush out during the Queen. Appeals, pleading, threats and standing in their way to be trampled hadn't worked. Then one day not a single kid left during the Queen. What did they do? They simply put it on at the beginning of the show. It was a great bit of lateral thinking. I don't know if it was Sheriff Ambrose's idea. He went on to become Mayor of Brighouse.

One day I was first in a queue of two standing at the Savoy paying kiosk. The woman in the kiosk was waiting for Deputy Harold's signal to let us in. Meanwhile she had a cup of tea, which had a string hanging out of it with a paper tag. She held the tag and lifted up the string; on the end of it, a soggy little bag appeared out of the cup. I was fascinated. I asked her what it was. She said it was a tea bag. I asked her where she got it. She said, 'It's a sample'. It was the first time I'd seen anything like it. I asked her how much it cost. Whereupon the bigger kid behind me said, 'Don't be stupid, it's a sample, they're free'. I never heard of a sample or free tea. Free apples from Canada, yes. I forgot all about the tea bag sample until one day Russell Whitely told me a joke. It went like this: A woman went to the doctors, the doctor said, 'I can't tell you what's wrong with you unless you bring me a sample'. (Strange, I thought, why would the doctor want a tea bag. I'd heard you could tell if a girl was a virgin with a lettuce leaf or a nicotine stained finger, but a tea bag?) The woman went home and said to her husband, 'What would you be thinking a sample would be?' He replied, 'Indeed to goodness Kathleen, I do not know. You'd better go next door and ask Mrs O'Flaherty.' Half an hour later she returned in a terrible state. Her hair was ripped out in clumps. She had a black eye, a missing tooth and her dress was ripped to shreds. Her husband was shocked. He said, 'What happened Kathleen?' She replied, 'I went next door and I said to Mrs O'Flaherty, nice as can be, I said, what would you be thinking a sample would be? She said to me 'Piss in a bottle'. I said, shit in your hat, and the fight was on'. I laughed politely, but I didn't get it. This joke made me even more confused about what a sample was.

It's interesting how these completely pointless memories stick with you. In later years I'd combine them to create a new idea. The combination of a urine sample and tea bag doesn't look promising. I was asked for an idea for a simple cheap fancy dress for a toddler. What could be easier to make than a tea bag costume, two squares of cloth with holes for arms and legs? The advantage is, if the kid pisses itself it adds to the look of the costume, particularly when steaming. It's now a used tea bag. While I was at art school I got a job as a projectionist at the Savoy. There were supposed to be two of us in the box to work every thing. The only records we had to play were *Swedish Rhapsody*, *Charmain*, *Stranger on the Shore* and the Queen. After we'd seen the film a few times, it would get boring waiting to just change the reels every 20 minutes. If it was a cinemascope film, I had to swing an extra lens in front of the projector; this enlarged the picture. It was great fun to swing it away during the film. This caused the picture to suddenly become very tall and thin, then back to normal. This alarmed the audience, who for a second thought their eyes had gone. The other trick was to move the sound on the stereophonic system. We'd turn the speakers off at the front of the cinema, then the middle. The sound would only be coming from the speakers at the back. These we would slowly turn down. The audience would be leaning over the backs of their seats straining to hear the sound whilst looking forward trying to watch the film. If I was really brassed off, I'd just join the audience. On some occasions the other projectionist would join me. We'd both sit there determined not to go back to the box first. The film would run off and the audience would shout and stamp their feet. We'd join in the stamping. I wasn't bothered, I'd seen the film anyway. It was a game of 'Chicken' till one of us lost our nerve and rushed to sort it out. One evening Deputy Harold told me I had to do the show alone. The other projectionist had come in to say he couldn't come. I looked through one of the projection windows. It looked mucky to me, so I thought I'd clean it. I must have pressed on too hard, because the glass fell out onto the balcony. This was the balcony that no one to my knowledge had ever been on. I went and told Deputy Harold what had happened. He gave me a hammer and told me the way to the balcony. I retrieved the glass with its wooden frame and started nailing it back. I hadn't put *Swedish Rhapsody* on so the cinema was silent. I could hear voices. I stopped hammering and went to look over the edge of the balcony. Deputy Harold had let the audience in. They were all mumbling it was very strange to be in a completely silent cinema. So, by way of explanation, I leaned over the balcony and shouted jocularly, 'Don't panic, I'm just nailing the balcony back on'. A very small audience viewed the show that evening. After the show, Sheriff Ambrose sacked me. Apparently the audience had ignored my instruction not to panic and they'd just gone ahead and panicked any way.

The last time I went to the Savoy was to watch every single episode of the *Batman and Robin* serial. At the beginning of every episode, they showed the end of the preceding week's episode to remind you what had happened. At the end they showed all the good bits of the next week's episode to make you come again. Watched over many weeks, it wasn't too bad, but end to end it was a brainwashing nightmare. I watched the lot; I had, after all said and done, paid to get in. A film inspired the first joke I ever made up. It was *I was Monty's Double*. I first saw it in April 1959. The joke went like this. I would say, 'Have you seen 'Monty's double'?' They say they had or hadn't, then I'd say, 'I was Monty's treble' (A treble is a soprano). I would then sing in a high-pitched voice, 'Oh yes I was'. It didn't get any laughs but I liked it. There's a difference between smart arse and funny.

I should have learned my lesson about music jokes; I didn't. Whilst doing a television series called *Patently Obvious* I was standing with Peter Cook outside the studio. The producer, Colin, asked Peter if he would go in first and warm up the audience. Peter said he didn't want to do it. To save embarrassment I jumped in and said, 'I know a good joke, I'll go in'. 'No, no', said Colin, 'I'd like Peter to do it'. Peter said, 'No, I think Wilf should do it'. I said, 'I know, I'll tell you both the joke now and see what you think of it'. Peter said, 'No, no, you tell the joke in there and I'll laugh'. This agreed, we all went into the studio and sat down on the set. Colin introduced us all to the audience and I proceeded to tell my joke. It went like this. 'Did you hear about the French horn player who couldn't kiss a girl without putting his hand up her skirt?' I paused, waiting for the laughter. Silence, nothing, not a titter. I turned to Peter and said, 'You said you'd laugh'. He replied, 'I didn't get it'. A faint titter went round the room. Perhaps it is the way I told it.

Two bins Lunn

When Granny Annie died the family on her side all met at Auntie Lizzie's house on Lillands Lane. Our godparents, Auntie Ethel and Uncle Tommy, weren't there. I was 9 at the time and Mam and Dad took me along to translate the proceedings. The meeting was about dividing up Granny's property, namely the house. We were completely ignored; no attempt was made to draw us into the proceedings. I stood up and said, 'What about us?' I was told it was nothing to do with us and to sit down. I said, 'It's where we live'. I was informed I was too young to understand and told to shut up. They argued amongst themselves, I can't remember what they decided, but we all know 'Where there's a Will there's a way'. There was a will; Granny left the house to Mam. They never spoke to us again.

The house at Thornhill Road was sold and we moved from our cellar across town to 9, Crown Street, Lightcliffe Road, Brighouse. It wasn't quite salubria, the house was just round the corner from Albion Street where Granny had moved to live. I thought it was a pity we hadn't moved earlier and saved her all that walking to our house. It was also much nearer to my school but still far enough away for a free bus pass. Dad was really proud of my bus pass and the school uniform. You see the pass was official. He used to mime to me how to use it. He'd mime taking the pass out of my top pocket and showing it to the bus conductor. He'd then stick his thumb up, as if to say 'Yes that's a real official bus pass, very few people have one but my son's got one and that's good'. The government had given it to his son personally. He would borrow it from me to show visitors and repeat the mime, whether they knew what it was for or not. The only time he'd been given a kind of a pass was in the war when he went to work at Blakeborough's. Going to work one morning he was nearly shot. He couldn't hear the armed guards asking for the password and he couldn't have answered anyway. I was told he wore a luminous badge with 'DEAF AND DUMB' written on it so the guards wouldn't shoot him. Or maybe it was one of 'Valentine's Globrite Buttons for Blackouts 3d each'. Years later I remembered Dad's luminous badge. I was at a party where there were a lot of teenagers. Many of them deaf. The hearing ones wanted the lights dim. The deaf ones wanted the lights on so they could see their chat-up hand signing. It could have been solved with a ultraviolet light and fluorescent gloves.

The new house was a terrace house, not a back-to-back but a proper through house. With a front and back door. This was considered very important. The lowest in the hierarchy was back-to-back, steps and in. That is a terrace house with another behind it and without a garden; you entered straight from the street. Next was a back-to-back with a garden. Followed by a steps and in through house. Then a through house with garden. This was all very important. I knew a chap who'd worked his way up to being a millionaire. He lived in a through house but unfortunately it was so situated that you could only get to the back door by going through the house. This was all right till he got his Rolls Royce and uniformed chauffeur. It wasn't the done thing for the chauffeur to go though the front door and he couldn't get to the back door. The solution was simple: another back door was put in the front. The millionaire would enter by the front door. The chauffeur would drive the Rolls into the garage, which had mock Tudor hinges on the 'Up and over door'. Then he would enter the house by the less ostentatious, back/front door, to the left of the main door.

Ours was a similarly placed house but you could get to the back door by walking down the street and through a backyard. In the backyard was a row of outside brick toilets, the doors facing away from the houses. Along the backs of them we all had two dust bins, yes two. This was class. One bin was the ordinary type, the other was painted white with 'WASTE FOOD' stencilled on it in red. The owners of each brace of bins were extremely territorial. If your bin was full or you had some embarrassing rubbish you didn't want the bin man to spot, you'd slip it into someone else's bin. One fellow up the yard thought he'd solved this illicit dumping problem. He'd painted 'OUT OF ORDER' on his dustbin.

At the front we had a tiny garden with a grand crop of chickweed. Under it was a cellar, which we used as a cellar, not to live in. The garden had a low stonewall that originally had a iron gate and railings on top. These had all been removed in the war. People think Feng Shui is new in the West but we inadvertently evoked it in the 40s with the removal of the 'Bad luck' spiked iron railings. They were all carted away, it was said for the war effort. Later we learned they had all been dumped in the North Sea. We didn't know it at the time but this, of course, brought the good Chi that won the war. So now you know. But did you know why rich people are content, tall, fit, healthy and happy? It's not just the money. Oh no! It's because they have always known about crystal therapy. They've all got loads of crystals in their chandeliers. We were on our way; we were passing the mammon milestones. We'd jumped a few rungs up the ladder of life and a few steps up the stairs.

At the far end of the street was a park at the other side; over to the left was a small road leading past an exotically named house, the Villa Bellisima. Down the hill at the bottom was The Bradford Dyers' Association, past this you could go up the hill to Southowram and the Southowram nudist colony. Little was know or said of that, but the Bradford Dyers Association, the BDA, was infamous. All the local kids knew the initials BDA. It was written on the side of Bradford Dyers' Association green vans. When you spotted one, you immediately, very vigorously, touched the nearest person and shouted 'BDA, no touch back'. Why? The only reason I can think of is it is very satisfying to be able to belt someone with impunity. Being a kid who frequently failed to spot these BDA vans, I was often very vigorously touched and it was very annoying, particularly if it was a smaller kid. 'Vigorously touched' would be considered a violent assault anywhere else. I therefore have a deep-seated hatred of the use of initial letters and acronyms, which are fast becoming a language of their own. I'm now the founder of GROAN, which stands for 'Get Rid Of Acronyms Now'. To irritate me further, my name has become an acronym, WILF or WILFING: 'What Was I Looking For'. In other words, aimlessly browsing the internet.

Mam's favourite initials were HP, not the sauce, hire purchase. Hire purchase restrictions were lifted in 1954. The letters HP were my first experience of the use of initial letters instead of words. Although in my case HP applied to Houses of Parliament sauce. The label on this bottle was also the first time I'd seen written French. I mentioned this before. Early bottles also had the maker's name, Garton's, on it. To the discerning eye, Garton's is, of course, snotrag backwards. Later I heard of TB, followed by FFF (Fish Friers' Federation). Then FMF, the Fs were joined to the M, the first F being reversed. This logo stood for Ministry of Food and Fisheries, it was on the bottom of most jam jars. We had to collect only these jars for school. I heard much later that you could pay to get into the cinema with one of these FMF jars. One lad whose Mam hadn't an empty FMF jar sent him with a very large Shaw's pickle jar. He thought they wouldn't let him in. He was amazed when they not only let him in, they gave him three jam jars as change. I suspect this story is apocryphal. Fiscal foolishness?

Anyway, back to HP. It was very popular because the best way to hide your poverty is to have lots and lots of stuff, and stuff could be got for 'The best room' on the so-called 'Never never'. You were still poor but what was important was you didn't look poor. 'The best room', was the front room, with good wallpaper that stayed on the wall, the china cabinet with the coronation mugs from Uncle Tommy, a three-piece suite and, eventually, a tiled fire place with a companion set, that is a poker, small shovel and coal tongs with little claw hands, all hanging on a purpose-made stand. The one I liked was the one shaped like a man in anodised armour, but that was beyond our pockets. Some lucky people had the 'Rolls poker'. This was a poker with a black rubber ring just below the handle, so if it was dropped it didn't crack the tiles. The same chap from Huddersfield invented the 'Four edge razor blade'. Edward Greenhalgh of Standard Fireworks first told me of these inventions, made by a friend of his. Try as I might I couldn't interest him in my ideas until I mentioned my air-cooled toasting fork, cat and lady tormentor. He thought this might be a

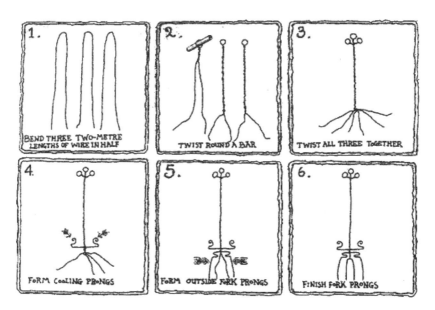

How to make an air-cooled toasting fork, cat and lady tormentor.

goer made from old sparkler wire. He always had three pieces of advice. The first was 'Always make a start'. I can't remember what the second was but I'm sure it was equally wise and indisputable. The third was 'Brown paper cures anything not malignant'.

Advert four edge and toasting fork

I didn't quite believe Edward Greenhalgh's story about the 'Four edge razor blade. Later I found a full packet in Leeds. My toasting fork was put into production. I like to think it was the lack of real fires that made it a total failure.

The best room was sometimes so good that it was only used on special occasions, such as funerals. Some people didn't even use the room for that, because their best rooms hid a secret. If you looked through the window you couldn't tell what it was. They had cheated, putting the best wallpaper only on the wall opposite the window to create a look of opulence, but only when viewed through the window.

We still had the stone floors and unfashionable, unflushed doors. All that had to wait until August 19th 1961. The lav was still outside but we were one up on the neighbours, we had a bath in the house. Not only was our bath flushed round the sides, it was flushed on top, in other words it had a lid. The bath was in a big box. The bath, and probably a toilet, had originally been upstairs. The previous owners, unlike everyone else who aspired to turn bedrooms into bathrooms, had turned their bathroom into a bedroom. The bath was now under the window in the back living room cum kitchen. The chimneybreast had an alcove on each side. In the right-hand alcove there was a Belfast sink and draining board. This was concealed by two large folding doors. The tap end of the bath was under the sink draining board and it stuck out in front of the window. The whole thing was flushed in or, if you want to be technical, boxed in. To get in the bath you opened the Fablon-covered lid. This effectively blocked off the window, so you couldn't be seen through the window. To stop the lid falling back on your head, you opened the big folding door in front of the sink and folded it back on itself, like closing a book. This held the lid up. Because the boxing was working-top height, you still had a raised flap board round the bath. This wouldn't fold down until you opened the little door under the sink because the flap hit the little door handle. So you had to open the little door, fold the flap down and then close the little door. You were now ready to fill the bath. This involved reaching under the sink draining board to the bath taps. The hot water came from a fireback boiler. Despite all this modem convenience, I could only face having a bath once a week.

Getting into the bath

1. FIRST OPEN LID 'A'   2. OPEN DOOR 'B'   3. OPEN SMALL DOOR
                         RIGHT BACK TO HOLD 'C' PULL DOWN FLAP
                         UP LID 'A'   'D' CLOSE SMALL
                                             DOOR 'C'

4. FILL BATH AND GET IN

The box lid stopped you being viewed from outside the house. Your modesty in the room, which was also a living/kitchen, was catered for by using the 'clotheshorse'. The clotheshorse was two simple wooden frames joined together on one side by wrap-over cloth hinges. Why it was called a horse I haven't any idea. Some called it a 'winteredge', country folk I suppose. 'Winteredge' with the 'H' dropped was the local pronunciation of 'winter hedge'. I assume that in summer the clothes were hung on the hedges to dry and in winter indoors on the 'winteredge' or, as we called it, the 'clotheshorse'. The only hedges round our way were in the park and any underwear hanging on bushes wasn't there because it was drying.

I once met an American touring Britain. He was lecturing on his invention and its use in theatre set construction. He was not amused when I pointed out we'd been using it for years on the clotheshorse. This cloth hinge opens both ways and doesn't rust.

When opened like a book, the clotheshorse is freestanding. The clothes are hung on the crossbars to dry. It also made an excellent frame for a tent when tipped on its side and covered with a sheet. The clotheshorse also had its use in household diplomacy. When we were living with Granny Annie, Dad returned home one evening 'Worse for drink'. He smashed the clotheshorse to smithereens with the poker. I suppose it was his version of the severed horse's head on the pillow, an implied threat. You see the clotheshorse belonged to Granny Annie. In the morning, when she saw the broken wood on the rag rug, her first angry thought was we were being unbelievably extravagant with wood for lighting the fire. Then the slow realisation came that she was looking at the remains of her clotheshorse. It had obviously not collapsed on its own. The poker ominously lay on top of a ration book. It was all something to do with Granny pinching our ration coupons.

My school chum Edward Graham Dyson Smith, when threatened, used to say, 'He who resorts to violence has lost the argument'. Then again, smashing a clotheshorse gives you a very satisfactory feeling. It also pisses the owner off and makes a point, Although you're left with nothing to hang the clothes on, you do have something to light the fire with. All this aside, on bath night, the clotheshorse was the modesty screen. Friday night was always bath night, which struck me as bad planning because Monday was clothes washday so you were lucky if there was anything to hang on it. So, before undressing, I would spend sometime carefully arranging my modesty screen. This involved strategically placing things on the clotheshorse, usually items that couldn't be hung outside for pride's sake (things with holes etc.) or my clean clothes for after the bath. (It was like being a painter placing the leaves on an Adam and Eve picture. These skills can lead to careers in window dressing.) Then, when I was happy with the arrangement, I would quickly undress, filling the gaps with my dirty clothes. Once, whilst I was in the bath, there was a knock on the door. Mam was sitting alone in front of the fire reading her *Red Letter* magazine. I waved at her over the clotheshorse. The water from my hand splashed her and she looked up. I indicated there was someone at the door. Why! Oh why! Did I do that? If I'd ignored it they would have gone away and she would never have known. I suppose I thought she'd go to the door and send them away. No, she came behind my modesty screen and, before I could do anything, she put her hand on my head and pushed me down into the bath. Just like the police do to stop you banging your head on their car and later claiming compensation for violence. She shut the lid and closed all the flaps. Leaving me in the dark. The knocking on the door stopped. She opened the door; the door closed, then, nothing. I listened, not a sound. I waited. The water got cooler. Many thoughts went through my head. Was Mam in the room? Had she gone off with the person at the door? Had the black man she was always running away with eventually turned up? Had she come back in alone and was waiting for me to get out? Had she completely forgotten I was in the bath? Was she with someone in the room? I couldn't hear talking. Could it be a deaf friend! You can't hear sign language, especially if you're boxed in a bath. I strained to hear the sound of slapping fingers. The water got colder and colder; should I put more hot water in? No! I must keep absolutely still in case someone was there. I didn't relish any gasmen laughing at me. I listened for the sound of shillings being counted, nothing. Perhaps the wooden box was blocking out the sounds? There could be a party going on for all I knew. I listened; my ears were getting keener. Odd sounds but nothing I could recognise. I waited. The water was getting colder. She'd forgotten me

My eyes started getting used to the dark. The soap in the water had separated and formed a scum, like the fat in an old chip pan. My imagination was taking over. I thought maybe the room was full of silent people all looking at the boxed-in bath, waiting for me to come out, Lazarus Lunn. John 11:37–43. The water got colder. I started forgetting my life before I got into the box. Maybe if I lifted the lid just a bit I could see what was going on? Oh no! What if I looked out and they were all there looking back with slight smirks on their faces? Rubbish, I must, I must, look. I reached up and pushed the lid. My god, it didn't move. The bastards had nailed it down. No! I'd have heard. Crafty swine, they'd quietly screwed the lid down. I was trapped. Stop being silly, it couldn't be screwed down. They could be sitting on it. I pushed again; did it move? Perhaps it was only the weight of the lid holding it down. If I put both hands on it and pushed I could maybe open it just enough to look out. I then realised that lying on my back I wouldn't be able to see through the open crack. I must slowly and quietly get into a crouched position, like Atlas with the World, then push up with my head and shoulders. When the lid moved my eyes would be in the right position to look through the opening. Slowly I got myself in the crouching position below the lid. The cold scum from the water was sticking to me. I braced myself and started pushing. My body was in a state of dynamic tension. The muscles were pushing hard but being held back, like a spring under tension, slowly being released, pushing against the lid as if it was a ton weight

Suddenly the lid burst open. I shot up like a Jack in a box into the light. I was dazzled. I couldn't see. Panic! Who was there? My eyes adjusted to the light. Mam had opened the lid and was repositioning my next week's clothes on the clotheshorse and hanging a towel. Modesty was preserved. I couldn't be seen. I removed my hands, which had instinctively covered my crutch. I don't subscribe to the logical eastern idea that, when caught in the starkers, you don't cover your crutch. You cover your head so no one knows who you are. Who else could it be in our bath disporting ginger pubic hairs? Which is what I thought they should have meant in the TV advert when they said 'Your Weetabix is showing'.

Nothing could be seen anyway. The cold water had caused me to suffer from the frightened tortoise effect, willy wise. The long immersion in cold water had turned me dead-body white with a slight hint of pink; the pink was an embarrassed blush struggling through. I looked like a pewter-pink wrinkled prune. Looking over the clotheshorse I could see the cause of all my misery. Mam's deaf friend Doreen. She was smiling; she then knowingly put her forefinger to her temple. Which either meant 'You've missed a bit'. Or, the meaning I would have preferred, 'Big boys are wearing their sideburns longer this year'. I suspect she really meant 'I think you're crackers'. I was furious with my Mam for putting me through the humiliation. But it was my humiliation and she didn't feel it. I had caused her embarrassment by unthinkingly having a bath when Doreen called. She forgot she forced me to have the bath because it was Friday. Friday was bath day. Why? Because Monday was washday. Why? Because the clothes had to be washed and ironed for Friday. Why? Because Friday was bath day. This was how it was and how it would always be. Why? Cos for. She pointed out I was lucky she'd remembered I was in the bath. Forgetting that she'd shut me in in the first place, I should thank her.

She had this ability to forget I existed. Little things like not buying any food for me. Food was bought almost meal-by-meal because there were lots of small shops around and no one had a refrigerator. In the past all were vegetarians till God ordered Noah to eat meat and he made rainbows to remind us. Genesis 9:1–3. Hitler was a vegetarian. So does this mean Jews and Christians should only eat meat when a rainbow appears? We didn't get fresh meat at home even as infrequently as the appearance of a rainbow. The cupboard was always full of tinned meat but it was dog food. Sometimes there'd be a Heinz tin of what I'd said I liked. When I ate it, it was always replaced by the same thing till I was sick of it. There was tinned salmon but I daren't touch it. The salmon was eaten only on Sundays. Mam would recreate the miracle of Jesus feeding the 5000 people with 5 loaves and 2 small fishes. John 6:1–5. Mam mixed the small tin of salmon with a lot of bread to make it go much further, much much, further. A final touch was a splash of vinegar to kill the germs. It was really flavoured bread mush. Mam considered this a treat. I quite liked it. To this day I'll eat anything as long as it comes out of a tin, and I often eat meat when there isn't a rainbow.

One summer I went away to a youth drama course for a week. I painted scenery with Walter Spradberry, who did the London rising from the ashes Phoenix posters. Mam completely forgot about me. At the end of the week, I came home in the afternoon. It was a really hot summer's day. The neighbours were all out in the backyard sitting in deckchairs, sunbathing. They were all wearing cotton frocks with knotted handkerchiefs or 'Kiss me quick' hats on their heads. It all looked very weird because they were all in a straight row, as if on the deck of an ocean-going liner. I think that's where they imagined they were when they closed their eyes. When they opened their eyes they were back in Brighouse looking at the back of the outside toilets. I lugged my suitcase past this seated rank of inspectors. As I passed, each one saying the obvious, 'Been away?' Then, 'Anywhere nice?' As if you'd admit to going somewhere horrid. They all knew where I'd been. They just wanted me to say it. So they could say 'Drama school, you don't need to learn about drama. I'll tell you about drama. I went to the University of Life'. Or words to that effect. I could, of course, have used a stock evasive reply, 'There and back to see how far it is'. These women were my elders and what I considered wit they called cheek, to which their stock reply was delivered in Morse code on the head with the flat of the hand. If you were lucky the hand was not an arthritic one. Which was like being hit with a bag of nuts, very painful, and then you were accused of hurting them with your head. I passed this gauntlet.

To my surprise, where Mam would have had a reserved deckchair there wasn't a deckchair and there wasn't a Mam. I went up to our back door and it was locked. I looked at the window, the curtains were drawn. This could mean only one of two things, either it was night, which it most obviously wasn't, it was definitely day, or, the only time curtains were drawn in daytime was when someone had died. Apparently daylight was not suitable for dead bodies, perhaps it made them fade. I also think this was a spin off from the Yorkshire work ethic. Which was if it was daylight you really should not be lying down. You should be up working and unhappy. The neighbours were sitting up and now showing interest. They had been facing the back of the lavs so they hadn't noticed the drawn curtains till now. The obvious conclusion was that someone was dead. They immediately showed a ghoulish sympathetic concern. 'Hadn't I a key?' they asked. 'Of course you haven't. You're not 21 yet.' Then the question on everyone's lips was 'How's he going to get in?' They didn't seem realise that, if there was a possibility of finding a dead body, I might not want to get in. No one seemed to want to invite me into their home to wait. They were all, technically, out. They were out for the day, sunbathing. It didn't matter that they were only 6 foot from their back doors. They were all, as the butler would say, 'Not at home'.

Anyway, it looked decidedly dodgy inviting me in with my bag already packed. I might just turn out to be an orphan and never leave. They were determined I had to get in somehow. I refused to go down the coal grate. Mrs Wood decided to forgo her day out and went home, returning with a kitchen knife. I took the knife and climbed onto the windowsill. The window was the sash type. By pushing the flat blade into the gap between the top and bottom window frame, it was possible to lever the catch open. I did this, then pulled the top window down. The neighbours were all lined up, admiring my cat burglary skills. With window now open, I put the knife into my mouth, pirate style, and faced the closed curtains. So, for effect, wasn't I just back from drama school, in front of my first audience? With the knife clenched in my teeth, I dramatically whipped both curtains open. Then, for the first time in my life, I heard my Mam's natural voice. It was in the form of a high-pitched scream and it was coming from the bath under the window. I immediately looked up from her into the room.

Dad was sitting in front of the fire trying to read the *Daily Mirror* in the dim light. Unaware that I was at the window and totally engrossed, he adjusted his paper, tipping it towards the window to take advantage of the extra light I'd let in.

I closed the curtains to no applause. I turned to my audience, they were all gone. They were back sunbathing, with that 'We know nothing about this' look on their faces. I was approached later and asked to return the knife; apparently they were having company for tea. There's posh!

On another occasion I returned to find myself locked out once again. It was raining slightly, what we called locally spitting, an allusion to what we thought our God thought of us. It looked like it might start to pour down or, as we termed it, 'sile it down'. I thought it would be a good idea to avoid God's greater displeasure and get shelter. I'd ask Mrs Bass next door if she knew where my Mam was and hopefully she'd invite me in. It worked like a charm. Mrs Bass didn't say the usual, that Mam had run off with a black man, which made a nice change. She said Mam had just gone out for a minute and wouldn't be long and would I like to wait in her house out of rain till she got back? I couldn't, of course, refuse this kindness, so I went inside and she sat me down to watch the television. My attention was soon drawn to the noise in the corner of the room, where there was a large birdcage on a pole. Not so unusual, but what was in it was unusual. I couldn't believe my eyes; instead of the usual budgie Mrs Bass had what appeared to be a crow. Strange, but not the most peculiar thing I've seen in a budgie cage. I once visited the house of the Mayoress of Brighouse, Mrs Mona Mitchell; she had two dead lobsters in her budgie cage. I was just pondering that perhaps Mrs Bass was not all she appeared to be. She could be involved in the black arts and this bird was her familiar. Mrs Bass, somehow sensing my feelings, turned from the telly and spotted me looking at the bird. She said, 'He's called Simon, he's a mynah bird'. This, of course, could have meant he was a bird that belonged to a coal miner, the bird actually dug tunnels itself or it was a minor bird, that is not an adult bird. In which case it would soon need a larger cage. This bird was an extremely messy eater, tearing up grapes and flicking the pips and skins all over the place; he didn't give a toss about the expense. You had to be pretty sick in our house to be given grapes. Mrs Bass ignored the bird and concentrated on the television. The bird was a novelty, but the telly was more so and Frankie Howard was on doing a monologue. He suddenly produced a large pair of pink lace-up corsets and said, 'Are these yours Mrs?'

I was embarrassed, sitting alone with an older woman while underwear was being flashed around. Mrs Bass looked uneasy; she felt, perhaps, that this was corrupting a youngster and, to deflect attention, she turned to the mynah bird. I thought 'It's not me she's worried about it's the bird'. Then she said, 'Dirty bird, dirty bird'. The mynah bird is, of course, well known as an excellent talker and mimic, and quick as a flash he replied, 'Ergogert im, ergogert im, ergogert urn'. I thought 'Someone's flogged her a duff bird, it can't talk properly'. Then I realised the intonation sounded very familiar, perhaps the poor chap was deaf. I looked at Mrs Bass; she looked at me despairingly and said, 'Yes, yes, he's copying your father calling in the dog'. 'Sounds just like Dad', I said enthusiastically, thinking this might make her feel better about it. She brightened up and said, 'Oh! Yes, and you should hear him do your Dad coughing'. I felt sorry for her; all that expense and the bird had decided to mimic my deaf Dad. I daren't say 'I don't suppose there's any chance of teaching him sign language'.

I never saw Simon again but learned later from a neighbour, Susan Wood, that he did learn to speak very well, without a trace of a Yorkshire accent. Mrs Bass's son Rodney had been a musician in the Guards down south so he could have had some influence. I suspect Simon acquired his 'Received pronunciation' from strict elocution lessons. Where he learned his long 'A's, such as in barth for bath, parth for path, grarse for grass and, what about, garse marsk, I don't know. I wonder if Simon called Mrs Bass, Mrs Barse. There are so many arses in this form of pronunciation I always find it strange when they actually pronounce 'Arse' itself: they say 'Ass'.

I understand sometimes Simon found it all too much and would lapse into an occasional therapeutic loud and joyful 'Ergogert'. Then he sadly had to return to his elocution exercises

> 'Farther's car is a Jaguar and Par drives rather farst.
> Carsels, farms and drarfty barns we go charging parst'.

Or my elocution poem.

The Southern pasty poem.

> Hair lair thair. I do declare, a stall that' selling parsties.
> Well I'm agarst; they're selling farst. I wonder what the corst is?
> Hay say young Miss, may hay arsk is that your ver' larst parsty?
> And is it larst becors it's parst its tame and it's gorn narsty?
> Or is it cors you've scoffed the lort? I see you've increased varstly.
> Please examine your ass in a looking glarse, you'll find it's facking
> garstly.

I like to tell people 'I'm an Anonist'. They look worried and are not sure that I should admit to such a thing. It sounds suspiciously like something to do with the anus. Not as much as 'Arsonist' does, or should it be pronounced 'Assonist'. Anyway, everyone knows what an arsonist is but not so an Anonist. Christians and Jews assume it's a perversion. They dimly remember the first 'Onanist', The son of Judah, Onan, who spilled his seed on the ground. Genesis 38:9. By Anonist I mean, of course, I write poems and don't put my name on them, so they are simply 'Anon'. Thus I'm an Anonist; for good reason. Here's one of my poems.

Advice.

Do not go out late at night.
There's mugging, rape and bashing.
Never sit on window sills
when men are pebble dashing.

Uncle Fred and Auntie Molly Mann lived just outside London at a place called Staines pronounced, 'Stines.' Founded, I think, by a chap who was a very messy eater. They had two sons, Terry and Edward. When we stayed with them for a week I had great difficulty communicating with my two cousins because of our different accents. My cousin Edward baffled me when he said 'We're going to the barfs at free'. Not only long 'A's but 'F's for 'Th's. It was quite a while before I figured out what a 'Vjoiner' was.

Uncle Fred was a civil servant and he was completely different to any adult I'd ever met. He would read the stories in the *Hotspur* or *Wizard* comic to us. He took us to see Guy the gorilla at London Zoo. Guy showed what he thought of us by filling his mouth with water and spitting at us. Later Uncle Fred told me how he led the rescue when the first 'V' bomb was dropped, for which he didn't get any recognition. He also got a sabre slash when he was involved in a demobilisation riot. Uncle Fred and me were together in the gallery shortly before the *Duke of Wellington* portrait by Goya was stolen. The day after, at lunchtime, in Piccadilly Circus, I was stopped as a suspect. Thinking about it later, I thought I'd probably been recognised as having been in the gallery but actually it probably had more to do with the large oblong parcel I was carrying. The police over-reacted. I was made to lean against the wall, arms and legs outstretched. This method of searching is quite common now, but then I'd never seen it. This all took place under the Guinness clock, with hundreds of tourists circled round, watching. The parcel, a small hessian sack, contained my sketchbook. They let me go. I think people may have thought I'd made the story up if Uncle Fred hadn't confirmed it. Uncle Fred always said when he retired that he would run away with me and we'd become film extras; alas it was not to be.

It's always useful having an extra witness like Uncle Fred to confirm the more bizarre incidents. I was waiting to board a plane to Boston USA. My companion on the flight was Dave Blackburn, the artist. Suddenly an American, further up the queue, interrupted our conversation. He said, 'Excuse me I was just admiring your moustache, is it real?' At that time I had a waxed moustache, 1 foot from tip to tip. 'Yes', I replied, and, trying to be a smart-ass added, 'But the nose is false'. To my amazement he replied, 'That's interesting, so's mine'. It transpired his nose had been rebuilt by plastic surgery after being ripped off with a claw hammer. How? I never asked him. I still envisage him, a claw up each nostril, and puzzle how it could possibly have happened. My father-in-law suggests he may have been using the claw hammer to remove a particularly tight pair of false teeth. I thought of Mam's cautionary tale of the blind man undoing the knot in his shoelace with a fork.

I found out recently that animals use sign language. There's a frog that lives near waterfalls and, because of the noise of the water, they can't hear each other croaking, which apparently is very important in the mating season. Girls in the textile mills had the same problem because of the noisy looms. I mean difficulty hearing, not mating. The girls solved the problem by carefully articulating their mouths and lip-reading. The frogs obviously decided that carefully mouthing croaks and lip-reading were not for them, so they communicate by semaphore using their back legs as flags. The 'Semaphore frog' is quite happy with this system, apparently there's never any confusion because of regional accents. Talking of strange animals, I hear the Volcano rabbit is becoming extinct. I wonder why?

Me and Shirley Wood. In the background, high on the wall,
The funeral director's tiny door.

Beware people on the other side

Nine Crown Street is a terrace house. When I lived there it was on an unmade cul de sac. At the far end is a playing field; at the near end, across the road, on an upper floor there was a strange tiny door in the wall. This was there because the funeral director who worked upstairs had put his circular saw too near the wall. Consequently he had to push his longer planks through this little door to get them on his saw table.

Part way on Crown Street, on the left, is a large passage going through the row of houses. By going down this passage and turning right you could get to our back door. Through the passage to the left you would pass Fish Harry's house in the corner. Fish Harry was that day's equivalent of the 'Hell driver'. His job was to get the fish from the coast to the shops, as fast as possible, no matter what. He did this in a small blue open-backed pick-up truck that had an aroma even this speedy truck couldn't leave behind. He probably brought the crabs to the crab dressers on Pong Alley. Next door was Mrs Bolton, with her little West Highland White dog called Candy. Mrs Drew's house was in the other corner. Back across the yard, next to the passage, was Mrs Wood's then Mrs Bass's. The houses were always called after the lady of the house. So it was Mrs Wood's at number three, Mrs Bass's at number seven and we were at number nine. Nobody knows why there wasn't a number five. A small flight of stairs went up to our back door, through which was our living room/kitchen/bathroom. Diagonally across the room was the door to the cellar. Straight in front of you, at the opposite side of the room, was the door to the bedroom stairs. Past the bottom of the stairs was another door, into the front or best room. At the other side of the best room was the front door, leading to the tiny front garden, with its excellent crop of chickweed, and then the gate to the street. The front and back door had Yale locks. I was not allowed a key to either. Is it not written in stone and said at bingo 'Key to the door, 21'. So until I was 21 years old, no key for me.

Mam and Dad went to bed early. If I was still out, they would leave the back door unlocked. One night I returned late. I went down the passage, turned right up the backyard and entered through the back door. Without bothering to put the light, on I dropped the latch, thus locking the door behind me, and I crossed the kitchen to the stairs door, to go to bed. Gripping the doorknob, I turned it and pulled it towards me. Usually when I did this the door opened and I walked through. On this occasion I automatically stepped forward, smacking my face into the door. It hadn't opened. Rubbing my head I turned and tried the knob again. The knob turned but I could feel it was not engaging the latch and pulling it back. The thing was worn out; no amount of turning would pull the latch back. I considered forcing the door with my shoulder. That wouldn't work because it opened towards me and I would be ramming it against the doorframe. I gave it up as a bad job and decided to sleep in front of the dying kitchen fire. I took my shoes off, attempting to fool my body into thinking it was bedtime, and I lay down on the rag rug. By the fire glow I examined the many coloured rags that made up the rug. A rag rug in Brighouse was like Wampum to an American Indian. It told the history of the tribe and was made by the tribal elders, in our case Granny Annie. The khaki bits spoke of the war. Uncle Tommy's escape to Switzerland, Uncle Clifford's service in India. The few brown pieces, rescued from my old short trousers, brought back terrible memories. I was on the baby swings playing parachutes. Swinging high and jumping off, shouting 'Geronimo'. The swings were like small chairs. You could hook a chain across the front to stop toddlers falling out. We, of course, didn't use this. The idea was to leap off the swing at it highest point over Germany. Unbeknown to me the hook on the chain was up my trouser slot. I flew through the air. Pulled the ripcord on my imaginary parachute. The hook on the chain tightened and ripped my trousers from bottom to top. I fell on my face with only one complete right trouser slot and a flap round my left leg. No underpants, it's the stuff of nightmares! It was like wearing a transient garment that was a cross between trousers and a kilt, without the benefit of a kilt pin. Holding my trousers up with my right hand and clutching my torn left leg where the kilt pin would have been, I made my way home wounded to Mam. Germany was safe for another day but I wasn't. Back on the rug, in amongst these brown scraps of my short trousers were the grey scraps, the remains of my first long trousers. The green bits looked like Doreen's dreaded green Mackintosh, and the navy blue my miniature gasman's Mac. Suddenly the stair door rattled and from behind it I heard 'Ergogert Whiff'.

It was Dad. Although he was stone deaf he must have felt the vibrations when I tried to open the door. Either that or he'd come down for a smoke. I rushed to the door and started frantically turning the handle and flicking the stair light switch, which was on my side of the door. Frustrated I shouted, although I knew he couldn't hear a thing. Dad knew I was there. He must have thought I had somehow locked the door but there wasn't a door lock. He couldn't work out what was going on. So he did what all great thinkers do, he went back to bed to think about it. I couldn't believe he'd gone back to bed! Really fed up, I returned to reading the rag rug. I was trying to find Doreen's green Mac bit when the stair door rattled again. This time I heard my Mam saying in her fashion, 'Open door Wifherd'.

Dad had obviously thought he couldn't sort it out so he'd brought in a higher authority, namely Mam. I rushed to the door and found myself carefully mouthing explanations before I realised even an Olympic lip-reading champion couldn't lip-read through an inch-thick unflushed door and 20 coats of paint. So now they were both behind the door, one deaf and dumb, the other deaf and lip-reading. Mam was getting angrier and angrier. She wanted the door open and she wanted to know what I was doing. I don't for 1 minute think she thought I had a girl in the kitchen. She probably thought it was more serious. I'd perhaps got the tin opener and, mad with hunger, I'd opened a tin of salmon. She raved and raved. I, of course, heard everything she said. She only felt the door moving. I couldn't go back to sleep with her carrying on. I even tried Morse code, flicking the lights in the kitchen on and off. Three long, three short flicks, SOS. This only made her more angry. This was fun. When she switched the light on, at her side, I could switch it off, with the two-way switch on my side. To a Mam, being in the dark was the same as me putting my fingers in my ears. You can't tell what anyone's saying in sign language if you shut your eyes or it's dark. I never did make those fluorescent gloves for dark, deaf, disco parties. She was steaming. Suddenly it went all quiet. There was a pause and she said, very deliberately, 'I'm sending father round'. Just like they say to little kids, 'Wait till your dad gets home'.

I listened to the silence of sign language. My father's grunt of assent followed shortly by the opening and closing of the front door. He was on his way down the street, past Mrs Bass's then Mrs Wood's, on through the passage, past the back of Mrs Wood's and Mrs Bass's. Up the yard, to our back door, where I was waiting to calm him down. He was not a happy man in his pyjamas, undone boots and raincoat. Dressing gowns were unknown to the likes of us. The recognised procedure on rising was straight from night attire to fully dressed or, if it was a particularly bitter time of year, fully dressed to extra dressed. I led him to the stair door and let him try the handle. That was easier than trying to explain. All this time

Mam, not knowing he'd arrived, was behind the door chanting, 'He's coming, he's coming, he's coming'. More of a threat than a promise of parousia.

Dad quickly grasped the situation. I mimed that I would go back the way he'd come and charge the door from the other side. He nodded, fully understanding the mechanics of forceful door opening. Then, firmly pushing him back from the door, I mimed that he must stand well back, so he wouldn't get hit when the door flew open. I then left him there and set off in my stocking feet. Through the back door, down the yard, through the passage. I turned left up the street, arriving at the front door with my socks soaked right through. The front door was locked. Dad, the gormless clot, had shut the door behind him, on the Yale latch, and it was now firmly locked. I couldn't believe it. I opened the letterbox to look through. There was Mam; I could see her talking to the door, 'He's coming, he's coming'.

I tried waving my hand through the letterbox. She was turned away from me, chanting to the door, and my deaf dad on the other side. Waving was a waste of time. I decided it would be better if I went back to tell Dad what an idiot he'd been, locking the door behind him. Cursing him, I set off down the street. Past Mrs Bass's, past Mrs Wood's, right down the passage, left past the back of the houses, to our back door. Which was locked. I'd cursed my Dad and I'd done the same thing. When I shut the door on the latch I'd locked myself out. I'd called Dad an idiot but he was locked inside. I was outside cold and miserable with wet stocking feet. Off I went back past Mrs Bass's, past Mrs. Wood's, left through the passage, right down the street. Hoping Mam had come to the front door. No, she hadn't, I looked through the letterbox, there she was still chanting, 'He's coming, just you wait, he's coming'.

I think she'd sort of forgotten what was going on, because the chanting was sounding slightly religious. Dad was waiting on the other side of the door, oblivious to her messianic mumblings.

Tensely waiting for the door to burst open, like watching a firework when the flames gone in the top and nothing's happening. At least he was warm. Outside, where I was, lights were going on up and down the street. Bedroom curtains were being carefully opened, just little. When they realised the incident was obviously going to continue for a while, the lights went out but only so they could open the curtains more and carry on watching, unobserved. They could also deny all knowledge of the event and not feel too bad about not helping, should it prove serious. It was looking like I would have to put into action the last resort plan. The plan was to climb down the coal grate. This was a lift-up metal flap in the front garden wall. I'd often had to furtively stand at the front room window counting the coal bags tipped through it. Mam trusted no one. There was a chain fastened to the back of the grate so it could be padlocked. It was never locked; only someone desperate would climb down it. This would get me into the cellar and from there I would climb the stairs and end up back where I started in the kitchen with Dad. At least I would be inside for the night. I was reluctant to do this because it was an extremely filthy way to get into the house. The only other time I'd done it I'd come up in Mrs Bass's house. She wasn't pleased. This time I'd count off the houses and coal grates and to be sure I'd get the right one. I took a last look through the letterbox at the light and warmth. Mam was looking upwards chanting, 'He's coming'.

Then she must have thought, hang on, he's taking a hell of along time coming. She turned to look at the front door. I quickly stood up and pushed my hand through, waving frantically. Fortunately she had her specs on. I think she thought the night had gone and the *Daily Mirror* had arrived. She walked to the door and realised it was a hand. Bravely she opened the door and let me in. Before she could start berating me, I took her back to the kitchen door and carefully mouthed that it was stuck. I was going to bash it open. She was alarmed; she stood back and,with out more ado, I shouted 'Geronimo' and threw myself at the door.

Meanwhile Dad had forgotten what the plan was. He had one of his deaf ears to the door. He'd seen hearing people do that. Whereupon the door burst open, knocking him to the ground. Mam, ignoring Dad, stepped over him to have a quick look round to see if it was all a complicated ruse to cover naughty activities. She saw nothing amiss. Not totally convinced, she had a quick look in the cellar head pantry to see if I'd been at the tinned salmon. Every thing in order, she turned her attention to Dad. Dad was stunned. I help him to the armchair. He smiled weakly, his false teeth had stayed in. Why had he put his teeth in to come down stairs? Who the ummer did he think I had in the kitchen to smile at; or was he going to bite a burglar?

Mam rubbed margarine on Dad's bump. We all had a cup of tea and went to bed. Fortunately none of the noise woke Doreen, she slept through it all. I still wasn't given a key to the door; in fact I never got one. I left home before I was 21. I was reminded much later of the door incident when I saw a sign on a door that said 'Beware people on the other side'.

Mam and Dad died within a week of each other, Dad on the 18th of July 1990 and Mam on the 22nd. He was 74 and Mam was 68. Dad left lots of Reader's Digest books. I suspect he only bought them for a chance to win the prize. One of them is *The Right Word at the Right Time. A Guide to the English Language and How to Use it*. When I visit their grave I particularly remember Mam because I walk past the grave of 5-year-old Rob Roy, who died March ~ 1899. On his grave stands a white marble cherub with one hand raised. Mam always told us that the cherub used to hold a silver sixpence in its fingers, the very sixpence that had killed the little lad after he swallowed it. Of course the sixpence had been pinched long ago and the fingers were empty. This story had useful lessons. One, not to put a foreign object in your mouth because the germs might get you or, two, you could swallow it and die. This was particularly aimed at Doreen, because at home, nestling in Mam's Gladstone medicine bag, was a steel ball bearing, which she'd swallowed. Mam would on occasions take it out and show it to us whilst telling us how, in a panic, she had fed Doreen on milk and cotton wool till, eventually, with a dull clink, Doreen parted company with it, into Granny's best potty, and lived. No marble cherub holding a ball bearing for our Doreen. The third lesson was, of course, not to leave your money lying around, even in graveyards, because it was sure to get pinched. When I visited, with my children, the cherub's fingers had been broken off, like a chip-shop man's. I returned recently to find the complete hand had been broken off. Is someone maybe stealing it a bit at a time and rebuilding it at home? Let's hope there's some of it left so my kids can recount Mam's tale to their children or, maybe because it's hard to swallow a credit card, they'll have to change it to a cautionary nail-biting story.

T' end

Rob Roy.